From Pews to Politics

Does religion influence political participation? This book takes up this pressing debate using Christianity in sub-Saharan Africa as its empirical base to demonstrate that religious teachings communicated in sermons can influence both the degree and the form of citizens' political participation. McClendon and Riedl document some of the current diversity of sermon content in contemporary Christian houses of worship and then use a combination of laboratory experiments, observational survey data, focus groups, and case comparisons in Zambia, Uganda, and Kenya to interrogate the impact of sermon exposure on political participation and the longevity of that impact. *From Pews to Politics* leverages the pluralism of sermons in sub-Saharan Africa to gain insight into the content of cultural influences and their consequences for how ordinary citizens participate in politics.

Gwyneth H. McClendon is Assistant Professor of Politics at New York University and the author of *Envy in Politics* (2018). She has published numerous articles on political psychology, religion, and political participation in the *American Journal of Political Science*, the *Journal of Politics*, the *Quarterly Journal of Political Science*, and *Comparative Political Studies*, among other journals.

Rachel Beatty Riedl is Associate Professor of Political Science, Director of the Program of African Studies, and a faculty fellow at the Institute for Policy Research at Northwestern University. She is the author of the award-winning *Authoritarian Origins of Democratic Party Systems in Africa* (2014). Riedl is the chair of the Comparative Democratization section of the American Political Science Association and member of the Council on Foreign Relations.

From Pews to Politics

*Religious Sermons and Political
Participation in Africa*

GWYNETH H. MCCLENDON
New York University

RACHEL BEATTY RIEDL
Northwestern University

 CAMBRIDGE
UNIVERSITY PRESS

CAMBRIDGE
UNIVERSITY PRESS

University Printing House, Cambridge CB2 8BS, United Kingdom

One Liberty Plaza, 20th Floor, New York, NY 10006, USA

477 Williamstown Road, Port Melbourne, VIC 3207, Australia

314-321, 3rd Floor, Plot 3, Splendor Forum, Jasola District Centre, New Delhi - 110025, India

103 Penang Road, #05-06/07, Visioncrest Commercial, Singapore 238467

Cambridge University Press is part of the University of Cambridge.

It furthers the University's mission by disseminating knowledge in the pursuit of education, learning and research at the highest international levels of excellence.

www.cambridge.org
Information on this title: www.cambridge.org/9781108707978
DOI: 10.1017/9781108761208

© Gwyneth McClendon and Rachel Beatty Riedl 2019

First published 2019
First paperback edition 2022

A catalogue record for this publication is available from the British Library

Library of Congress Cataloging in Publication data
NAMES: McClendon, Gwyneth H., author. | Riedl, Rachel Beatty, author.
TITLE: From pews to politics : religious sermons and political participation in Africa / Gwyneth H. McClendon and Rachel Beatty Riedl.
DESCRIPTION: Cambridge, United Kingdom ; New York, NY : Cambridge University Press, 2019. | Includes bibliographical references and index.
IDENTIFIERS: LCCN 2019015913 | ISBN 9781108486576 (hardback : alk. paper) | ISBN 9781108707978 (pbk. : alk. paper)
SUBJECTS: LCSH: Christianity and politics–Africa, Sub-Saharan–Sermons. | Political participation–Africa, Sub-Saharan. | Political participation–Religious aspects. | Africa, Sub-Saharan–Religion.
CLASSIFICATION: LCC BR1430 .M385 2019 | DDC 261.709676–dc23
LC record available at https://lccn.loc.gov/2019015913

ISBN 978-1-108-48657-6 Hardback
ISBN 978-1-108-70797-8 Paperback

Contents

Figures

Tables

Acknowledgments

This book has benefited from the support, input, and feedback of many people and organizations. We are indebted to the British Institute in Eastern Africa and to the Busara Center for Behavioral Economics for their help in implementing the research. At the Busara Center, we are especially grateful to Jennifer Adhiambo, Peninah Mukai, James Vancel, and Lornah Wahome. We are most grateful to the churches that opened their doors to us, and to the members who spoke with us about their experiences and explained their views of citizenship and politics. When Gilford Kimathi was at the Youth Agenda, he helped us coordinate the measure of political participation for the first experiment. We are also most grateful to Mwongela Kamencu, Julie Santella, Alice Xu, Eddine Bouyahi, Malitt Ishmael, Nelson Ngige, Brenda Ochieng, May Koko, and Esther Kerubo, as well as to Amalia Bersin, Jack Furness, Carina Kaplan, Nicole Kempis, Ahmad Keshk, Kennedy Mmasi, Elvira Salgado, Adelina Pak, Michelle Ki, and Mert Salur for invaluable research assistance.

The Eric Mindich Foundations of Human Behavior Initiative at Harvard University; Northwestern University's Equality Development and Globalization Studies program, Program of African Studies, Institute for Policy Research, Buffett Institute for International Studies, and Department of Political Science; the Fulbright Scholars Program; and the Department of Politics at New York University generously provided funding that facilitated the research and also ensured time to write the book.

Many people provided comments on the project throughout its development, and we are appreciative of the rich intellectual communities of which we have been a part. The project began when we were both in residence as fellows at the Yale Program on Democracy, with many thanks to

Sue Stokes for making that time a productive one. We thank participants in workshops at the British Institute in Eastern Africa; the Busara Center; Boston University; Columbia University; Cornell University's Institute for African Development; Georgetown University; Harvard University; the Massachusetts Institute of Technology; New York University; Northwestern University; Texas A&M University; the University of California, Berkeley; the University of California, Los Angeles; the University of California, San Diego; the University of Chicago; University of Illinois Champaign–Urbana; the University of Michigan; the University of Rochester; the University of Southern California; the Midwest Working Group on African Political Economy; and Vanderbilt University, as well as participants at the Midwest Political Science Association, Evidence in Governance and Politics (EGAP), the African Studies Association, Northwestern University's Global Politics and Religion Research Group, and the American Political Science Association meetings, especially to Scott Abramson, Sheri Berman, J. J. Carney, Alex Coppock, Kim Yi Dionne, Paul Djupe, Salif Jaiteh, Kimuli Kasara, Cecilia Kim, Dat Nyugen, Guadalupe Tuñon, Leo Villalon, and Anna Wilke, who served as discussants at these seminars and conferences. We thank Ruth Marshall for helpful conversations at the start of the project. The support of our colleagues at Northwestern University, Harvard University, and New York University gave us time and energy to complete the project.

Kathleen Thelen generously supported a book manuscript workshop at the Massachusetts Institute of Technology, and we are extremely grateful to Melani Cammett, Paul Djupe, Evan Lieberman, Phillip Martin, Dan Posner, Leah Rosenzweig, Rachel Sweet, and Lily Tsai for their feedback during that workshop. Gina Giliberti, Elizabeth Shakman Hurd, Brannon Ingram, and Martha Wilfahrt also provided comments in a book workshop held by the Global Politics and Religion program at Northwestern University. Anna Grzymala-Busse, Tracy Kuperus, Timothy Longman, Jeremy Menchik, and Richard Nielsen separately took the time to provide comments on parts or all of the manuscript. The Chicago Women in Comparative Politics group, and an informal reading group of women political scientists in New York, also provided comments on various portions of the project, with thanks to all members, including Monika Nalepa, Allison Carnegie, Alisha Holland, Ana Arjona, Sarah Daly, Thania Sanchez, and Jaimie Bleck. We also thank two anonymous reviewers and Robert Dreesen at Cambridge University Press for advancing this project through review to production.

Parts of Chapter 3 originally appeared in an article published in *African Affairs* in 2015: "Individualism and Empowerment in Pentecostal Sermons: New Evidence from Nairobi, Kenya," 115(458): 119–144, published by Oxford University Press on behalf of the Royal African Society. Many of the results from the first lab experiment described in Chapter 4 were originally published in *The Journal of Politics*, 77(4): 1045–1057 ©2015 by the Southern Political Science Association under the title "Religion as a Stimulant of Political Participation: Experimental Evidence from Nairobi, Kenya." The brief discussion of sermons in South Africa in Chapter 3 draws on data collected in collaboration with Maria Frahm-Arp at the University of Johannesburg and her students, including Yvette Angoma, Mpho Bengu, Gerrit Berrimann, Desree Mekgwe, Fikile Mosola, Lerato Motsau, Sally Phago, and Matshepo Sikhulu, for whose efforts and willingness to share the data we are deeply grateful.

Throughout the life course of a book, many momentous things happen in real life. We thank Scott Hartman and Drew Riedl and our amazing daughters Eleanor, Adelaide, and Amelie for sharing their lives with us.

Religion as Metaphysical Instruction, and Its Influence on Political Participation

There is a popular view that religious teachings motivate political participation. In Kenya, Margaret Wanjiru and other political candidates announced their decisions to run for office with reference to their journeys in the church, arguing that the content of their faith was leading them to seek positions in political leadership. Beginning in 2016, Pastor Evan Mawarire of Zimbabwe delivered a series of sermons, online and in church, for which he was arrested. The pastor's words, the Zimbabwean authorities and media argued, were causing people to take part in protests against the current political leaders. In Ghana, citizens, reportedly moved by sermons, pledged to take action to resist and report petty bribes (Ghanian Times, 2016). In every case, journalists and other observers linked religious teachings to political action.

Similar claims about the influence of religious teachings on political participation have been made around the world. In June 2011, CNN ran the headline "Prayer and Politics: How Friday Became the Middle East's Day of Protest" (Mackay, 2011). The article posits that the religious ideas communicated in Friday sermons in the Middle East help drive political mobilization. Gathering to hear sermons, and then to pray, "can be a way of preparing to go to battle," an expert on the Middle East is quoted as saying. "It gives the people … strength." In 2014, the Egyptian Ministry of Religious Endowments began mandating that imams discuss only a government-assigned weekly topic in their Friday sermons precisely because of concern over sermons' mobilizing influence (Maher, 2014). In the United States in the 1960s, ordinary participants in the civil rights movement, and many of its leaders, were reportedly driven by the "re-imagination of Christian thought" delivered in the sermons and messages of black clergy and religious activists (Harvey, 2016). "That is what empowered the rank and file who made the movement move" (ibid). In 1980s' Poland, the sermons of some Catholic priests "provid[ed] the moral center that emboldened [members of the Catholic Church] to peacefully and yet forcefully challenge the reign of the regime imposed by Moscow" (Time, 2005). And, today, journalists and other public commentators often argue that exposure to jihadist sermons and online teachings by prominent clerics influences individual participation in political violence (Cottee, 2016).

In contrast to the popular willingness to attribute patterns of political participation to religious teachings, political science scholarship has typically been more cautious in making such links (cf., Harris, 1994; Wielhouwer, 2009; Glazier, 2015).[1] Indeed, political scientists often dismiss cultural and ideational explanations for political behavior as either epiphenomenal or overdetermined (cf., Collier, 2017; Martin, 2018). Studies of the link between religiosity and political participation often focus instead on the material resources and skills (Verba and Nie, 1972; Verba, Schlozman, and Brady, 1995; Jones-Correa and Leal, 2001; Campbell, 2004), the habits (Chhibber, 2014), the attachments to social identities (Wilkinson, 2006; Longman, 2009), or the social networks (Wald, Owen, and Hill, 1988; Lewis, MacGregor, and Putnam, 2013) that accompany religious practice, rather than on the content of religious teachings or ideas. Recent analyses of the causes of suicide bombing dismiss the role of religious teachings and instead stress the strategic logic and organizational structure involved (Giles and Hopkin, 2005; Pape, 2005). To the extent that social science scholarship ever analyzes the impact of religious ideas and beliefs on behavior, it has usually been to try to unpack the drivers of generosity and prejudice (Shariff and Norenzayan 2007; Sachs 2010; Norenzayan 2013; Ben-Nun Bloom, Arikan, and Courtemanche 2015; Warner et al. 2015) or to explain attitudes toward specific issue areas (Djupe and Calfano, 2013b; Glazier, 2013; Masoud, Jamal, and Nugent, 2016) rather than to explain decisions about whether and how to engage in politics.

---

[1] We focus in this book on political participation as the outcome of interest. But important research in American politics explores links between religious communication and other political attitudes and behaviors (e.g., Djupe and Gilbert, 2009; Djupe and Calfano, 2013a; Ben-Nun Bloom, Arikan, and Courtemanche, 2015). Djupe, Calfano, and Glazier are notable for their work in this area. In addition, new research considers the implications of religious communication for left–right views in Latin America (Tunón, 2017).

There are good reasons to be skeptical that religious teachings would drive political participation. Nothing requires people to listen to and absorb messages from the pulpit. People might hear what they want to hear (Huckfeldt and Sprague, 1995). They may project their own views onto clergy's words (Krosnick, 1989; Krosnick et al., 1993), ignore ideas that contradict their own prior beliefs (Djupe and Calfano, 2013a), or simply tune out altogether. They may choose to attend worship services less frequently and limit their exposure to certain ideas. In addition, especially within large faith traditions (Christianity, Islam), people have some degree of choice over their place of worship, selecting particular denominations, sects, or religious leaders who "speak to them." As a result, any relationship between exposure to religious messages and political participation may be spurious. Exposure to religious messages and political participation may both be a function of people's prior political inclinations.[2] People may show up to Friday or Sunday sermons because they are already inclined to participate in protest; they may attend houses of worship that preach disengagement from politics because they are already inclined to do so. Alternatively, people may try to separate their religious beliefs from their analyses of politics. They may consider religious leaders' purview as limited to the spiritual realm (Güth et al., 1997; Beck, 2008), and discount or delegitimize explicit political directives from the pulpit.[3] Religious messages could go in one ear and out the other, be simply a symptom of people's political proclivities rather than a cause, or be divorced from understandings of politics.

Yet the dissonance between these two perspectives raises important questions. *Do* religious teachings influence how people think about and engage in politics, or are they merely symptomatic of people's preexisting political leanings? If religious teachings do influence political

---

[2] In some cases, political changes and preferences may even drive religiosity, as Margolis (2017) shows happens in the United States.

[3] Of course, in many contexts, the leaders of churches and other houses of worship are prohibited by law from endorsing specific candidates or engaging in explicit partisan politics. This book concentrates much of its empirical analysis in Kenya, where "Public Benefit Organizations," or PBOs, enjoy tax-exempt status so long as they are "autonomous, non-partisan and nonprofit ... and engage in public benefit activities." A PBO can be a "religious organization which is primarily devoted to religious worship or propagation of religious beliefs." But prohibitions need not necessarily be legal. Grzymała-Busse (2015) argued that European churches historically lost influence over their congregants when they visibly joined the political fray and were unable to appear "above politics." Choosing sides in political contests, or mobilizing people around partisan issues, often seems to diminish churches' moral authority.

behavior, *how and under what conditions* do they do so, and *what is the extent* of their influence? These contemporary and politically salient questions touch on old debates. In the early twentieth century, Weber's *Protestant Ethic* argued that Calvinist and Catholic teachings influenced economic behavior. Just a few years later, Durkheim's *Elementary Forms of Religious Life* instead characterized religious teachings as symptoms rather than drivers of individual and social thought and action. In one view, religious teachings directly shape behavior; in another view, religious teachings reflect but do not drive our social and material conditions. These debates remain pertinent today. The world remains, overall, deeply religious. Houses of worship are ubiquitous, and attendance is regular. Religious messages appear on billboards, in magazines, and in leaflets. Religious programming travels radio airwaves and occupies television channels. *How, in this era, do religious teachings shape political participation, if at all?*

In this book, we take a new look at whether, how, and to what extent religious teachings, even when not explicitly political, might shape the mindsets and behaviors of citizens and thereby influence their political participation. We focus on the influence of sermons, and use contemporary Christian sermons in sub-Saharan Africa as our empirical vehicle for exploring that influence. We take social scientists' cautions about making causal claims about religious teachings seriously, and, through a mix of experimental and observational methods, we seek to advance our understanding of these important questions.

ARGUMENT

We propose that exposure to religious teachings, through sermons, can influence political participation by providing metaphysical instruction that influences how listeners respond to political opportunities. Consider two individuals we spoke to during focus group discussions with congregants in Nairobi, Kenya. The first, whom we will call David, told us that he is considering running for public office, and that he is taking leadership and other training courses to that end, to learn how to be the best leader he can be. He participates in forums with public officials in order to help guide them on the challenges facing ordinary citizens, and makes gentle appeals to them to follow Christian values. His orientation toward politics is active but largely uncritical of existing institutions and formal rules. Instead, he is eager to pursue change through his own internal transformation and those of others. He seeks *personnel* change in politics: to get more people of faith and character into office, and to encourage the internal transformation of those already there. The other individual, whom we will call Leon, admits feeling overwhelmed at times, but when he feels absolutely fed up, he participates in social media criticism campaigns, directed at calling out widespread poor governance and the need for institutional reform in order to force politicians to behave better; he contributes to efforts to get campaign finance law enacted, since he thinks the structure of current laws makes corruption more likely. His orientation toward politics is hesitant but highly critical of institutions and structures. He assumes most politicians will behave badly unless the proper constraints are put in place and enforced. When he engages, he seeks *structural* reform.

On most indicators, David and Leon are similarly situated: employed, with some higher education, from the same ethnic group (which as we discuss later in the book often indicates partisan leanings in this context), and living in the same neighborhood; it is not readily apparent why one would be more eager to work through existing political institutions, seeking change in people rather than in structures, while the other would take a more critical stance toward that system, seeking change in structures more than in the personal characters of citizens and leaders. Indeed, both David and Leon could choose to stay out of politics altogether. Instead, they take actions (in Leon's case, occasionally) down different political paths.

We propose that exposure to religious teachings, through sermons, explains important divergences in political participation. Sermons are sources of metaphysical instruction, informing people's understanding of how the world works. Sermons regularly tackle deep questions about the causes of the problems of this world, the possibilities for change, and the nature of human agency. Answers to these questions can inform citizens' subsequent assessment of what kind of political change is necessary and whether that political change can be made. Sermons need not be explicitly political to have this influence. Whether a sermon depicts the state of the world as one shaped fundamentally by people's characters, or instead as one fundamentally shaped by structures and the sets of extrinsic incentives in which people are embedded, can affect how listeners diagnose and respond to political problems, even if the sermon names no specific political policies, candidates, parties, or debate. Likewise, how sermons discuss the nature of human agency can shape listeners' sense of internal and external efficacy – whether they think their individual actions can affect material outcomes – making them feel more pivotal and inclined to participate in political collective action, *even if the sermons made no explicit call for political engagement*. All else equal, sermons have the potential to shape political participation, even when they are not explicitly political, because they provide interpretative maps for understanding cause, effect, and possibility in the world.

David and Leon – the first focused on leadership change, the second on structural reform – were also each frequently exposed to sermons that provided different views about how the world works. David was primarily affiliated with a Pentecostal church in Nairobi. When he spoke with us, he had just attended a Pentecostal service, in which the pastor preached vividly about the world's problems being due to a pervasive lack of faith, and about the material change that would come if more people embodied strong faith. This left David energized about bringing his own strength of faith to leadership positions and about helping to guide the character development of sitting public officials. Leon, on the other hand, was primarily affiliated with a Catholic parish. When he spoke with us, he had just attended Sunday mass, in which the priest's sermon discussed people's cultural incentives to mistrust and neglect each other as sources of the world's problems. The sermon encouraged listeners to change social norms around caring for one another, to sanction those who were inhospitable and mistrusting, but offered no firm promise of the possibility of success in changing these dynamics, leaving Leon focused on extrinsic incentives and structural solutions (e.g., new legislation to constrain politicians) but cautious about presuming he could make a difference. The sermons provided guidance on metaphysics: how cause and effect operate in the world, what the nature of human agency is, how change happens. These lessons could straightforwardly be applied to grappling with political questions and opportunities.

David and Leon self-selected into these houses of worship, so their exposure to these sermons might simply be a reflection of their preexisting inclinations to pursue political participation in these ways. Yet, it is plausible that, even if people choose a house of worship because they find its teachings appealing, their political views and inclinations may still be susceptible to shaping and sharpening. Indeed, people may attend religious services precisely *in order* to receive metaphysical guidance and direction – that is, to have their viewpoints changed, clarified, or bolstered. These questions (what causes the world's problems? will my action make a difference?) are difficult ones to answer. Houses of worship are one place people turn for help in answering them. In highly religious places, houses of worship are a very common place for people to go to answer these questions. And, as with any training or instructional endeavor (physical, mental, spiritual), although individuals may choose to attend based on their prior expectations about what they will develop there, engaging in the training itself can still have an independent effect.[4] As with exposure to other forms of cultural and media communication, exposure to religious messages might prime predispositions or change underlying opinions, even though there is a process of self-selection into exposure (Tesler, 2015). Untangling the independent influence of religious teachings on behavior from the influence of preexisting views is thus challenging, but it is an empirical problem, not a theoretical impossibility. We grapple with this challenge methodologically in later parts of the book.

Indeed, sermons may have the strongest effects on the people who are inclined to self-select into hearing those messages. In contexts where social boundaries between houses of worship are fluid,[5] religious listeners may be open to and intrigued by sermons no matter their primary affiliation, and exposure to less familiar religious teachings may influence all listeners' understandings of the world to some degree.[6] But communications research generally finds that people are more likely to pay attention to and absorb elite communication that is in line with their prior views than communication that is not as familiar or conforming (Kunda, 1990; Taber and Lodge, 2006; Leeper, 2016; Adida et al., 2017). Thus, people who have already chosen a particular place of worship because they find its messages appealing or credible may be the most likely to listen carefully. Listening to a familiar type of sermon may also revive memories of previous sermons, generating a cumulative influence on a person's metaphysical understanding of the world. That is, those who are inclined to

---

[4] We thank Rich Nielsen for this point. In a study of young men listening to sermons in Egypt, Hirschkind (2001) notes that the words used by his informants to describe listening to sermons conveyed much more than passive hearing – they talked about "inclining one's ear," "being silent in order to listen" (p. 633). A preacher explained to him, "A sermon must lead an audience beyond mere hearing to where they pay close attention, such that the words actually turn over their behavior" (p. 634).

[5] By socially fluid, we mean that it is common for people of different congregations and denominations to socialize with and marry members of others congregations and denominations, as well as to attend worship services in congregations and denominations other than their primary one. We also mean that a person's sense of political and social identity is not threatened by socializing with people from other congregations and denominations or by attending worship services in other congregations or denominations.

[6] By contrast, in places where social identity boundaries firmly divide some houses of worship from others (*not* characteristic of the context in which we work), people may ignore or even defy religious teachings from the out-group in order to affirm their affinities with the in-group (Djupe and Calfano, 2013a).

a particular type of sermon, like David and Leon, may be most likely to listen carefully and to weave that message together with previous religious teachings they have heard.

We also propose that the influence of sermons on political behavior is recurrent: activated and reactivated. Many scholarly discussions of religion assume that the connections between religious world views and political attitudes are deep-seated and relatively unmoveable.[7] But we argue that the effects of exposure to sermons, like the effects of exposure to other forms of elite communication, are subject to decay and then reactivation. Religious messages are susceptible to memory failures, and they may be diminished by encounters with countervailing experiences and arguments if not recharged.[8] Scholars have made many arguments about why belief in divine beings may be part of our cognitive infrastructure as human beings (see Norenzayan, 2013, for a review), but any "naturalness" (McCauley, 2015b) in religious world views does not mean that human beings are able to hold an understanding of the spiritual world at the forefront of their minds at all times (Luhrmann, 2012).[9] Doing so takes repetitions and reinforcement (Luhrmann, 2012). Because religious teachings rely on claims that cannot be based on, and may seem to contradict, empirical patterns (Grzymala-Busse, 2016), their resonance may quickly decay when listeners return to everyday life. Absent reinforcement (frequent reexposure to the metaphysical ideas communicated in a sermon), it is plausible that religious beliefs would recede as individuals engage in quotidian activities during the course of the week. And in pluralistic religious settings, the metaphysical ideas communicated in a particular sermon are likely quickly to encounter countervailing arguments,

---

[7] Tesler (2015) gives religious world views as one example of a deep-seated predisposition. Inglehart and Norris (2011) argue that religious world views constrain attitude changes caused by economic development.

[8] Scholars of other types of elite–citizen communication have made similar arguments about those forms of elite communication. For instance, a literature on campaign advertisements finds that the persuasive influence of those political attempts at persuasion decays rapidly (Gerber et al., 2011; Hill et al., 2013). In one large study focused on campaign advertising, the average half-life of attitude change after exposure was four days (Hill et al., 2013). In a study conducted on the duration of campaign advertisements by Gerber et al. (2011), "only trace effects of the ads survived as long as a week" (Tesler and Zaller, 2017). In other words, the influence of these other forms of communication decays in a matter of days.

[9] In fact, through fascinating ethnographic research in two churches, Luhrmann (2012) shows how much consistent and regular practice is required before congregants develop a stable feeling of a relationship with God.

as worshippers are exposed to contrasting metaphysical ideas in other religious practices, either incidentally (through radio or TV programming, or preaching on public transportation) or purposefully (through attending services in other houses of worship or having conversations with friends and family who worship elsewhere). These countervailing messages might make the original one recede from the forefront of the mind and lose its influence over a short period of time.[10]

The short duration of a sermon's influence does not mean that influence is unimportant. Opportunities for political action often occur in close proximity to religious services. For instance, it is quite common for political rallies in Kenya to be held on Sundays, and (recently) for street protests to be organized on Mondays (Munro, 2010; Manson, 2014). Likewise, in the Muslim world, as mentioned, calls to political action are frequently delivered immediately after Friday sermons (Chhibber and Sekhon, 2015). Other types of elite communication (ad campaigns, media spin) also exhibit vulnerability to decay (Gerber et al., 2011; Hill et al., 2013), and so we try to understand how short-term influences are exploited and sustained (Tesler and Zaller, 2017). The duration patterns yield additional implications for understanding how religious messages – and other types of metaphysical instruction – work. Instead of viewing religion as a force that constantly exerts behavioral influence, we should study the *work* that churches, parishioners, and other ideological institutions have to do in order to sustain the influence of their world views. The patterns give us insight into why houses of worship expend effort seeking ways to encourage frequent, fervent religious practice (and thus frequent, repeated exposure to their messages), especially in places and times when they are surrounded by countervailing evidence and messages (Iannaccone, 1990).[11] In the current era, such efforts take the form of organizing worship and prayer services throughout the week, and creating television and digital resources that parishioners can rely on for repeated message exposure in between worship service attendance. The short duration of religious messages' effects also gives insight into how religious cultures change and new movements arise. If religions had only static, long-lasting

---

[10] However, as we discuss in the conclusion, in places where strong identity boundaries coincide with the circulation of particular religious messages, we might instead expect backlash against countervailing messages – that is, a reinforcement of the influence of religious teachings to which people were previously exposed, rather than a decay, in response to the countervailing perspectives (Bechtel et al., 2015).

[11] Iannaccone (1990) built on the insights of Adam Smith to argue that places with higher religious competition would be the places with more fervent and demanding faiths.

influences, there would be little room for such change absent major demographic shifts. Instead, the short duration of religious teachings could level the playing field between incumbent and newer faiths.

Notably, these arguments about sermons' political influence through metaphysical instruction and about charging/recharging are not unique to sermons. Other forms of elite communication can provide metaphysical instruction as well. Educational courses, popular media, works of literature, and the like all provide narratives and cognitive understandings of the way the world works and of individuals' place in it (Martin, 2018). People self-select into these forms of communication, too, seeking guidance, and may be more susceptible to their influence if the messages align with their existing views. The influence of such secular communication may also be vulnerable to decay when not reinforced as the messages recede from memory or are confronted with conflicting observations or countervailing arguments in everyday life. In a larger sense, then, we argue that religious teachings can be understood as a case of ideological communication, or of culture, as we discuss later. Many secular ideological forces share a family resemblance with sermons, even though they typically do not deal as directly in discussions of the spiritual and the occult. The sermons we describe "hang together" because of the ways they link the spiritual with the physical, and because they address the extent and nature of God's role in the world. But the contours of our main arguments are more general. Learning about the political influence of religious teachings should help us understand more about the broader subjects of culture and ideology as well.

FOCUSING ON CHRISTIAN SERMONS IN AFRICA

Our contention that sermons can influence political participation through their metaphysical instruction is general. So why focus the empirical analyses in sub-Saharan Africa? To start, most people living in sub-Saharan Africa are highly religious and are frequently exposed to sermon content. In the 2014–2015 Afrobarometer survey wave, only 3 percent of respondents said they have no religion. Fewer than 10 percent reported either not having a religion or never attending religious services. In the 2011–2013 wave, 84.5 percent of all sub-Saharan African respondents said that religion is "very important" in their lives.[12] Most people regularly go to a house of worship.

---

[12] The same could be said of many parts of the world outside of Western Europe and parts of the United States.

Yet we know fairly little about the political consequences of these highly personally salient, regular experiences across the continent. With the exception of rich ethnographic and case study research (e.g., Ellis and Ter Haar, 1998; Gifford, 2009; Longman, 2009; Marshall, 2009; Villalón, 2010) and some recent survey and experimental work (Sperber, 2016; McCauley, 2017), religious content – and even religion more broadly – has not often been a central component of political science research in the region. The absence is particularly striking in studies of Christian-majority countries, which make up more than half of the continent's largest countries.[13] In the few instances when political scientists have paid attention to religion in Africa, they have tended to focus on the organizational resources of churches or on the politicization of group boundaries (Grossman, 2015; Sperber, 2016; McCauley, 2017; McCauley and Posner, 2017), rather than on the content of religious teachings.

Our hope is to bring greater attention to religion and politics in sub-Saharan Africa, and this is one reason we concentrate our empirical analyses in this book there. There are also other reasons for this geographic focus. There is great diversity in official doctrine and theology across prominent religious denominations in Africa, including within Christianity and Islam.[14] Such diversity makes it likely that we would find variation in locally delivered sermon content in order to test whether differences in content have an influence on political participation. It is also the case that reformist strands of Islam and Christianity in sub-Saharan Africa share important sermon themes (as we discuss in the concluding chapter), making it possible to propose broader generalizations across world religions. Empirically, we focus exclusively on Christianity in sub-Saharan Africa in order to expose citizens to different types of religious messages while staying within the bounds of what they might be exposed to in daily life, through self-selection or through incidental exposure. Indeed, social boundaries between Christian denominations are relatively permeable in much of sub-Saharan Africa (Ngong, 2014), which means that there is a high likelihood that individuals would be exposed to various religious

---

[13] At least twenty-five of the region's forty largest countries are majority-Christian today (Johnson and Zerlo, 2015).

[14] Such diversity characterizes anglophone sub-Saharan Africa in particular because of the legacy of colonialism, wherein the French gave greater preference to Catholic missionaries while the British were more permissive to many types of Christian missionaries. We are better able to research the implications of different religious teachings on political behavior specifically in anglophone African countries, where there is a greater diversity of Christian messaging (Sundkler and Steed, 2000).

ideas within Christianity, and to different Christian sermons, even as they self-select into primary houses of worship.[15]

The *content* of religious teaching demands careful consideration in sub-Saharan Africa precisely because sub-Saharan Africa couples a ubiquity of religious belief and practice with a diversity of official doctrine and theology. In this sense, it is emblematic of a global reality: the vast majority of the world population is religious, and yet the set of messages they hear, beliefs they hold, and practices they engage in vary dramatically. Where almost everyone is religious, explanations for variation in political behavior are less likely to come from distinctions between theists and nontheists, between those who pray and attend church and those who do not, or between those who have access to religious communities and those who do not (cf., Scheve and Stasavage, 2006; De La O, and Rodden, 2008; Lewis, MacGregor, and Putnam, 2013; Shariff, Piazza, and Kramer, 2014). With a few notable exceptions,[16] religious groups are also not the primary source of citizens' political identities in many parts of sub-Saharan Africa and the rest of the world, so explanations for variation in political behavior cannot necessarily come from religion as "in-group" and "out-group" cue. Yet the ideational content of the religious world views to which citizens are exposed is a crucial part of religious practice for most people and does vary significantly. With the spread of democratic institutions and the rise of new technologies disseminating religious messages widely, much of the world – including sub-Saharan Africa – has become increasingly religiously diverse. The formal separation of religion and state has divorced religion from the coercive arm of the state in many parts of the world (Warner, 2000). Instances in which religious leaders command their flocks with absolute authority have become relatively rare (Gill, 2008; Trejo, 2009; Toft, Philpott, and Shah, 2011). This separation, and the formal protections for religious freedom that often accompany it, has meant increased religious diversity in many countries and generated variation in the content of religious teachings within the same polity. Most people attend a house of worship, but the content of what they hear there varies significantly. Unbundling religious

---

[15] In some parts of sub-Saharan Africa, boundaries between Islam and Christianity are also fairly permeable (Trinitapoli and Weinreb, 2012).

[16] For instance, there are some highly politicized interreligious conflicts, e.g., between Muslims and Christians in Nigeria or Côte D'Ivoire – see McCauley and Posner (2017); Scacco and Warren (2018) – and some instances in which religious leaders have explicitly politicized ethnic identities (Longman, 2009).

practice and experience to explore differences in religious content offers one avenue into understanding religion's influence over variation in political behavior in sub-Saharan Africa and elsewhere.

Another reason to focus on contemporary Christian sermons in sub-Saharan Africa is that the rise of new Christian denominations, particularly Pentecostalism, in sub-Saharan Africa and throughout the world, is a major sociological phenomenon of interest to the general public and scholars alike (Woodberry, 2006, 2013; Miller and Yamamori, 2007; Gifford, 2009; Marshall, 2009; Comaroff, 2012; Freston, 2013; Boas, 2014; Grossman, 2015; McCauley, 2015a; Smith, 2017). Pentecostalism[17] has garnered attention because of how rapidly it grew across the globe in the four decades following the 1970s, particularly in majority Christian countries of the Global South. By some estimates, these churches globally doubled and tripled their numbers during this time (Miller, 2013). According to Pew (2006), as many as seven in ten Protestants can be classified as Pentecostals or Charismatics in Christian-majority sub-Saharan African countries today.[18] As Woodberry (2008) notes, we still know relatively little about the consequences of populations' increasing exposure to Pentecostal teachings.

In this book, we do not explain the rapid rise, or popularity, of contemporary Pentecostalism; instead, we attempt to shed more light on the *consequences* of its spread. There is already an interesting cross-disciplinary literature asking questions about the drivers of Pentecostalism's recent popularity across regions. That literature suggests that, although Catholic and Mainline Protestants had established advantages in institutionalization and public service delivery, and had developed a resonating message about eternal salvation and caring for others, Pentecostalism has been able to compete by providing a powerful, provocative, and appealing message about the possibility of individual transformation, the attainment of health, well-being, and security in the contemporary world (not just in heaven), and direct access to the Spirit (Martin, 2002; Gifford,

---

[17] As we note again in Chapter 2, we use the term Pentecostal to refer broadly to churches that are Pentecostal, Neo-Pentecostal, Charismatic, or Renewalist (Freston, 2001; Pew, 2006; Ranger, 2008).

[18] The World Christian Database estimates that at least 11–12 percent of the continent's total population is Pentecostal, a share that is increasingly rivaling the 17 percent of the population that is Catholic. Pew also notes that when its 2006 survey was conducted the Assemblies of God (Pentecostal) church had almost as many adherents as the Catholic Church in Zimbabwe and that the Church of Pentecost is the largest church in Ghana.

2009; Miller, 2013).[19] As Cooper (2006) suggests, successful evangelism occurred in many places because it rendered Christianity plausible within the local landscape, making the Holy Spirit accessible in the world. Thus, the very metaphysical ideas we highlight in this book may also help to explain the appeal of Pentecostalism, and Pentecostal pastors may have formulated and spread these ideas in order to grow their flocks.[20]

Yet, this literature on the rise of Pentecostalism, and on religious competition more generally, often assumes, but does not test for, the effects of religious appeals on ordinary adherents. Moreover, even if the *religious* appeal of Pentecostalism seems clear, there remains considerable debate about its *political* consequences. Some scholars of Pentecostalism have argued that Pentecostalism has the potential to generate social movements and political change (Martin, 1990; Patterson and Kuperus, 2016). These scholars point to the empowering aspects of Pentecostalism: that it is antifatalistic and encourages everyone to believe in their own capabilities. Martin (1990) argues that Pentecostalism is cultivating a "vibrant civil society," and Martin (2002) suggests that Evangelicals of the Global South, including sub-Saharan Africa, resemble de Tocqueville's picture of American Christians in the early nineteenth century: voluntarist, independent of the state, and assiduous practitioners of associational life. Patterson and Kuperus (2016) argue that Pentecostal churches are able to generate grass-roots movements where other churches have failed. Ranger (2008) suggests that the "evangelical ethic" in Africa promotes both the spirit of capitalism, through microlevel moral and cultural change, and the spirit of democracy, through faith-based civic engagement in a growing democratic ferment. However, other scholars are skeptical, viewing Pentecostal churches as unlikely to make contributions to movements for social change (Woodberry, 2006, 2013; Miller, 2009; Freston, 2013).

---

[19] More generally, there is an important literature explaining the drivers and exploring some of the consequences of religious competition, particularly in Latin America (Trejo, 2009; Gill, 2004). For example, Trejo (2009) argues that the Catholic Church in Latin America changed its position on supporting the needs of indigenous peoples in part to compete with the growing popularity of Protestantism. In the empirical context we examine, we did not observe as much Catholic or Mainline Protestant adoption of Pentecostal messaging as we thought we would, given Pentecostalism's competitive rise, but Trejo (2009)'s argument suggests that we might observe adaptation and message adoption in the future in the face of persistent religious competition.

[20] Methodologically, we circumvent questions about where these sermons came from and why they are appealing by focusing the book largely on citizen reactions and by leveraging random assignment or by controlling for factors that might predict selection into particular types of sermon content. See Chapters 4 and 5, especially.

These scholars point to the relative paucity of successful Pentecostal parties (Freston, 2013), to Pentecostals' unwillingness to create conflict with civil authorities (Miller, 2009), or to the deference of Pentecostals to "big man" authoritative figures (McCauley, 2013, 2014).[21]

Media coverage of Pentecostals exhibits similar tensions. Some stories tout the mobilizing potential of Pentecostal churches, noting that Pentecostals report feeling highly capable and willing to participate in political life (Washington Times, 2007), that Pentecostal churches are reaching and empowering large numbers of people in marginalized and forgotten areas (Gonzalez, 2007), and that incumbent politicians are watching their numbers closely (Economist, 1999). Other accounts note that Pentecostals nevertheless do not support radical social change (Economist, 2006).

The problem, as Marshall (2009)'s seminal ethnographic study of Pentecostalism in Nigeria points out, is that any argument that sees Pentecostalism, or another variant of Christianity, as strictly pro- or antidemocracy, or pro- or antipolitical participation, misses the complexity of Pentecostal and other Christian teachings. Each variety of Christianity has dualistic potential to contain the seeds of either prodemocratic civic engagement and political participation (Ranger, 2008; Elolia, 2012; Fantini, 2013; Woodberry, 2013; Sperber and Hern, 2018) *or* authoritarian acquiescence and reluctance (Haynes, 1996; Gifford, 1998; Longman, 2009).[22] As discussed in Chapter 3, contemporary Pentecostal teachings contain promises of dramatic material change in this world, and argue that the change can happen for anyone who has the right strength of faith and embodies that faith in action. This element of contemporary Pentecostal teaching may be empowering and perhaps conducive to prodemocratic forms of civic engagement. But Pentecostal teachings also locate the sources of earthly problems in individuals. This element of the messaging may lead listeners to be relatively uncritical of political systems or institutions and instead to seek political change through the internal transformation of citizens and leaders. In other words, the

---

[21] All of these accounts agree that Pentecostalism is no longer an "otherworldly" religion. Before the 1970s and 1980s, there was a view that Pentecostal churches advocated that members keep their hands clean of "dirty politics." All scholars agree that Pentecostal churches have pivoted from that position in more recent decades, but they disagree as to the form of participation encouraged by the churches (Burgess, 2015).

[22] As Haynes (1996) suggests, "Christian religious exposure both draws believers into democratic, open-ended and largely egalitarian religious communities, *and* produces clear distinctions between individuals, resulting in differentiated, hierarchical structures" (215, emphasis added).

teachings may be empowering but lead to action that largely works within existing institutions, rules, and structures. In order to understand the political consequences of contemporary Christian teachings, we need to pay attention to their consequences both for *whether* and for *how* citizens engage in politics.

Fantini (2013)'s case study of Pentecostals in Ethiopia parallels Marshall (2009)'s observations in Nigeria, demonstrating how the laity find an empowering world view in the context of radical insecurity–material, political, ideological, and ontological security linked to neo-liberal globalization. Citizens combine a political imaginary of the public space (related to the 'modern' themes of good governance, leadership, and so on) and the 'force of the invisible' (the power of the spirits, healing, and miracles) to connect a metaphysical understanding of the world to their political orientations within it. In doing so, citizens use religious teachings to cultivate a social imagination and to understand their appropriate role in the political world through both 'modern' and 'tradition' frames (Kalu, 2008; Elolia, 2012; Katongole, 2012). This social imagination may be neither strictly pro- or anti-democracy, pro- or anti-social, but nevertheless it influences how citizens engage in the public sphere.

This book builds on insights from this rich ethnographic work, further develops those insights, and tests them with new, wide ranging data and a mix of methods. We bring together a new collection of sermon observations, a set of expectations about the consequences of these teachings for individual- and group-behavior, and a diverse set of methodological tools for probing those expectations at different levels of analysis and across different contexts. As we show in later chapters (particularly Chapter 6), across a variety of contexts, Christians of all denominations share similar goals: national development, state building, and improving human welfare. Yet the routes to achieving these goals have been different. We do not focus on what gave rise to different religious content, nor do we ask simply whether the consequences of contemporary religious practices are pro or anti-democracy, modern or traditional. Instead, we investigate the mechanisms through which sermons influence people, shaping their political orientations of what is possible, and their conceptions of appropriate political action.

Generally, the findings of this book support the notion that religion *per se* is neither "good" nor "bad" for democracy. We find that one set of sermons we examine emphasizes individual efficacy, energizes citizens to be engaged with their representatives and encourages them to "buy into" political institutions. At the same time, that set of religious teachings depresses citizens' inclinations to assert any institutional critiques of the state – encouraging them instead to focus on self-mastery, individual character, and getting the right people into positions of power. We find that the other set of sermons we examine increases skepticism of political institutions and authority. But that set of teachings also does little to energize listeners as individuals or to ensure their willingness to engage at times within the political system. Each of these sets of sermons enhances some aspects of democratic culture while ignoring or detracting from others. Looking explicitly at lived religious content, and testing for rather than assuming its influence on political behavior, forces us to adopt a more nuanced view of religion's political influence in the world.

DIFFERENCES IN SERMON CONTENT

In an examination of Christian sermons in sub-Saharan African cities (through an empirical strategy we describe in Chapter 3), we found stark thematic differences in metaphysical instruction *between* Pentecostal sermons, on the one hand, and Mainline Protestant and Catholics sermons, on the other, and remarkable consistency in metaphysical instruction *within* those groupings. Pentecostal sermons tended to locate the source of earthly problems primarily inside the individual, whereas Catholic/Mainline sermons tended to locate the source of earthly problems in the relationships between people and in community structures and institutions. Pentecostal sermons asked listeners to transform their mindsets and to embody that transformation in their actions – to live as if the material change had already happened. "It's how you see yourself that matters most," one Pentecostal sermon argued. "You can do without systems. You will rise without systems ... [Act in] faith," another argued.[23] The Catholic and Mainline Protestant sermons were much more focused on factors external to the self. "We have a culture of not trusting one another," argued a Catholic sermon. "Why do powerful people ignore the plight of others?" asked another.

The sermons also differed in their portrayal of the possibilities for creating change in this world. The Pentecostal sermons were consistently optimistic, indeed uplifting, in this regard: they promised imminent material change if people would strengthen their faith, think positively, and

---

[23] In her ethnographic study of Pentecostalism in Nigeria, Marshall (2009) calls this the location of problems in "the work of the self on the self." It entails both a change in thinking and action that reflects (embodies) that way of thinking.

embody that mindset in every action they take: "All things are possible to those who believe ... a faith declaration from one's heart greatly determines the outcome of a person in this life." This finding is in keeping with the characterization of Gifford (2009) and others that Pentecostals in Africa propound a "gospel of success" – both in terms of personal achievement and in terms of national progress. The Mainline and Catholic sermons, on the other hand, promised no high likelihood of an end to earthly problems or material change in this world. "We are limited ... our realizations are few because of our limitedness," one said explicitly. We found the differences in these particular themes to be apparent throughout the year and in both election- and nonelection periods. We made efforts to pay attention to diversity in messaging *within* major church categories but found that these differences in content were largely inter- rather than intradenominational.

Building on these specific instances of variation in sermons' metaphysical instruction, we can think broadly about two dimensions along which sermons could differ more generally: (1) in whether they identify the sources of problems in this world as located in the self or also in factors external to the individual (relationships and structures and institutions), and (2) in whether they portray the probability of enacting change in this world as high or low.

Figure 1.1 provides an illustration of these dimensions. Along the horizontal dimension, sermons can differ in the extent to which they blame the characters and intrinsic motivations of individuals for earthly problems or blame the institutions and extrinsic incentives in which people are embedded. Along the vertical dimension, sermons can differ in the extent to which they describe a high possibility for material improvement on this earth or characterize the possibility of change as quite low. As we discuss in Chapter 3, we would place contemporary Pentecostal sermons in sub-Saharan Africa in the upper-right quadrant, and contemporary Mainline Protestant and Catholic sermons in sub-Saharan Africa in the lower-left quadrant.

It is not difficult to think of examples of religious teachings that might fill in the other quadrants of Figure 1.1. In the upper-left quadrant would be sermons that locate responsibility for earthly problems in relationships between people and in collective institutions and structures but that promise the possibility of change. Liberation theology, associated with black Protestant churches in the United States and with Catholic churches in Latin America in the mid- to late twentieth century (Levine, 1986), fits this description. It located the roots of earthly problems in the systemic

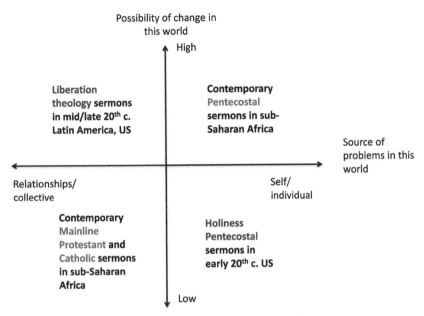

FIGURE I.I Illustration of sermon content dimensions.

treatment of the poor; and yet it offered the possibility of salvation from injustice not just in heaven but on earth, through purposeful action and fellowship.

In the lower-right quadrant are religious teachings that locate responsibility for earthly problems inside individuals while promising little possibility of material change. "Holiness" theology, associated with Pentecostal churches earlier in the twentieth century (e.g., at the turn of the century in the United States), provides an example. The teachings emphasized a focus on purifying individual thoughts and actions – decrying personal impurity as responsible for the ills of the world. And yet the teachings were rather fatalistic in their outlook – promising no material change in this world, only salvation in the next (Gifford, 1991; Marshall, 2009). Similarly, the Amish in the United States view problems and solutions in this world as rooted in individual thought and practice but propagate a "belief in the futility of political action" to create change in this world (Yoder, 2003).

Figure I.I is not an exhaustive representation of the politically relevant ways sermon content can differ. In other contexts, sermons might offer a different configuration of answers to metaphysical questions about the sources of earthly problems or about human agency. They might also do something altogether different: e.g., make explicit endorsements of political candidates or issues, offer explicit selective incentives for political action, portray particular forms of political action explicitly as moral obligations, or play on social identity cleavages (Longman, 2009). Nevertheless, our general approach and specific arguments should offer a framework for how to conceptualize and test sermons' influence on political behavior beyond the empirical context we examine.

CONNECTING SERMON CONTENT TO POLITICAL PARTICIPATION

To conceptualize the influence of the types of sermons in Figure 1.1 on political participation, we have to think not just about the dichotomous difference between political engagement and disengagement but also about different *modes* of political engagement. Discussions of the sources of earthly problems have implications for listeners' views as to what needs to change politically; discussions of possibility and agency have implications for listeners' sense of efficacy – whether they think that their actions can be successful in enacting change (Niemi, Craig, and Mattei, 1991; Valentino et al., 2008; Caprara et al., 2009; Holbein, 2017; Lieberman and Zhou, 2017). The sermons may thus affect what is sought (individual vs. structural transformation) by listeners' political engagement *as well* as whether listeners take political action at all. Figure 1.2 outlines these expectations. Sermons can have this influence without being explicitly political themselves.

By indicating that one should focus on changing personal characteristics, not on changing systemic or structural factors, the Pentecostal sermons we observe lend themselves to focus on changing government personnel and the character of citizens and leaders, rather than on changing institutions and structures. The object of critical attention is the individual and her intrinsic incentives and relationship with God, not the institutions, structures, or set of extrinsic incentives in which she is embedded. Pentecostal sermons may inspire critique of individual leaders, combining the emphasis on leadership with a set of criteria that focus on personal characteristics, such as honesty, integrity, morality, and so on, but leave aside the broader set of conditions and structures that bring people to power.[24] At the same time, in indicating that material change

---

[24] Attributing the world's problems to a lack of strong faith in individuals lends itself, we argue, to a focus on leaders' characters, rather than to a focus on the institutions that brought them to power and constrain them. Further, in much of sub-Saharan Africa and

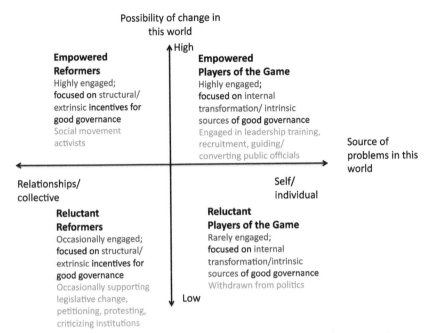

FIGURE 1.2 Connecting sermon content to modes of political participation.

in this world can be achieved by anyone who transforms her mindset and embodies strong faith, Pentecostal sermons increase listeners' sense of self-efficacy, making it more likely that they would enter intimidating arenas of life (including politics) when given the opportunity, even if such action might seem, outside of that world view, to be of little likely consequence (McClendon and Riedl, 2015). The teachings make listeners feel empowered to act boldly – to embody the change they want to see in the world; they also indicate that such change should happen through the betterment of individual characters rather than through reform of political institutions.[25] We thus call those exposed to Pentecostal teachings

in other parts of the world, material and social advancement often happens through access to the state and its resources. Where overlap of social action, economy striving, and political engagement is high, empowering messages of enacting change through self-transformation may find themselves inevitably bundled up with decisions about political action.

25 To be clear, in suggesting a high possibility for change, the Pentecostal teachings do not indicate that such change will be handed down from above without any need for human action. If change happens on earth, it will be through the actions of people who have strong faith and embody that faith, and through divine rewards from those actions.

empowered players (of the game): confident in their own efficacy but inclined to play by the existing rules of the game while seeking change through individuals.

Our arguments here are similar to the observations Marshall (2009) made in her ethnographic study of Pentecostalism in Nigeria, which we referenced earlier. Marshall (2009) draws attention to the contemporary Pentecostal "program of conversion" and to its potential political significance. As she explains, it presents "conversion as a means of creating the ideal citizen, one who will provide a living incarnation of the nomos of an ordered political realm" (211). The Pentecostal project is political insofar as political change, under its lens, centers around conversion, around the bettering of citizens and leaders – their internal lives, characters, and strength of faith. "For Pentecostals," Marshall (2009) writes, "political structures in and of themselves are neither more or less legitimate" (209). The route to political change is through personnel change, not structural change. And that route is direct and readily available. "Conversion promises not only 'everlasting life,'" Marshall (2009) writes, "but also 'life more abundant' in the here and now" (13). Our findings support and extend these observations – that the messages preached in contemporary Pentecostal churches in Africa promise imminent change through personal and personnel transformation and that they can lead individuals to seek personnel change in government.

In contrast, exposure to the Catholic and Mainline sermons, even when not explicitly political, lends itself to a very different mode of political engagement – one that focuses more on the structures and incentives in which people are embedded than simply on the internal lives and characters of individuals. By locating the source of earthly problems in other people, in relationships among people and in community structures, rather than primarily in the self, such sermons are likely to color people's responses to political questions and opportunities for political action by making criticism of factors external to the self (other people, elites, institutions) more salient. At the same time, Catholic and Mainline sermons offer little promise of imminent material change and so do little to boost listeners' sense of self-efficacy, leaving dilemmas of the collective action problem (whether to take on the personal costs of engaging instead of freeriding off of the efforts of others) more salient. We thus call those exposed to the Catholic–Mainline sermons *reluctant reformers* – people with a critical posture toward existing institutions, structures, and systems but who are hesitant to take political action.

We outline these expectations in Figure 1.2. In this book, we do not observe sermons falling on the other diagonal of the two-by-two,[26] but we would expect the political consequences of exposure to the other diagonal in the two-by-two to follow a similar logic. Locating responsibility for earthly problems inside the individual should lower the chance of critical attitudes toward the political system and existing institutions, since any critical energies of listeners should be turned toward seeking the internal transformation of individuals; absent a boosted sense of efficacy to engage in the world, this attention to the self should result in a retreat from politics – the kind of behavior that has been associated with "quietist" religions in the past (Quinley, 1974). We call those exposed to such teachings (e.g., to the Pentecostal teachings of the early twentieth century) *reluctant players of the game.* On the other extreme, in the upper-left quadrant, we would expect those exposed to teachings locating responsibility for earthly problems in relationships and collective structures to be more likely to be critical of the political system and existing institutions, but unlike those exposed to contemporary Catholic and Mainline Protestant teachings in sub-Saharan Africa, the possibility of change through action promised in the teachings they hear should increase a sense of efficacy and ameliorate the collective action problem to a greater degree. We call those exposed to such teachings (e.g., to Liberation theology) *empowered reformers.* For those most willing to take on potentially costly – even deadly – repercussions for political engagement, we suggest that they are oriented by both a belief in the capacity for earthly change, and the source of earthly problems located in relationships and institutions that must be addressed.

Religious teachings can help explain both whether people engage with or disengage from politics and their different *bents* of political engagement. This implication becomes most clear when looking at the lower-left to upper-right diagonal in Figure 1.2, as we do in this book. Popular conceptions of religion's influence on political participation often focus on only the upper-left to lower-right diagonal of this figure – that is, on the difference between messages promoting no political action and those promoting more radical action and social movements. A famous

---

[26] We do not find examples of such messages in the churches we examine, and, for the sake of ethical considerations and to preserve mundane realism, we do not introduce new religious messages into this environment simply to see what their effects might be. See the discussion in Chapter 4.

quote from Martin Luther King Jr.'s writings is often used to illustrate this point: "I prayed out loud that night … And it seemed at that moment that I could hear an inner voice saying to me, 'Martin Luther, stand up for justice, stand up for truth. And lo I will be with you, even to the end of the world'" (cited in Garrow 1986). Judging by this quote, Martin Luther King, Jr., engaged in politics the way he did because his religious understandings gave him both a clear view of the factors responsible for the world's ills and a feeling that God was behind him, enabling material change. Other scholars focus largely on the distinction between preaching that encourages opting out of politics and preaching that gives people a clear sense of what needs to be changed and a sense of efficacy (Quinley, 1974; Harris, 1994).[27] But we need not stop there. Focusing on the lower-left to upper-right diagonal of Figure 1.1 helps illustrate the possible implications of sermon exposure for both people's level and their mode of political participation.

The evidence we present later in the book suggests that individuals are affected by the content of religious messages in the immediate aftermath of hearing them, and the influence of sermons generates divergences in political attitudes and behaviors. But, after only a few days, any divergences in behavior across people exposed to different sermons begins to converge again. We argue that these patterns are consistent with religious messages' influence decaying as listeners come into contact with countervailing messages and countervailing daily experiences. Sermons describing a high possibility of imminent change may be difficult to hold at the forefront of one's mind if one does not encounter positive feedback in daily life. It may be difficult to sustain an expectation of material change if none immediately occurs. Similarly, the messages locating earthly problems in structures and relationships may also be difficult to sustain since it is difficult to "see" the structural and institutional sources of suffering, poverty, and inequality. Scholars of system justification have also found that, psychologically, most people have a hard time maintaining perceptions of the world as systematically unjust – that is, as structurally problematic (Jost et al., 2014). Jost et al. (2017) explain that human beings have existential needs for safety and security and therefore are

---

[27] Harris (1994) points to possible different "modes of political action" that might result from different configurations of belief and practice across black and white Americans, but in the end the study's discussion focuses on the ways in which cognitive and organizational religious resources promote higher levels of political participation for both groups.

epistemologically motivated to maintain a sense of order and predictability in order to function and feel comfortable.[28]

This kind of decay does not undermine the importance of sermons' influence. Their influence can be "recharged" when people are exposed to sermons again on the following Sunday or during midweek services if they attend. Political opportunities (the organization of meetings, the holding of rallies, efforts to recruit candidates or enroll people in leadership institutions) that take place soon after worship services can translate short-term religious influences into concrete political actions. The influence of sermons – even when not explicitly political – on political participation is demonstrable but has a temporal dimension that is worth paying attention to.

SERMONS AS A WAY OF STUDYING RELIGION AND CULTURE IN POLITICAL LIFE

Religion is an instance of culture, and the effects of culture on politics are difficult to study for a variety of reasons. Culture encompasses "the meanings and values which arise amongst distinctive social groups and classes ... and the lived traditions and practices through which those understandings are expressed and in which they are embodied" (Hall, 1980, 63). Scholars often recognize the difficulty of studying cultural influences in the abstract, but in practice, attempts at cultural arguments are sometimes plagued by essentialism, claiming that a particular group of people share a fixed set of consistent, systematic meanings and practices.[29] Cultural arguments can be overly deterministic and tautological, linking a certain outcome to a set of ideas that must accompany it (Martin, 2018).[30] It can be difficult to identify the causal effects of systems of belief and meaning, not least because adherents might select into particular systems of meanings and values to which they are already predisposed.

---

[28] Most people achieve this sense of order and predictability by ignoring or downplaying claims of structural problems and focusing on things they themselves can control (e.g., their own thoughts and actions), especially when they are focused on the daily business of basic survival. It is not implausible that the effects of both types of religious teachings would lessen over time, absent reinforcement.

[29] Despite these challenges, cultural explanations are coming to the fore again, reflecting a general desire to understand cognitive and social processes shaping individual behavior (Collier, 2017; Enke, 2017; Lowes et al., 2017; Paluck and Ricart-Huguet, 2019; Tunón, 2017; Bryan, Choi, and Karlan, 2018; Martin, 2018).

[30] See also Collier (2017) for a review of the difficulties of studying culture as a political variable.

Or everyone in a particular place and time might be embedded in the same system of belief and meaning, such that, without variation, the counterfactual is difficult to assess (Paluck and Ricart-Huguet, 2019).

One solution is to disaggregate cultural systems into component parts.[31] These component parts often do vary, and can sometimes be randomly assigned by nature or the researcher, allowing scholars to overcome concerns about selection bias. Religion is a bundle of things. It is not a singular, transhistorical, transcultural analytical category (Hurd, 2015). Even in its varied forms around the world, religion typically combines many different elements: ideational content, rituals and practices, organizational resources, hierarchies, social networks, social identity categories, social insurance, service delivery, and so on. See Table 1.1. Some religions combine all of these elements; others involve only some. The frequency and degree of exposure to any one of these elements can vary across adherents of any given religious tradition. One Christian might attend a church that is hierarchically organized, while another attends a congregation with flatter authority structures. One Muslim might hear a sermon with explicit political instructions, while another hears a sermon that says nothing about politics. The sermon content a worshipper hears might also vary from week to week, service to service. These empirical realities mean that exposure to individual components of religion is variable and potentially manipulable. For instance, as-if random processes might alter the leadership of a particular house of worship, and thus its governance or service content (Tunón, 2017). Or, as we do in this book, particular components of religion (e.g., its sermons) can be brought into the lab and randomly assigned by researchers without stepping too far outside the bounds of what would happen in the real world.

In this book, we illustrate one way to study the political influence of religion as culture by focusing on sermons. Exposure to sermons is a core part of lay religious practice in many faith traditions. Most obviously, sermons are a core part of religious practice for most Christians, Muslims, and Jews. Sermons are not the only way in which religious teachings are conveyed, even in these faith traditions,[32] but they are a core and

---

[31] See Sen and Wasow (2016) for a similar discussion of disaggregating race and ethnicity to overcome methodological challenges to studying the effects of immutable characteristics.

[32] For instance, religious teachings are also conveyed through scripture, through written addresses from clergy to congregants, and through formal clerical training and instruction.

TABLE I.I *Unbundling religion across political science studies*

Focus	Example Studies	Advantages
Sermon content/teachings	This book: Weber (1934); Toft, Philpott, and Shah (2011)	Highlights a core part of lay religious experience in many faiths that is also easily mutable; connects leaders' actions/ interpretations to lay behavior without assuming lay receptivity; varies in highly religious contexts and where religion is not primary social identity; highlights connection to ideology and media-effects literatures
Social network	Durkheim (1912); Wald, Owen, and Hill (1988); Wittenberg (2006); Djupe and Gilbert (2009); Lewis, MacGregor, and Putnam (2013)	Gives insight into communal dynamics among laity; highlights connection to social organization and social capital literatures
Social identity	Varshney (2003); Wilkinson (2006); Cammett (2014); Ben-Nun Bloom, Arikan, and Courtemanche (2015); Dancygier (2017); Margolis (2017); McCauley (2017); McCauley and Posner (2017)	Gives insight into relations between religious groups; highlights connection to ethnic/identity politics literatures
Interest group	Kalyvas (1996); Warner (2000); Grossman (2015); Grzymala-Busse (2015)	Gives insight into leaders' strategies; highlights connection to issue politics literatures
Firm competing for members	Iannaccone (1990); Gill (2008); Trejo (2009)	Gives insight into elite incentives and strategies; draws attention to competition among religions; highlights connection to political economy literature
Organizing skills	Campbell (2004); Harris (1994); Brady, Verba, and Schlozman (1995); Jones-Correa and Leal (2001)	Offers direct connection between activities in church and in politics; connects to social capital literature
Patronage linkages	McCauley (2013a)	Draws attention to power dynamics within religious institutions; highlights connection to clientelism literatures
Source of social welfare	Cammett and Issar (2010); Jennings (2014); Thachil (2014)	Focuses on core historical function of many religions; highlights connection to redistribution/ welfare state literatures
Elite directives/ mobilization	Brass (1997); Guth et al. (2002); Wilkinson (2006); Glazier (2015)	Offers direct connection between religious communication and political behavior; highlights connection to endorsement/political entrepreneur literatures
Set of practices	Chhibber (2014)	Applies well to religions in which sermons/messages are not a core part; connects directly to behavior; highlights connection to literatures on performance, ritual; focuses on local variation
Set of beliefs	Harris (1994); Scheve and Stasavage (2006); Driskell, Embry, and Lyon (2008); Glazier (2013, 2015)	Can differentiate between religious and non-religious people or among religious people; takes seriously whether people have absorbed religious world views; highlights connection to political values

regular way in which religious teachings and interpretations of doctrine are communicated by religious leaders (clergy) to congregants. Following Laitin (1986) and Wittenberg (2006), we set aside official theological doctrine articulated by the founders of a faith or by the holders of the highest positions within that faith, and focus instead on sermons delivered by clergy and received by ordinary laity at the local level. This focus more aptly captures "the practical religion of the converted" (Laitin, 1986), and also captures an element of religious experience that in fact varies across individual adherents and over time for any given adherent.

Our approach has much in common with a view of culture as "toolkits" – resources that can be cued and used in particular contexts (Swidler, 1986). The nature of culture as variable has been contested. In one view, cultures are seamless and robust. Geertz (1973) called them "webs of significance" – sets of symbols and meanings that are coherent and sticky and that embed individuals within them, shaping their decisions and behavior. People are socialized into a particular way of understanding and interpreting meaning in the world – often as children – and this web of meaning in which they are suspended exerts powerful influence over them across different domains and situations. In contrast, an alternate view sees people holding multiple toolkits in their heads. Swidler (1986) argued that "all people know more culture than they use."[33] In this view, individuals are not socialized into one coherent culture that then holds them within its grasp but are instead exposed to different interpretive maps that they selectively draw on or are moved in and out of by cues in their environment. Similar to this second view, we allow in this book that people may be open to multiple religious (and secular) world views and these different world views can come to the forefront of or recede from their minds, depending on the messages (sermons) to which they have recently been exposed. In pluralistic settings, such as where multiple Christian traditions are practiced side by side, where people are regularly exposed to messages from different religious denominations and traditions, this approach to studying culture seems particularly appropriate – providing a richer description of the environments people actually experience.

---

[33] DiMaggio (1997) points out that this perspective is consistent with research in cognitive psychology, which suggests that people hold many cultural referents and images in their memories, that these referents and images may contradict one another and be called upon separately, and at different times, by different cues in a person's physical and social environment.

An advantage of our approach is that it avoids treating religion and, more broadly, culture, as a singular, transhistorical, transcultural analytic category (cf. Huntington, 1997; Hurd, 2015). The approach allows that the content of religion varies greatly, even within the same time period and place. Rather than assuming, for instance, that Pentecostals throughout the world, and throughout history, share the same world views and engage and have engaged in the same type of political participation, our approach demands that we know something about the particular teachings to which people have been exposed at the local – even individual – level, and how recently they have been exposed. It allows for individuals to participate in more than one religious tradition, and it allows for the possibility of change in individual exposure, views, and behaviors, even within relatively short periods of time.

Although they have not focused on sermons, other researchers have also opened up the bundle of religion in order to examine theoretically relevant parts. Table 1.1 provides some examples. Some authors have focused on religion as social network or social identity, as interest group or firm, as a set of organizational skills imparted on active members, as a set of patron–client relationships, or as a vehicle for the delivery of social services. For instance, in his account of the persistence of right party support in post–communist Hungary, Wittenberg (2006) focuses on local Catholic parishes as places for people to interact socially and thereby to gird their own convictions and resistance to communism. For him, religion provides "focal points for mutual interaction" (237); religion is community and social network. Taking a different approach, Warner (2000) treats the Catholic Church in her study as a type of interest group, one that lobbies for particular protections and issues to find their way into secular law and institutions. In Wilkinson (2006)'s or Dancygier (2017)'s approaches, religion plays a role in political violence or political inclusion insofar as it demarcates boundaries between in- and out-groups.

Some other work has drawn attention to religious communication but focused largely on explicit direction from the pulpit. For instance, Philpott (2007); Toft, Philpott, and Shah (2011); and Glazier (2015) focus on religions' explicit political visions and views about the state – what Toft, Philpott, and Shah (2011) call "political theology." Toft, Philpott, and Shah (2011) argue that what a religion explicitly says about whether religious leaders should hold office, whether religion should be joined with the state, and whether the state should offer freedoms for all religious groups or not is what matters for religion's intersection with politics. Glazier (2015) argues that religious teachings influence political behavior insofar as they connect theology to specific political projects. We share the attention of these studies to differences in the content of religion. But we argue that this content need not be explicitly political in order to have a political influence.

The way other studies have conceptualized religion may explain some of the inattention to it, particularly in political scientists' research on Africa. Consider religion as social identity. Important work on African politics (Posner, 2005; Habyarimana et al., 2009; Lieberman, 2009; Robinson, 2016) scrutinizes the role that social identity (tribal, linguistic, racial, and regional) plays in influencing political behavior. But in many places in sub-Saharan Africa, religious affiliation is not the most salient political identity cleavage (Laitin, 1986), so focusing on group identity attachments as explanations for political behavior tends to sideline religion.[34] Other aspects of religion that social scientists tend to emphasize depend on distinctions between "theists" and "nontheists." For instance, some social scientists have argued that religions generate tight social networks of committed individuals, who can then mobilize each other and provide each other with social insurance (Lewis, MacGregor, and Putnam, 2013), which can generate differences in political participation between people who are religious and those who are not.[35] But such distinctions are less helpful in explaining variation in political behavior where belief in God, high levels of religiosity, and high levels of access to religious networks are central components of life for nearly all citizens.

In fact, in our empirical work, we discovered (often to our surprise) that many aspects of church experience were quite similar across houses of worship, even though sermon content differed starkly. As we detail in Chapter 3, Pentecostal, Mainline Protestant, and Catholic churches organized similar types of small groups within congregations, cast similar roles for religious leaders in interacting with those small groups, asked

---

[34] The exception that supports the rule is that in places where the religious cleavage is highly politicized (e.g., the Christian–Muslim cleavage in Nigeria or Côte D'Ivoire), religion has been a firmer focus of research. See Scacco and Warren (2018) on Nigeria. See McCauley and Posner (2017)'s study of the salience of religious identity in Côte d'Ivoire.

[35] Not all work on religion in American and European politics focuses on differences between religious and nonreligious people. Important work that examines differences across different faiths includes research by Djupe, Gilbert, Calfano, Glazier, Campbell, Barro and others, who, building on traditions in sociology going back to Durkheim (1912) and Weber (1993), examine how both the social structure of churches and differences in their associated belief systems yield differences in political attitudes among religious people.

for similar levels of donations to the church, and differed little in their involvement of laity in social welfare provision, even as their larger social welfare activites differed.[36] Churches of all categories tried to involve their members in weekday prayer and outreach activities and to embed them in tight social networks ("Small Christian Communities," to borrow the Catholic terminology) outside of Sunday worship service. The relationship between these groups and church leaders was consistently nonhierarchical, giving right of organization and initiative to laity rather than clergy. Congregants in all three categories had access to social insurance. Furthermore, as we describe in more detail in Chapter 6, when we looked across time in three countries (Kenya, Uganda, and Zambia), we found that patterns of political engagement across Pentecostals, Mainline Protestants, and Catholics lined up better with the content of their religious teachings than with their extent of social service provision.

Our treatment of religion as repeated exposure, through sermons, to religious teachings is analytically useful where almost everyone is religious, where religious social identities are not highly politically salient, and where other aspects of church experience are quite similar across houses of worship or otherwise do not correlate with patterns of political engagement. In such contexts, whether people believe in the divine, whether they attend places of worship, and whether they have access to religious social networks, small group communities, and social welfare, may not do much work to explain variation in political behavior. Where social identities other than religion are highly politicized, people are unlikely to use religion as a hard distinction between in-groups and out-groups. Nevertheless, there may still be variation in religious teachings. Investigating religion as repeated exposure through sermons to metaphysical instruction thus gives us leverage over individual variation in political behavior in those contexts.

---

[36] The big difference in social welfare provision, as we describe later in the book, is that Pentecostal churches do not do it on as grand a scale as Catholic churches and most Mainline Protestant churches do. Consistent with their sermonic focus on individual transformation, Pentecostal churches routinely offer psychological counseling and seminars, though some are also building schools and running medical camps. Some Catholic and Mainline Protestant churches do little poverty relief, and most do not heavily involve the laity in social welfare provision, but such churches do frequently run hospitals or clinics, schools, nutrition programs, and the like. In Chapter 6, however, we exploit variation in Mainline Protestant and Pentecostal involvement in social welfare provision in order to argue that differences in social welfare provision are not necessary explanations for political engagement.

Indeed, the most fruitful way to disaggregate religion, or culture more generally, might depend on the context. In contexts of lower levels of religiosity (e.g., Western Europe, parts of the United States), the distinction between "theists" and "nontheists" can be useful. In contexts where conversion from one faith to another is unthinkable, barriers between religious groups are high and there is littly fluidity in membership across groups, isolating religion as politicized social identity may be most analytically useful (Varshney, 2003; Wilkinson, 2006).

Furthermore, where multiple aspects of religion vary in a given context, it may be most analytically useful to theorize the *interaction* among components of religion and how that interaction influences political behavior. For instance, one might examine how in-group and out-group boundaries amplify or depress the influence of sermon content on political behavior. This book largely seeks to draw attention to the influence of one component of religion (sermon content), because it is analytically useful, a core part of religious experience, and often overlooked by scholars of politics. But in the conclusion of the book we discuss ways one might investigate the interaction among different components of religion in future research.

THE BOOK'S EMPIRICAL APPROACH

To answer our research questions, we employ a multimethod approach, leveraging different methods in order to examine the observable implications of our argument with varying degrees of internal and external validity. Our aim is "integrative" (Seawright, 2016). That is, we aim to "use each method for what it is especially good at, and to minimize inferential weaknesses [in a given method] by using other methods to test, revise, or justify assumptions" (Seawright, 2016, 9).

For instance, before investigating the effects of exposure to religious teachings on political behavior, we first sought to collect and describe sermon content in our research sites. We wanted to be sure that we understood what clergy–congregant communication across a range of contemporary churches actually looks like, without prejudgment. Therefore, we sampled churches of different denominations and conducted church-level surveys and participant observation in sub-Saharan African cities where a diversity of churches is concentrated. Along with a team of research assistants, we collected texts of Sunday sermons, observed worship services and other church activities, and collected information on congregation characteristics. We compare the churches' social organizations, weekday programming, and social welfare activities but find that churches are fairly similar in many of these respects. We then present results from a combination of computer-assisted text analysis and hand coding of the sermon texts and show that Pentecostal sermons consistently answer metaphysical questions quite differently than Mainline Protestant and Catholic sermons do: Pentecostal sermons locate the source of earthly problems in factors internal to the individual and promise imminent change in this life; Mainline and Catholic sermons locate the source of earthly problems more often in factors external to the individual and promise no imminent change in this life. We describe focus group conversations in which congregants recall and interpret sermons in these ways as well.

Having made descriptive claims about some of the ways in which religious messaging varies in contemporary sub-Saharan Africa, we then use laboratory experiments to test for causal effects of exposure to these differences in content on individual political behavior. The laboratory allows us to randomly assign exposure to sermon content and thus test for effects of exposure on political efficacy and participation while circumventing issues of self-selection into exposure. This experimental part of the research design builds on the descriptive analysis of sermon content by using the real-world sermon content we collected to create realistic treatments. We integrate both behavioral and attitudinal measures of political participation into the experiments in order to measure outcomes of interest at the individual level after randomly assigned exposure. Through these studies, we find that exposure to Pentecostal sermons increases listeners' sense of internal self-efficacy and prompts a willingness to enter into intimidating arenas of life, including politics, in order to offer oneself as a good leader or to request opportunities for leadership development. Further, we find that exposure to Mainline Christian messages increases the incidence of criticizing institutions and the government as a whole, and it also increases citizens' willingness to participate in forms of sanctioning politicians for not acting in citizens' interests–that is, it increasing their inclination to create institutions to constrain politicians' behaviors regardless of their internal characters, particularly among those already familiar with the messages.

We then leverage nationally representative surveys conducted by Afrobarometer and the Pew Forum in many sub-Saharan African countries in order to examine whether individual-level patterns of political orientation and participation outside of the lab and across a wider array of contexts are consistent with our main arguments. The surveys provide a wider array of relevant measures than we used in the lab: e.g., of whether people view the system as unfair, whether they view it as appropriate to criticize political institutions, whether they are inclined to make requests of public officials or to challenge the system through refusal of taxes, and so forth.

The surveys also offer opportunities to examine the duration of the patterns generated by exposure to religious teachings. Because respondents in these surveys were interviewed on different days of the week (and thus at differing intervals of time since Sunday services), we can document how long divergences in political outlooks and activities between Pentecostals and Mainline Protestants/Catholics persist after Sunday. After accounting for observable differences between people who select into these different categories of churches and among people interviewed on different days of the week, we find that the effects of religious teaching exposure on orientations toward political engagement are not long-lasting: a couple of days if not reinforced midweek. We also conducted focus groups with Pentecostal and Catholic congregations at different points in the week in order to explore whether, and for how long, people's own words would reflect the outlook and orientations of the sermons to which they had been exposed. There, too, we find that citizens expressed their views about the political world and their own possibility to implement change in very different ways depending on the proximity of their last church attendance. Those who had recently attended services readily had words in mind that resonated with their approach as reluctant reformers or empowered players, whereas those who had not been to church for nearly a week – on Friday or Saturday evening – expressed less specific views on causal attribution or of their role in politics and more easily felt overwhelmed by the circumstances they were facing.

We also explore evidence of group-level forms of political participation by looking at the historical record across several sub-Saharan African countries, and within countries over time, to further demonstrate the external validity of our arguments across different political contexts. We use a mix of historical case comparisons in Kenya, Uganda, and Zambia, along with a unique newspaper database, to demonstrate that patterns described in previous chapters at the individual level are consistent with group-level patterns outside of surveys and the laboratory. In this way, we provide a rich description of modes of participation by religious actors, as groups, in extremely different political contexts, with different degrees of access to the core resources of the state, and different degrees of political freedom to articulate critiques or run for office. One might suppose that any group-level patterns in forms of participation across denominations are due to variation in the denominations position vis-à-vis the state, or to the organizational features of denominations, rather than to the content of metaphysical ideas that those denominations express. In order to address these possibilities, we maximize the differences across countries as well as within each country's regime and government transitions, to ensure variation in regime type, religious affiliation of the incumbent, and the strategic position of the churches. We also exploit organizational differences (e.g., levels of hierarchy, degree of ties to international church bodies) across Mainline Protestant churches to see whether their modes of public engagement vary with their organizational features or not. In both the newspaper database analysis covering all Anglophone countries over the past decade and in the case study comparisons, we find consistently different patterns of public engagement from Pentecostals, on the one hand, who are engaged in the pursuit of personnel and personal change within government, and from Mainline Protestants and Catholics on the other, who are sporadically, or hesitantly, engaged in the pursuit of structural reform, despite variation in political context and church organization.

This integrative mixed-methods approach yields a combination of evidence, which suggests that the role of metaphysical ideas in general and of sermons in particular helps to account for patterns of political engagement across incredibly different contexts. This research design as a whole yields a picture greater than the sum of its parts, as each of these methods helps us explore some piece of our overall argument. Each data collection strategy also helps to alleviate some of the concerns that might be raised by the weaknesses of the others. We are also able to point to the generalizability of the arguments while being attentive to vast differences and nuance in empirical content and context.

PLAN OF THE BOOK

In the next chapter, we provide background and context for the rest of the book. Chapter 2 briefly describes the religious and political landscape in contemporary sub-Saharan Africa, with a focus on Christian anglophone Africa. It discusses the arrival of missionary churches on the continent during colonialism, their activities after independence and into the contemporary period, as well as the rise of more recent Christian movements. It discusses who tends to belong to Pentecostal, Mainline Protestant, and Catholic churches and the permeability of social boundaries across denominations. It outlines some of the different political contexts in which these churches operate.

Chapter 3 turns to the content of contemporary sermons. The chapter draws on original surveys of Pentecostal, Mainline Protestant, and Catholic churches in important African cities (Nairobi and Johannesburg), as well as on smaller-scale sermon collection in Accra, Lagos, and Lusaka and on sermon notes collected by others in rural Malawi. The chapter demonstrates that, even when the social organization and programming of these churches are similar, as they are, broadly speaking, in Nairobi, their sermons differ. Based on some computer-assisted text analysis as well as hand coding, the chapter outlines thematic differences in sermon content, which we find fall largely across broad church categories – specifically between Pentecostal churches, on the one hand, and Catholic and Mainline Protestant churches on the other – rather than within them. We examine sermons in both election and nonelection periods but find that the sermons are rarely explicitly political. Instead, the sermons regularly discuss deep metaphysical questions: What are the sources of earthly problems (poverty, violence, suffering)? What is the nature of human agency? The sermons' answers provide different metaphysical takes on the world: Pentecostal sermons tend to locate the sources of earthly problems inside individuals (in their characters, intrinsic motivations, strength of faith) and promise material change in this life for those who engage in personal transformation. Mainline Protestant and Catholic sermons tend to locate the sources of earthly problems more often in factors external to the individual (in relationships, culture, institutions) and make no promises of material change in this world. Discussions with focus groups of congregants illustrate that ordinary congregants interpret the sermons in these ways.

Chapter 4 begins to examine the influence of exposure to these sermons on the political attitudes and behavior of ordinary citizens. The chapter presents the results of three laboratory experiments conducted in Nairobi at the Busara Center for Behavioral Economics. In those experiments, Christian participants, of various denominations, were randomly assigned to listen to recordings of different real-world sermons drawn from our descriptive survey of sermons in Chapter 3, or to secular control messages. We then measured participants' psychological states, political views, and political participation. We found that those exposed to a sermonic message typical of a Pentecostal church were more eager to participate in politics, but the focus of their participation was on cultivating leaders' intrinsic incentives to work in citizens' interest. Those exposed to a sermonic message typical of Mainline Protestant and Catholic churches were less eager to participate, but the focus of their participation was more on creating extrinsic incentives for leaders to work in citizens' interests. The effects of exposure were often strongest among those already affiliated with the relevant churches.

In Chapter 5, we investigate whether these individual-level patterns extend outside of the lab, and we also investigate the temporal patterns of sermons' influence. We turn to Afrobarometer and Pew survey data, collected across a range of sub-Saharan African countries, as well as to focus groups conducted with congregants of a Pentecostal church and a Catholic church. These data allow us to see whether the same patterns (Pentecostals' exhibiting high levels of political efficacy, focused on individual rather than structural reform, and Mainline Protestants' and Catholics' exhibiting lower levels of political efficacy but focused on structural rather than individual reform) hold outside of Kenya or, as in the focus groups, when people are allowed to describe their reactions to sermons in their own words and to relate those reactions to social and political life. We staggered the focus groups at different points in the week (just after or almost a week after Sunday sermons) and randomly assigned participants to early or late in the week, and the survey data provide information on the day of the week on which respondents were interviewed, allowing us to explore whether divergences between Pentecostals, on the one hand, and Mainline Protestants and Catholics, on the other hand, vary during the course of the week, in between exposures to Sunday sermons. We find that the lab results extend across countries and find parallels in focus group discussions. We also find that the influence of religious teachings is short-lived but recharged with additional exposure. The starkest differences in political inclinations appear across denominations early on in the week, when the religious world views communicated by sermons are freshest and more amenable to political mobilization. For those who attend church more frequently, differences in political inclinations appear again later in the week, after midweek services.

In Chapter 6, we examine whether *group*-level patterns of political engagement are descriptively consistent with the individual-level findings in previous chapters. Through interviews and primary and secondary sources, we conduct case studies across regimes in Kenya, Uganda, and Zambia. We chose these countries for their variation in the political positions of each denomination vis-à-vis the state, the degree of centralization of the churches in different denominations, and the access of different denominations to international networks and to resources for service provision. We leverage a "most-different" case comparison design to show that, despite variation in political-strategic environments, church organizational features, and church access to international resources, the forms of political engagement by members of Pentecostal and Mainline Protestant/Catholic denominations remain consistent across countries and time periods, with Pentecostals consistently focused on leaders' characters and strength of faith and Mainline Protestants and Catholics consistently focused on institutional critiques and reform. We also collect an original database of newspaper reports of religious actors' political activities throughout anglophone Africa in the last decade and show that the group-level patterns in the case studies appear across a wider set of countries.

We conclude in Chapter 7 with a return to the debates presented at the start of the book. We discuss the implications of our argument and findings for understanding the conditions under which sermons, *and ideological world views more generally*, influence politics. We discuss the political trends portended by our interpretations of Pentecostals and Catholic/Mainline Protestant sermons, describing the likely trends in democracy and governance on the continent they suggest. We also discuss other faith traditions in which one might expect to find similar differences in religious communication content and thus possibly also differences in modes of citizen public engagement. We address questions about generalizability of the book's findings and offer directions for future research on religion as metaphysical instruction, particularly on how exposure to religious teachings might intersect with other aspects of religious practice and organization and on the consequences of those intersections for religious-political influence.

2

Christianity and Politics in Africa

Religious practice is robust and widespread across sub-Saharan Africa and dominated by the practice of various forms of Christianity and Islam. The vast majority of the population in sub-Saharan Africa is highly religious. In the 2011–2013 round of the Afrobarometer, 84.5 percent of all respondents said that religion is "very important" in their lives (Figure 2.1).[1] At the turn of the twentieth century, most people participated in some form of "traditional" religion rather than in "imported" religions (Christianity or Islam). Today, most people identify primarily as either Christian or Muslim. The share of people claiming traditional African religion as their primary religious practice is now quite small, somewhere between 3 and 10 percent (McCauley, 2017, 38), though many Africans who consider themselves Christians or Muslims incorporate some traditional practices into their religious lives (Isichei, 1995; Maluleke, 1997). For instance, in the 2008–2009 Pew survey of religion in African countries, 27 percent of Christians and 30 percent of Muslims surveyed reported believing that sacrifices to spirits or ancestors can protect them from bad things happening. These patterns are one reason to study *lived* religion, as we do in this book. Rather than assume that Christianity is unified and constant across time and space, we make no ex ante assumptions about sermon content but instead seek to describe contemporary sermons in local contexts before examining their consequences.

---

[1] Among the countries surveyed, South Africa exhibits the lowest share of the population reporting that religion is very important, but the percent of the population reporting that religion is very important is still quite high at 68.5 percent.

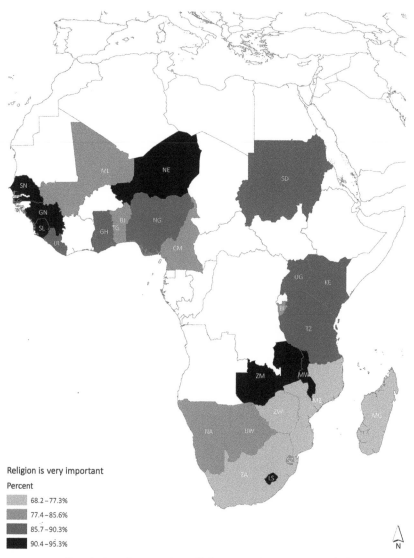

FIGURE 2.1 Population share saying religion "very important" (Afrobarometer).

Christianity has experienced sustained growth in Africa over the last century. According to the World Christian Database, Christianity increased from about 10 million adherents in 1900 to about 144 million by 1970, largely due to colonial-era missions. Today the continent's Christians are estimated at around 400 million, or 46 percent of the total population of the continent, including the predominantly Muslim North

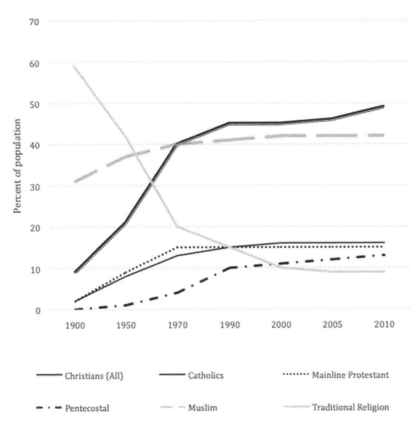

FIGURE 2.2 Religious change over time in sub-Saharan Africa.
Source: World Christian Database.

(Figure 2.2). Catholics grew from 13 percent of Africa's population in 1970 to 17 percent in 2005. Protestants very broadly defined constituted about 15 percent of Africa's population in 1970 but nearly doubled, to 29 percent, by 2005 (Pew, 2006). Pentecostal growth on the continent, often defined as a subset of the overall growth in Protestantism (Mainline and new movements), began in earnest during the second half of the twentieth century, and by 2005 represented 12 percent of Africa's population of 890 million, or about 107 million people (Pew, 2006).

There are several aspects of Christianity in sub-Saharan Africa that are important for understanding the arguments in this book. First, Christianity is widespread and denominationally diverse. The diversity of Christian denominations is particularly evident in urban centers of anglophone African countries, where we center much of our analysis in this book, but is also a feature of lusophone and francophone Africa, and of both rural and urban areas. Second, Mainline Protestants and Catholics arrived earlier on the continent than Pentecostals. This difference in timing has shaped differences in their social service activities and relationships with the state, although there is much within-Pentecostal and within-Catholic/Mainline-Protestant variation across countries in the latter, as we describe in more detail in Chapter 6. The differences in missionaries' arrivals may also explain some of the differences in sermon content across denominations that we describe in Chapter 3. Third, Christian denominations vary organizationally in Africa in ways that parallel their organizational variation elsewhere in the world. For instance, the Catholic Church is more unified and hierarchical than other denominations; Pentecostal churches are, relatively speaking, more decentralized and horizontal. But there is more within-denomination variation in organizational structure (especially among Mainline Protestant and Pentecostal churches) than one might think. We make use of this structural variation in Chapter 6. Fourth, the demographic characteristics of congregants vary considerably across countries. In some places, Pentecostalism has grown particularly among women, the urban, and the young, but this pattern does not hold everywhere. There is no predominant or single pattern of demographic characteristics distinguishing people of different church categories. This point is important because it means that the patterns of religious influence we find (particularly in Chapter 6) are unlikely to be driven solely by demographic differences across denominations. Fifth, the social boundaries between Christian denominations in sub-Saharan African countries are often quite fluid; people often attend services in houses of worship other than their own, or are incidentally exposed to content from denominations other than their own. It is thus substantively important to understand the effects of sermon content not only on people who identify with the houses of worship delivering that content but also on other Christians. The following sections turn to each of these five points.

DENOMINATIONAL DIVERSITY

As we describe in this chapter, conversion to Christianity began with the arrival of European missionaries before and during European colonization of sub-Saharan Africa. French colonial governments typically privileged Catholic missionaries, and British colonies exhibited some affinity for Protestantism (Adogame, Gerloff, and Hock, 2008). At the same time, the counter-currents of French anticlericalism in the metropole bled into colonial administration's secular agenda, giving it a religiously pluralist orientation (Daughton and Daughton, 2008). Likewise, despite British ties to the Anglican church, British colonies exhibited a broader infiltration of Catholic missions and other Protestant denominations, such as Presbyterian, Lutheran, Adventist, Baptist, Calvinist, and Methodist (Kiwanuka, 1970; Sundkler and Steed, 2000). The result is interdenominational diversity across much of Christian sub-Sahara Africa. The rise of Pentecostalism in the latter half of the twentieth century has added to this diversity.

Today, calculations of denominational fractionalization in each country demonstrate Christianity's diversity on the continent. Figure 2.3

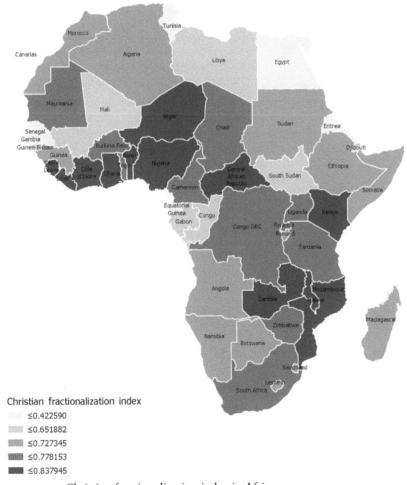

Christian fractionalization index

≤0.422590
≤0.651882
≤0.727345
≤0.778153
≤0.837945

FIGURE 2.3 Christian fractionalization index in Africa.
Data source: World Christian Database.

shades each country by its degree of denominational fractionalization among Christians, including Catholics, Evangelicals, African Independent Churches, Orthodox, Mainline Protestants, and Charismatics as subgroups.[2] Fractionalization scores represent the probability that two Christians randomly drawn from the same country population would belong to different denominations. A fractionalization score of 1 would mean that each Christian in that country belongs to a different denomination. A fractionalization score of 0 would mean that all Christians in that country belong to the same denomination. In countries at the high end of intra-Christian fractionalization (Nigeria, Ghana, Kenya, and Zambia), the Christian fractionalization score is about 0.83. The lowest levels of Christian fractionalization occur in North Africa, where Christianity is a minority religion, and Christian enclaves are more likely to be homogeneous, such as among Coptic Christians in Egypt. This pluralistic environment provides a useful context to investigate the influence of sermons on political participation. Denominational diversity likely means diversity in sermon content, allowing us to examine the consequences of exposure to different sermons on political behavior in realistic ways. We describe that diversity in sermon content in the next chapter.

TIMING OF ARRIVAL

Christianity spread most intensely in sub-Saharan Africa in the nineteenth and twentieth centuries, led by European Catholic and Protestant missions. Before the sixteenth century, prominent Christian intellectuals emerged in parts of North Africa, but Christianity reached relatively little of sub-Saharan Africa. During the sixteenth to eighteenth centuries, Portuguese slave traders and missionaries brought Catholicism to a few sub-Saharan African kingdoms. Christian court civilizations were established in Kongo Kingdom, and in Warri in the western Niger delta (Isichei, 1995). Then, in the late eighteenth century, Mainline Protestant missionary societies started to arrive on the continent, and in the nineteenth century both Catholic and Mainline Protestant missionaries spread throughout the continent. Major conversion began in the twentieth century, largely through Catholic and Mainline Protestant mission schools that drew pupils with the promise of economic mobility through education (Wantchekon, Klašnja, and Novta, 2014).

---

[2] These calculations underrepresent the full degree of fractionalization, because they omit a full disaggregation of Mainline Protestantism: Anglicans, Methodists, Baptists, Presbyterians, Adventists, Lutherans, Calvinists, and so on.

By the early 1900s, such Catholic and Mainline Protestant mission churches were widespread. This conversion period meant a significant decline in primary identification with traditional African religions (Figure 2.2). However, new religious organizations also emerged in response to the mission churches, ensuring some degree of syncretism. Among these new religious organization were the African Independent Churches (AICs): versions of mission churches established and run by Africans. Also known as African Indigenous Churches, AICs exist in every country but are most prevalent in western and southern Africa. The churches are not a distinct denomination but are instead found within the Anglican, Catholic, Orthodox, Pentecostal, and Methodist traditions. The AICs all place emphasis on including African cultural norms into their modes of worship, theology, and practice, to varying degrees, and are considered syncretic in that respect.[3] In a sense, the African Independent Churches continued the cycles of earlier modes of Christian inculturation, with each phase "moving churches forward in a new direction but displaying some continuity with the traditional past, embedding African Christianity into the deep structure of all African traditional religions" (Meyer, 2004; Kalu, 2013). A certain degree of syncretism also ended up characterizing white-founded mission churches. Although these missions were nominally linked to global denominations, in practice the mission outstations in rural areas were largely independent and autonomous (Isichei, 1995, 238). A central mission would typically be surrounded by a vast network of outstations, run by African teacher catechists and occasionally visited by the expatriate missionary or African priest. (This pattern still characterizes many Catholic parishes and Mainline Protestant congregations.) From the 1920s, white missionaries and upwardly mobile African clergy were primarily concerned with the administration of church schools or hospitals, and had little contact with their flock, leaving the pastoral care to the catechist (Isichei, 1995). The sheer number of African Christians also ensured some degree of autonomy for local churches, as there were never sufficient expatriate missionaries to cover all teachings and

---

3 Educated laity and catechist preachers who were disgruntled with the lack of leadership opportunities within the mission church often formed the AICs. Many independent churches were founded by Catholics. Many local laity were eager to join, if they had been expelled from the mission churches for continuing to engage in traditional practices. Isichei (1995) recounts a village headman in 1929 who said, "I am a Christian, but I am not a church member." Like many others, he had been suspended for beer-drinking and polygamy. Would-be Christians waited years for baptism. To people in these categories, the new churches offered immediate baptism and great attraction.

activities. Furthermore, following independence, mission churches also largely transitioned to African leadership. Although the number of white missionaries had continued to increase throughout the 1950s, church leadership positions were rapidly shifted to locals upon independence. Few mission church leaders had advocated sincerely for the end of colonialism or really wanted independence to come (Richard, 1987), and they left in large numbers once it did. (Note, however, that, by the early 1990s still some thirty thousand to forty thousand Catholic and Mainline Protestant missionaries continued to work throughout the subcontinent.)

Neo-Pentecostal, Charismatic, and Renewalist churches, which we term together "Pentecostal,"[4] started to arrive in the midst of this postindependence decline in Mainline Protestant and Catholic European missionaries. Pentecostalism originated with a revival meeting (the Azusa Street Revival) in Los Angeles in the early twentieth century, beginning a new Christian movement that emphasized the work of the Holy Spirit, including in healing and in moving people to speak in tongues. In the second half of the twentieth century, Pentecostalism spread throughout the globe, including to sub-Saharan Africa. From Brazil to Nepal, from the United States to Cambodia, membership in Pentecostal churches grew rapidly especially from the 1970s into the 2010s. In sub-Saharan Africa, Pentecostalism has seen growth in western, central, eastern, and southern Africa. At least 12 percent of Africa's total population now belongs to a Pentecostal church (Miller, 2013),[5] and in many majority-Christians countries, members of so-called mission churches (Catholic and Mainline Protestant) now comprise less than half of the population, with a significant share identifying instead with "independent" (often Pentecostal, Charismatic, and Renewalist) churches (Figure 2.4).[6] Although Pentecostalism began in the United States,

---

[4] Following the Pew 2006 survey, we use the term Pentecostal in the book to refer broadly to churches that are Pentecostal, Neo-Pentecostal, Charismatic, or Renewalist (Freston, 2001; Ranger, 2008; Grossman, 2015).

[5] Growth was particularly remarkable in the 1980s. In 1977, for example, Kenya had 210 Pentecostal churches established, and only seven years later, that number had risen to over 300. For a population of 20 million, that number compared favorably to the 700 denominations in the United States with a population of 200 million (Isichei, 1995).

[6] Unfortunately, the World Christian Database does not consistently distinguish between "independents" and "Pentecostals," nor does it always distinguish between Mainline Protestants and Pentecostals, who may also report being Protestant even though they do not identify primarily with a Mainline Protestant/mission church. Figure 2.4 may therefore underreport the share of the population of these countries who are Pentecostal,

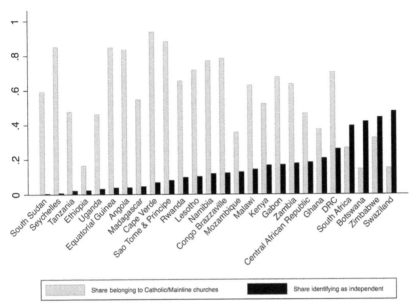

FIGURE 2.4 Share of population in Christian-majority countries belonging to different types of churches.
Source: World Christian Database 2015.

many present-day Pentecostal churches in sub-Saharan Africa were indigenously founded. African Pentecostal churches also "plant" (found) churches abroad, including in the United States, Europe, and Latin America, for the purposes of evangelization.

The difference in timing of arrival of these denominations – with Catholicism and Mainline Protestantism arriving earlier, and Pentecostalism arriving later – likely shaped the denominations' approaches to service delivery and possibly also their differences in sermon content. Colonial governments had little interest in investing in education and health care for Africans and either delegated (and subsidized) such activities to Catholic and Mainline Protestant missionaries or did not stand in the way of their providing such services. As a result, Catholic and Mainline Protestant missions came early on to be heavily invested in large-scale social welfare provision. In the postindependence period, Catholic and Mainline Protestant leaders clashed with new leaders

to the extent that some Pentecostals may here be counted under the general heading of "Protestant," which we group together with Catholics in the gray bars.

who nationalized, or attempted to nationalize, mission schools and hospitals (Sabar-Friedman, 1997), but for the most part Catholic and Mainline Protestant churches continue to play a significant role in social welfare provision through parochial schools and hospitals, as they do in many parts of the world. Pentecostal churches arrived later, after mainline churches had already monopolized these forms of social welfare provision (Seay, 2013). These newly arrived churches typically did not have established resources (monetary or organizational) to compete with the mainline churches on this front. So their approach to poverty alleviation has been somewhat different: typically focused more on financial and psychological counseling, rather than on large-scale social welfare provision. This is not to say that Pentecostal churches engage in *no* social welfare provision. In the next chapter, we document examples of Pentecostal churches' running nutritional, medical, and educational programs, or caring for orphans. Yet, relatively speaking, the denominations that arrived earlier are more heavily engaged in providing material handouts to the poor, and the denominations that arrived later are less engaged in those activities and more engaged in counseling.

In this book, we do not seek to explain the differences in sermon content we observe. Instead, we use methods (especially in Chapters 4 and 5) that allow us to focus on the *effects* of these sermons on citizen participation, whatever the factors driving the differences in content. However, it is worth noting that there are parallels between the denominations' approaches to service delivery, which may have been shaped by the timing of their arrival on the continent, and the themes that appear in their sermon content. For Pentecostals, possibilities for change lie within the individual. The Pentecostal sermons communicate that changes in faith and mindset can bring about material change in one's own life and in society at large. This theme is in keeping with the Pentecostal churches' focus on individual counseling as an approach to poverty alleviation. In contrast, the mainline churches (Catholic and Mainline Protestant) go beyond individual counseling in their approach to service delivery, and in their sermons, they draw attention not just to factors internal to the individual in accounting for poverty but also draw attention to larger, more systemic explanations. Although these larger, systemic causes of poverty are difficult to change, the sermons communicate that they must be tackled in the hope of eternal salvation (Shorter, 1985, 169–170). We further describe the sermons' metaphysical ideas about causal attribution and possibilities for change in the next chapter.

ORGANIZATIONAL FEATURES OF CHRISTIAN
CHURCHES IN AFRICA

In sub-Saharan Africa and around the world, the Catholic Church exhibits the greatest degree of centralized control and hierarchy among Christian denominations. Catholic leadership training, selection, and placement are standardized and centrally controlled; Catholic parishes around the world are governed by a set hierarchy, with the Vatican at the top, followed by regional cardinals, national or district-level archbishops, bishops, and then priests, deacons, and cathecists at the parish level. The liturgical calendar dictates scriptural readings to Catholic parishes around the world each week, providing priests and their staff with guidance on topic and approach, though sermons (homilies) are ultimately composed by the local clergy. The Catholic authority structure includes an administrative component that provides guidance about concrete activities such as foreign and home missions, produces Sunday school and other educational content, publishes religious tracts, administers pension funds, and helps to finance the building and other congregational projects; and a religious component oriented around legitimating the leader's and congregation's spiritual authority (Chaves, 1993). This leadership and authority structure guides the practice of African Catholicism in many respects, though it does not necessarily standardize all communication. Gifford (2015), for instance, argues that African Catholic theology offers little guidance on how to respond to political events, and that local religious leaders have taken the initiative to offer critiques of the state at key moments, as we discuss in greater detail in Chapter 6. Nevertheless, although local priests compose their sermons and take initiatives that deviate from or are not dictated by the Church center, the center retains the capacity to shuffle assignments and promote or punish local clergy.

Mainline Protestants, on the other hand, exhibit a vast array of organizational structures. For instance, the Anglican Church is less centralized than the Catholic Church but more centralized than other Protestant churches. Anglicans do not have an infallible central authority (such as the Pope), and the Anglican global communion does not have a governing structure that exercises absolute power over other Anglican parishes. Instead, the Anglican communion serves a supporting and organizational role, and offers a Consultative Council to provide guided recommendations. Each church is then free to adopt those recommendations or to make its own decisions. (And indeed, deep ideological schisms between Anglican churches in the West, on the one hand, and African Anglican churches, on the other, divide these member churches on many agenda items, such as same-sex marriage.) Selection of Anglican clergy occurs at the regional rather than central level, involving training by the diocesan bishop and screening by a regional committee.[7] Relatedly, there is no centralized institutional guidance for sermon content, but the Anglican churches do follow the liturgical calendar, as Catholic parishes do. Also close to this more centralized end of the spectrum, Adventists have a degree of central organization and a well-articulated hierarchy, wherein local churches send elected representatives to a local conference (field/mission), which then aggregates into a union conference, and ultimately into the General Conference, where all geographical divisions are represented. But these bodies are elected, aggregated from a single level of ordained clergy, and governed by the principle that "no man should be governed by the judgment of another."[8] In contrast, Lutherans, Presbyterians, and Calvinists exhibit middling levels of centralization and hierarchy. Lutherans, for instance, take part in the centralized governing global Assembly of the Lutheran World Federation but are not bound by its decisions. Instead, Lutheran churches are free to be pragmatic in their internal organization, and the international body encourages local churches to adopt forms that suit their particular historical and cultural circumstances.[9] Their leadership structure allows a combination of ordained ministers and lay leadership positions (such as "elder") to be charged with the institutional leadership of the church. Last, Baptists are among the least centralized of Mainline Protestant denominations. They are organized through competing fellowships, recognize equal participation and status of all members, and reject any hierarchy of bishops or priests.[10] Baptist congregations exhibit a great degree of variation in theology and structure, differing widely from one another in what they believe and how they worship, and in their understanding of what is important in discipleship (Shurden, 2018). The prevalence of different Mainline Protestant denominations varies greatly across sub-Saharan African countries – a pattern that we exploit in Chapter 6 to rule out the possibility that group-level differences in

---

[7] See information about the Anglican Communion here: www.anglicancommunion.org/structures.aspx.

[8] See information about the Adventist global ministry here: www.adventist.org/en/world-church/general-conference/.

[9] For information about the Lutheran Federation, see www.lutheranworld.org/content/structure.

[10] BBC Introduction to Baptist churches: www.bbc.co.uk/religion/religions/christianity/subdivisions/baptist_1.shtml.

political participation between Pentecostals and Mainline Protestants are due simply to differences in organizational structure.

Pentecostal churches are on the decentralized end of the organizational spectrum. The churches are often autonomous with no formal regional or global affiliation. There are low barriers to entry, and new churches arise without the sanction of a higher authority or organization. There are some federations (e.g., the Pentecostal Assemblies of God) that provide an overarching structure and an affiliation with a global communal body. Some Pentecostal federations (e.g., the Deliverance Church of Kenya) are purely domestic. Pentecostal churches, like Baptist churches, have an explicit evangelizing mission and often seek to grow through "planting" churches in other locations and countries, but, relative to the Catholic Church and to some Mainline Protestant churches, Pentecostal churches lack the level of centralized and standardized religious training and selection procedures for clergy, and also lack standardized requirements for starting a congregation that other categories of churches exhibit (Kalu, 2008; Bongmba, 2012; Burgess, 2015). Pentecostal churches as a category do not have formal mechanisms for coordinating messages, nor do they typically follow a formal liturgical calendar the way Catholic and Anglican churches do. However, there are online repositories of sermons from US Pentecostal preachers[11] and widely shared theological texts that pastors around the world may draw upon when composing sermons. Indeed, as we describe in the next chapter, there seem to be significant similarities among Pentecostal churches on the main metaphysical themes expressed in sermons, despite the churches' overall level of decentralization.

DEMOGRAPHIC CHARACTERISTICS OF THE LAITY

Who are the members of these different denominations? The perception in much existing literature is that Pentecostalism is largely an urban phenomenon that has drawn the poor, the young, and women away from Mainline Protestant and Catholic churches. However, using rounds 5 and 6 of the Afrobarometer and a 2008–2009 Pew survey of nineteen African countries, we find that the types of people who identify with Pentecostalism rather than as Mainline Protestant or Catholic vary quite a bit across countries within sub-Saharan Africa. There is no one demographic pattern. It is not always the case that Pentecostals are typically urban, young,

---

[11] See, e.g., www.sermoncentral.com and www.jimfeeney.org/morebibleteachings.html.

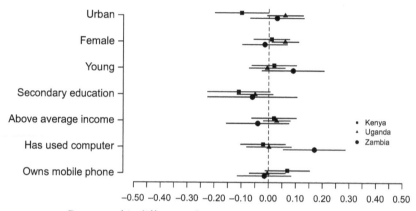

FIGURE 2.5 Demographic differences between Pentecostals and Catholics in
Kenya, Uganda, and Zambia.
Source: Pew 2008–2009 Survey.

poor, and female, while Mainline Protestants and Catholics are rural,
older, wealthier, and male. Instead, the profile of "typical" Pentecostals
varies across countries, and the features that differentiate Pentecostals
from more mainstream denominations also differ across countries.

Figure 2.5 compares attributes of Pentecostals to those of Catholics
in three countries, Kenya, Uganda, and Zambia, using responses from
the Pew 2008–2009 survey. Point estimates to the left of the dashed
line indicate that Pentecostal respondents were less likely than Catholic
respondents to exhibit that attribute. Point estimates to the right of the
dashed line indicate that Pentecostal respondents were more likely than
Catholic respondents to exhibit that attribute. Bars around the point estimates show 90 percent confidence intervals. We assess these three country
samples (squares point estimates are estimates from the Kenyan sample,
triangles from the Ugandan sample, and circles from Zambian sample)
in order to preview our historical examinations of these same countries
in Chapter 6.

There is no one pattern. In Kenya, Pentecostals are indeed less educated
than Catholics, but they are more likely to live in rural rather than urban
areas and more likely to own a mobile phone but no more likely to
be women or young. In Uganda, Pentecostals are indeed more likely
to be women, but they are no younger than Catholics on average, nor
are they on average worse off (less educated, less often employed) than
Catholics or more likely to live in urban areas. The elite in Uganda are just
as likely to be Pentecostals than the poor, which accords with the fact that

President Museveni's daughter runs her own Pentecostal church that caters to many elite politicians and businesspeople. In Zambia, Pentecostals are indeed younger on average than Catholics, but, if anything, they are better off economically than Catholics (more likely to have used a computer, to be employed), and they are no more likely to be women or to live in urban areas. The country-specific patterns hold for the most part in the two Afrobarometer rounds as well.

Table 2.1 summarizes characteristics of the average respondent from each denomination in different countries covered in the Pew survey. The profiles of typical congregants vary quite a bit across countries. Only in Uganda, Rwanda, and South Africa are Pentecostals systematically more likely than Mainline Protestants and Catholics to be female. Only in Ghana and Zambia are Pentecostals younger on average than both Mainline Protestants and Catholics. In the Democratic Republic of the Congo, the average Pentecostal is younger than the average Mainline Protestant but not distinguishable from the average Catholic in this regard. Only in Cameroon and Uganda is the average Pentecostal an urban resident whereas the average Mainline Protestant and Catholic is a rural resident. The patterns of wealth and education are also quite varied. In Botswana, the average Pentecostal *is* poorer than the average Mainline Pentecostal and Catholic, but the average member of all three denominations is female, urban, and young. Pentecostals do not stand out in this regard. In Mozambique, the average Pentecostal and Mainline Protestant both have *higher* levels of education than the typical Catholic. In Nigeria, the average Pentecostal is younger than the average Mainline Protestant and Catholic but also on average *richer* than the average Mainline Protestant and Catholic.

In broad strokes, these survey data highlight that, although when taking all countries together, Pentecostalism may largely be drawing poorer, urban, younger, and female congregants from the older, more mainstream denominations, these characteristics do not typify the average Pentecostal congregant or distinguish her from the average Mainline Protestant or Catholic in all countries. In Kenya, from where we draw our experimental data in a later chapter, there are very few observable characteristics that statistically distinguish Pentecostals from Mainline Protestants and Catholics on average.

In other words, despite the contention that Pentecostalism is drawing support particularly from the poor, urban, young, and marginalized, the empirical pattern is mixed and varies by context. To the extent that we find that modes of political engagement consistently differ across

TABLE 2.1 *Characteristics of an average Pentecostal, Mainline Protestant, and Catholic across countries (Pew 2008–2009).*

	Pentecostal	Mainline Protestant	Catholic	Significant differences
Botswana	Female, urban, 18–29 years old, some secondary school, average income, uses a computer, owns a mobile phone	Female, urban, 18–29 years old, some secondary school, (just) above average income, uses a computer, owns a mobile phone	Female, urban, 18–29 years old, some secondary school, above average income, uses a computer, owns a mobile phone	Pentecostals are less likely to be above average income than Mainline Protestants and Catholics.
Cameroon	Female, urban, 18–29 years old, some secondary school, below average income, does not use a computer, owns a mobile phone	Female, rural, 18–29 years old, primary/some secondary school, below average income, does not use a computer, owns a mobile phone	Female, rural, 18–29 years old, some secondary school, below average income, does not use a computer, owns a mobile phone	Pentecostals are more likely to be urban and less likely to use a computer than Mainline Protestants and Catholics.
DRC	Female, urban, 18–29 years old, primary/some secondary school, below average income, does not use a computer, owns a mobile phone	Male, urban, 30–39 years old, primary/some secondary school, below average income, does not use a computer, uses a computer, owns a mobile phone	Male, urban, 18–29 years old, primary/some secondary school, below average income, does not use a computer, does not own a mobile phone	Mainline Protestants are older than Pentecostals and Catholics. Pentecostals are somewhat less likely to use a computer than Mainline Protestants and Catholics.
Ghana	Female, urban, 18–29 years old, primary/some secondary school, below average income, does not use a computer, owns a mobile phone	Male, urban, 18–29 years old, primary/some secondary school, above average income, does not use a computer, uses a computer, owns a mobile phone	Female, rural, 30–39 years old, primary/some secondary school, below average income, does not use a computer, uses a computer, owns a mobile phone	Pentecostals and Catholics are more likely to be female than Mainline Protestants; Pentecostals and Mainline Protestants tend to be younger and more urban than Catholics.
Kenya	Male, rural, primary/ some secondary school, 30–39 years old, above average income, does not use a computer, owns mobile phone	Male, rural, 18–29 years old, some secondary school, above average income, does not use a computer, owns a mobile phone	Male, rural, 18–29 years old, some secondary school, above average income, does not use a computer, owns a mobile phone	Pentecostals are somewhat more likely to own a mobile phone and somewhat less like to have some secondary education.
Liberia	Female, urban, 18–29 years old, primary/some secondary school, below average income, does not use a computer, owns a mobile phone	Female, urban, 18–29 years old, primary/some secondary school, below average income, does not use a computer, owns a mobile phone	Female, urban, 18–29 years old, primary/some secondary school, below average income, does not use a computer, does not own a mobile phone	Pentecostals are somewhat less likely to have some secondary education and less likely to use a computer than Mainline Pentecostals and Catholics.
Mozambique	Female, rural, 18–29 years old, some secondary school, below average income, does not own a computer, owns a mobile phone	Female, rural, 18–29 years old, some secondary school, below average income, does not own a computer, does not own a mobile phone	Female, rural, primary/some secondary school, below average income, does not use a computer, owns a mobile phone	Mainline Protestants and Pentecostals are more likely to have some secondary education than Catholics.
Nigeria	Female, rural, 18–29 years old, some secondary school, above average income, does not use a computer, owns a mobile phone	Female, rural, 30–39 years old, some secondary school, below average income, does not use a computer, owns a mobile phone	Female, rural, 30–39 years old, some secondary school, below average income, does not use a computer, owns a mobile phone	Pentecostals are younger and more likely to have above average income than Mainline Protestants and Catholics.
South Africa	Female, urban, 30–39 years old, primary/some secondary school, below average income, does not use a computer, owns a mobile phone	Male, urban, 20–29 years old, secondary education, average income, does not use a computer, owns a mobile phone	Male, urban, 30–39 years old, secondary education, average income, does not use a computer, owns a mobile phone	Pentecostals are more likely to be female and less likely to have some secondary education than Mainline Protestants and Catholics.

denominations in many of these different countries, it is unlikely to be driven by the particular, observable characteristics of congregants in those denominations. Distinct Pentecostal modes of engagement are not due simply to the average Pentecostal's being younger, poorer, more urban, and female.

SOCIAL FLUIDITY ACROSS RELIGIOUS BOUNDARIES

In many sub-Saharan African countries, there is a high degree of social fluidity across denominations, meaning that individuals are relatively free to participate in multiple religious traditions and congregations over the course of their lifetimes, or even in the course of their day-to-day lives. As McCauley (2017) puts it when writing about Christianity and Islam, "Religion in Africa is a voluntary, not purely ascriptive, identity ... [And] changing from one confessional religion to another in Africa can be done with relative facility, owing to the fact that conversion is in many instances achieved on no more than personal profession and minimal doctrinal education (Rambo, 1993)" (34–35). Conversion across major faith traditions like Christianity and Islam is not unheard of (Gifford, 2004). In ethnographic studies from Nigeria to Malawi , scholars have documented examples of conversion from Christianity to Islam– and sometimes back again – over the course of a citizen's life, often in times of marriage, and in the event of a spouse's death (Marshall, 2009; Trinitapoli and Weinreb, 2012). Conversion is more frequent, and even common, across denominations within Christianity (Ngong, 2014; McCauley, 2017). One empirical observation of a Pentecostal South African church demonstrated a shockingly high churn rate: over a three-year period, a full 80 percent of the congregation left and was replaced by new members (Van Wyk, 2014). As McCauley (2017) notes, "This process of religious 'churning' (Putnam and Campbell, 2010) is not unique to Africa but suggestive of the general nature of membership in religious groups" in many parts of the world (35).

Short of conversion, many Christians attend services from time to time in other denominations of Christianity than the one with which they are primarily affiliated. Doing so does not generally come with high social costs. Congregants in Kenya explained to us that they often attend other churches with family members or friends. A given person may attend a Pentecostal service one Sunday and a Catholic service the next Sunday. This crossover attendance is common in midweek bible study and youth groups; it can also happen when urban residents return to rural areas and attend their family's church, which may be of a different denomination. In Sierra Leone, it is not uncommon for people to attend both church and mosque and to celebrate holidays of both religions (State, 2015).

Incidental exposure to religious messaging from other faiths and denominations is typical outside of church as well: e.g., on the radio, the television, billboards, and other public spaces. Long-distance buses leaving Nigeria for neighboring countries often receive a sermon before departure. City buses in places such as Lagos, Nairobi, and Accra tune into the local religious radio station, or witness street preachers boarding them to deliver sermons to passengers during the ride. Local restaurants, bars, and other public spaces show television programs that feature sermons. Religious messages are part of the "public culture" in sub-Saharan Africa (Englund, 2011), and that message content is quite varied.

All of this means that it is not unusual for highly religious people in sub-Saharan Africa to be exposed to sermons other than those espoused in their primary house of worship. Thus, most people may be somewhat open to the messages communicated by denominations other than their own, or at least open to messages from *within* their larger faith tradition. Where in-group/out-group cleavages between faith traditions or denominations have become socially and politically salient, people may not be so open. Under such circumstances, people may perceive social costs to adopting ideas from other traditions and denominations. For instance, long-standing divisions between Christians and Muslims in Nigeria may depress the possibility that Christians would be open to the world views communicated in Friday sermons, and that Muslims would be open to ideas communicated in Sunday sermons. In places such as Cote D'Ivoire and the Central African Republic, Christian–Muslim conflict and violence have similarly hardened interreligious boundaries. But in places where religious content does not demarcate rigid political identity boundaries, listeners are likely to be relatively open, and through myriad points of dissemination, they are likely to be exposed frequently to teachings from denominations other than their own. It is in this context that we explore the consequences of exposure to sermon content on citizens' political behavior.

THE POLITICAL LANDSCAPE

Five key themes, very broadly speaking, characterize contemporary African politics in ways that are likely consequential for understanding the impact of religious messages on forms of political participation that we explore in the rest of the book. First, because of the legacies of colonialism, churches typically play a relatively significant and fairly autonomous role in public life (Young, 1994; Englebert, 2002). Colonial states relied on mission churches to provide public services and relieve colonial governments of this burden. In this way, the state was dependent upon missionaries and their priorities, and had to provide them a significant degree of autonomy of action in return. Upon independence, some national elites tried to wrest control over the education and health sectors from religious authorities, but the infrastructure and administration the mission churches had already established remained a compelling substitute for the nascent postcolonial state. And many states retained the assistance of mainline churches in service provision over the subsequent decades. State retrenchment following neoliberal reform in the 1980s further weakened the state's role in service provision in most countries (Callaghy, 1987) and amplified religious organizations' role in providing an alternative source of poverty alleviation (Bassett, 2008; Botha and Maruping, 2013). There is still significant variation across countries, and within any given country over time, as to which denominations have been closest to the state – a pattern we exploit in Chapter 6. But the overall pattern is that churches are significant contenders in public life in most African countries, even as individual church bodies vary in how close they are to the state.

The second key theme is rising political pluralism, catalyzed by the end of the Cold War and the end of bipolar support for single-party regimes, and also spurred by domestic movements for reform. The move toward increasing political competition created new and weakly institutional-ized democracies, as well as competitive authoritarian regimes (Levitsky and Way, 2010) and instances of chronic regime instability (Bratton and Van de Walle, 1997; Young, 2012; Riedl, 2016). In new democracies, increased political competition was often accompanied by a proliferation of different types of Christian and Islamic associations. In competitive authoritarian regimes, the playing field remained significantly tilted in favor of the ruling party (Levitsky and Way, 2010), and important restric-tions were placed on opposition leaders, political parties, and the press in particular. But these regimes still held elections – even though freedoms and competition were limited – and the holding of elections provided new opportunities for religious organizations, religious leaders, and the laity to consider their partisan affiliations and the possibility of critiquing individual candidates, incumbent parties, or institutions and the political system as a whole. Certainly, the stakes were higher in more restrictive regimes. But elections and contestation over democratic institutions and procedures provided opportunities and focal points for citizens' political participation, either within the institutional rules of the game or in opposition to them.

The third key theme is the nature of state–citizen relations: the centralization in many countries of power around the presidency, the clientelistic relationships in many countries between the state and the citizenry, and control of the state's resources as the key prize over which zero-sum contestation and conflict are often waged (Van de Walle, 2003). The majority of sub-Saharan African political systems are presidential, and power is often personalized around the figure of the president. The executive controls lawmaking in many cases with supermajorities in the parliament or weak legislatures, directs a large portion of state finances with little accountability, and commands the military (Barkan, 2008; Opalo, 2014). Pervasive clientelism means that there is a systematic attempt to gain and maintain political support through patron–client exchanges, and that weak attachment to the "public" realm can mean that the strength of clan, ethnicity, language, region, or other subnational identities often structure dyadic exchanges (Ekeh, 1975). Because state structures and public expenditures are often limited (the civil service employs only about 2 percent of the population on average), clientelistic politics have become a mechanism for accommodating and integrating a narrow political elite (Van de Walle, 2003). The result is that interaction with the state (alongside interaction with religious organizations) is often at the heart of citizens' efforts to improve their livelihoods or that of their families and communities. It is rare to see citizens' demanding "smaller government" (as they might in the United States) or to see an individualistic or self-help approach to poverty alleviation completely eschew the state.

A fourth theme is that religion is infrequently the most salient political identity cleavage. Nigeria's regional and religious North–South, Muslim–Christian divide is the most obvious exception, and Tanzania's increasingly competitive party competition has recently taken on religious tones. Côte D'Ivoire provides another example. Yet the vast majority of ethnic and partisan mobilization in Africa is not based on a religious cleavage. Citizens often vote along ethnic (tribal, regional, or linguistic) lines, in the expectation of ethnic favoritism or psychic benefits, or because they expect that coethnics will defend their relative status and interests. But citizens rarely vote, or conflict, along religious lines. Religious leaders may at times be involved as brokers in clientelistic distribution (McCauley, 2013), and the roles of village elder and religious cleric may overlap

(Paller, 2014), but by and large, religion is not among the important set of politicized social identity cleavages in sub-Saharan Africa. Likewise, religious affiliation does not generally drive party affiliation, and political parties are constitutionally barred in most countries from claiming a religious mantle explicitly. Thus, to the extent that religion has an influence on politics in these contexts, it is unlikely to be through social identity (in- versus out-group) politics. Instead, we suggest that one way religion influences political behavior is through the world views (ideology) it communicates.

Fifth, a culmination of the four prior themes suggests that citizens might face conflicting incentives to engage directly in politics. In contexts of systemic political violence, high levels of uncertainty, and illiberal regimes, citizens might want to exit the political sphere. On the other hand, with state resources as a key means of economic improvement and contestation, citizens want to turn toward political engagement but may be unsure about *how* to best engage. It is in this context that we find such varied patterns of engagement, from reluctant pursuit of structural reform in key moments, to energized and empowered players pursuing leadership development and personnel change. The absence of class-based sociopolitical mobilization in general in Africa has perhaps furthered the influence of religious ideologies: "oppressed and defeated peoples turn to the metaphysical in pursuit of their struggle against outside control" (Haynes, 1996, 50). This turning to religion for guidance is likely not restricted to a particular historical period, either colonial occupation or postcolonial nationalist and developmental struggles, but in the following chapters we seek to shed light on it in the contemporary period.

3

Differences in Contemporary Christian Sermon Content

The pastor of a Pentecostal church in Nairobi stood in front of about eighty people under a large tent. Many attendees had come alone and, for the most part, they were sitting by themselves in chairs, listening attentively, singing, and repeating pastoral messages. The pastor asked attendees to repeat: "I have been empowered to prosper and never to fail; I am blessed everywhere I go, and in everything that I do. The works of my hands are blessed; I will stand out and succeed in everything that I do." The message was one emphasizing earthly victory and success – the power of individuals, through faith, to overcome everyday struggles, to make material change in their lives and also in society as a whole. The pastor stressed that believing strongly in positive outcomes in this life is enough to achieve them; that social and material change comes through faith, through a change in mindset and embodying that mindset in action. The message made no room for the concept of defeat: "We will not fail!" the attendees were encouraged to affirm out loud at several points. This Pentecostal service exemplified the kinds of messages we had been hearing in worship services in Pentecostal churches in this and other cities.

The service was uplifting – indeed, relentlessly positive. An assistant pastor stepped to the front and reminded listeners, "It is really important that you make declarations as if you have already received. Speak positively, think positively, dance positively. Just believe and you will receive it." The pastor was not simply encouraging listeners to change their mindsets. She was encouraging change in both mind and action. Attendees received a handout with declarations to repeat. One read, "The Grace of God is upon me. I move with divine enablement and great favour." Another: "I will stand out and succeed in everything I do." Another: "I can and will do all things through Christ." Another: "I am strong. My strength is renewed as I wait on God. Isaiah 40:31 Those who wait on the Lord shall renew their strength; they shall mount up with wings like eagles; they shall run and not be weary; they shall walk and not faint." Everyone took the handout and spoke the declarations together. They sang a hymn and then were encouraged to repeat the declarations individually. The woman assistant pastor encouraged people to pray at their own pace and "let the word of God manifest." The pastors' words thus affirmed the worth and strength of each participant to make change – change achieved through faith. Attendees then expressed these affirmations out loud, over and over again – both in chorus with other attendees and, at moments, alone at their own pace.

Throughout the service, pastors reminded listeners that change is imminently possible, not just in heaven but in this life, too, and that social and material change happens through the embodiment of strong faith. "You speak opposite to your situation. You speak antithesis to your situation," the pastor told listeners in the middle of the service. "If you cannot do it, you *say* I *can* do it. Because our situations are difficult. Make sure that every time you are in a situation you see the word of God that is changing your situation." "Whatever you decree and declare in the spiritual world will realize in the natural." Change is imminently possible. It happens as more individuals speak and embody faith, even in the face of contradictory material circumstances.

That same week, the Catholic and Mainline Protestant worship services we visited in the city exhibited a different emphasis. In a Catholic church across town, the priest spoke in general terms about poverty, corruption, and unfairness. A congregation of similar size, also sat largely separately from one another, listening intently, singing and praying where appropriate. "There are so many things in the world that seem good, but it is not good," the priest observed during his sermon. "We have reached a point where we embraced human corruption. But we need to put Jesus before every other thing ... Are we ready?" the priest asked. "Are we able to stand as a voice against injustice? This life is a life of struggle against evil. We continue to fight, so that one day, we can enjoy the peace. In order to one day enjoy eternal peace, we continue to fight now, so that one day we will be in the eternal light of Jesus." The priest's promise was *not* one of imminent change in this world. Indeed, the message was not particularly uplifting, certainly not relentlessly positive as the Pentecostal service had been. Instead, the message drew listeners' attention to systemic injustice, to deep problems embedded in the fabric of society and institutions. The sermon argued that struggling against these material and social circumstances might bring rewards in the afterlife ("the eternal light," "eternal peace") but is unlikely to yield change in the here and now.

In an Anglican Church that same week, the sermon was similarly trained on structural issues as the root of earthly problems and cautionary. The priest invited a leader of the congregation to deliver the sermon, and he began with the topic of Olympic runners. The summer Olympics had just begun, and many Kenyans had been watching and rooting for the country's talented runners. Congregants perked up at the mention of the topic. But the sermon did not encourage listeners to consider their own victory – to declare it, to embody it – as a Pentecostal sermon on the same subject might have done. Instead, the speaker proceeded in his sermon to make the argument that "in your race in life, there is a time to be defeated." He urged listeners to be sensitive to and to act against evil, suffering, and injustice because at the root of all of these are human limitations. But the sermon gave no promise of change, even if people fought against injustice. Instead, the speaker urged listeners to "run the race with perseverance," always cognizant that we are all limited in our own capacities. The reward for acting against injustice would be realized in the next life but not in this one.

* * *

The sermon differences described in the preceding are indicative of broader thematic differences in clergy–congregant communication between Pentecostal churches, on the one hand, and Mainline Protestant and Catholic churches, on the other hand, in many parts of contemporary sub-Saharan Africa. Throughout the year,[1] in election seasons and between election seasons, Pentecostal, Mainline Protestant, and Catholic sermons remained relatively apolitical across the board. But Pentecostal sermons, on the one hand, and Mainline Protestant and Catholic sermons, on the other, answered deep metaphysical questions quite differently. In answer to questions about what causes earthly problems, Pentecostal sermons turned to factors internal to the individual, and to each individual's relationship with God. And in answer to questions about whether earthly problems can be overcome, the Pentecostal sermons gave a resounding "yes!"

---

[1] The Catholic and Mainline Protestant churches follow a liturgical calendar. Many Pentecostal churches do not do so explicitly or formally. Nevertheless, even when discussing the same passages of scripture (as we discuss later in this chapter), these categories of churches provide very different interpretations of how the world works.

Sermons are a central and pervasive part of Christian practice, as they are of other important world religions, including Islam and Judaism. Sermons disseminate ideas that deal with deep existential and metaphysical questions and are likely to influence the levels and modes of political engagement of ordinary churchgoers. As we discuss later in the book, sermons are important because they activate and *re*activate world views that influence how people make sense of political questions, problems, and opportunities.

Throughout much of this chapter, we draw information on sermon content from Nairobi, Kenya, for reasons we will soon discuss.[2] We then corroborate that similar patterns occur in other anglophone urban areas on the continent. Cities tend to exhibit a diversity of churches and thus offer the opportunity to document a range of religious messages to which people are being regularly exposed.[3] In addition, cities in anglophone countries tend to have a greater diversity of Christian churches because the British maintained a more neutral policy toward Protestant and Catholic missionaries during colonialism than the French, Belgian, and Portuguese, which in some instances had policies favoring the Catholic Church (Gallego and Woodberry, 2010). We thus concentrate our descriptive work in this chapter on anglophone cities in sub-Saharan Africa but encourage scholars to pay attention to the political importance of religious ideas in a broader context.

SITUATING SERMONS WITHIN THE CHURCH EXPERIENCE

Sermons sit within a larger church experience, one that often complements and supports messages from the pulpit. Before delving into the differences in sermon content we found, it is worth describing the social organization, social welfare provision, and worship service experiences we observed in the Nairobi churches we surveyed. We were surprised to

---

[2] Deidentified sermon texts will be available in "From Pews to Politics: Religious Sermons and Political Participation in Africa." Qualitative Data Repository. http://doi.org/10.5064/F6NUVQRR. QDR Main Collection.

[3] That cities tend to exhibit more religious diversity than rural areas do is a pattern within and outside of sub-Saharan Africa. Within sub-Saharan Africa, colonial-era missionaries tended to move into interior areas that were not already controlled by other churches (and to follow the path of missionaries within their same denominations to similar areas so as to maintain connections from the interior to coast), and so rural areas tend to be more religiously homogeneous than cities for this reason as well (Nunn, 2010; Cagé and Rueda, 2016). These patterns possibly do have implications for the generalizability of the findings in later chapters, and so we return to these differences in the conclusion.

find starker differences in sermon content across denominational categories[4] than in these other social, organizational, and resource aspects
of the churches. Where we did find differences in social organization,
social welfare provision, and worship service conduct, we found them
to coincide with (and thus complement) sermon content differences. We
turn to a discussion of the interactions between sermon content and these
other aspects of religious organizations in the concluding chapter of the
book, but the similarities across churches along these other dimensions
and the potentials for synergies between sermon content and other church
activities only underscore the importance of our focus on differences in
sermon content.

In the following, we describe our approach to surveying a large number
of churches in Nairobi and other cities in sub-Saharan Africa. We also
collected more sustained and in-depth observations of four Pentecostal
congregations and four Catholic parishes to observe their activities and
messages during Sunday worship services as well as during the week. We
purposefully selected four Pentecostal congregations that, based on our
larger survey of church worship services, exhibited the range of demographic characteristics in the sample of Pentecostal churches. We selected
one megachurch in an affluent area of the city, one small congregation in
a slum area, and two mid-sized congregations in mixed-income (middle-
lower class) neighborhoods. In the latter category, we chose one Pentecostal church that belongs to an umbrella group of multiple churches
and that was started in the earlier waves of Pentecostal arrival to the
continent (in the 1950s); the other midsized congregation belongs to no
umbrella group and was started in the last decade. Research assistants
and we then followed these churches over a period of six to eight weeks,
attending weekday services, offering service provision efforts, and further
interviewing church staff about the social organization and activities of
the churches. The following year, we observed four Catholic parishes: a
large Catholic cathedral with a largely upper-class congregation, a mid-
sized parish in a wealthy suburb, a midsized parish in a lower-middle-class
neighborhood (the same neighborhood as the umbrella group middle-
class Pentecostal congregation we had followed), and a small parish in a
slum area. We collected information on their extra-Sunday services, social
welfare activities, and informal organization through interviews and focus

---

4 "Denominations are collections of ideas, individuals, congregations, small groups, and
   communities" (Kellstedt and Green, 1993: 53, quoted in Djupe and Gilbert, 2009: 82).

groups with congregants and interviews with informal group leaders. We focused on Catholic churches rather than Mainline Protestant churches for these comparison follow-ups because we suspected ex ante that they might be the most different from Pentecostal churches in their approach to service provision and to social organization.

We found communication in other parts of Sunday worship services and in weekday services to be consistent with the messages communicated in Sunday sermons. In Pentecostal Sunday services, it was common to have members of the church testify to the material differences that faith had made in their lives, underscoring the sermonic promises of the possibilities of imminent material change in this world and the sermonic attribution of earthly problems to the individual. In Catholic services, it was not uncommon to have (nonpolitical) speakers about topics related to systemic issues (accommodation of people with disabilities, cultures of inhospitality, structural sources of poverty), underscoring the sermonic attribution of earthly problems to factors outside of the individual. Both Pentecostal and Catholic churches of all types had weekly services (morning prayers, evening prayers – sometimes called "boot camps" by the Pentecostal churches, Wednesday or Thursday evening services, youth services, and youth group meetings). As far as we could detect, the content of these services reflected and complemented the content of clergy–congregant communication on Sundays. In recognition of the "recharging" function of these midweek services and activities, one pastor described these weekly services as the church's effort to "make people remember what was preached last Sunday since people forget. We try to make them remember."

We were surprised to find that the Catholic and Pentecostal congregations were not very different in the ways they organized social interactions among lay members. At the outset, we expected to find that membership in Pentecostal churches would demand more intense and frequent participation and involve tighter social organization among congregants.[5] However, we found that churches of both denominations offered robust opportunities for informal social gatherings and message renewal throughout the week.

---

[5] In other country contexts, e.g., the United States, scholars have sometimes described Pentecostals has highly socially organized – emphasizing frequent service attendance throughout the week and participation in informal small groups, with the opportunity to gain skills. By contrast, Catholics are sometimes described as relatively less committed and offered fewer opportunities to participate in small groups or build skills within the church (Verba, Schlozman, and Brady, 1995; Jones-Correa and Leal, 2001).

The Pentecostal churches we observed organized informal groups of congregants called "home cells" or "home fellowships," and the Catholic churches we visited all also had what they called "small Christian communities" (or SCCs), or jumuiyas ("communities" in kiSwahili) – small groups of parishioners who met in each other's homes once a week or twice a month for prayers and discussion. In the contemporary period, we learned from focus groups and in-depth conversations with group leaders that these small group activities are organized and operated very similarly. Members of a given congregation or parish are all encouraged to participate in the small groups, which were typically organized by neighborhood (members who lived close to one another would be part of the same group), with occasional thematic groups as well (e.g., for single people or for young couples). Informants in both Pentecostal and Catholic churches estimated that only a fraction (maybe 10–20 percent) of their congregations actually participated regularly. Small groups would meet in one of the members' homes, eat together, pray, and discuss scripture. Pastors and priests were invited to attend in both types of churches, should they wish to, but in both types of churches clergy usually did not attend; were they to attend, in both instances they led the meeting as a service (mass). Otherwise, in neither case did clergy direct the order or content of the small group meetings. Explicitly political topics were reportedly uncommon in the small groups. However, such topics came up from time to time, in a more informal and unexpected way. In both denominations, these kinds of informal, dense social groupings appeared common.[6] The social organization of congregations was surprisingly consistent across church categories.

In their 2009 book, Djupe and Gilbert caution against assuming that sermons and other clergy cueing will have an influence over listeners. Instead, they argue that clergy cueing is likely to have an influence only where people are deeply embedded in their churches socially and also

---

[6] In focus groups with congregations outside of the eight designated follow-up churches, we did find examples of congregations that did not organize these kinds of small groups. However, we found these exceptions among both Pentecostal and Catholic churches. Focus groups in two Pentecostal megachurches, for instance, informed us that their church either does not organize home cells (instead it has only "Departments" that focus on organizing categories of congregants, e.g., the youth or the women – a form of organization that is also common in Catholic churches that have Catholic Women's Association branches and so on) or that there are not enough congregants living in any one area, so to the extent that there are home cells in the church, they happen informally and in combination with neighbors who attend other Pentecostal churches. In a Catholic parish we observed, SCCs, though established in name, did not actually appear to be a vibrant part of the memberships' experience. But we found no evidence to suggest that these exceptions occur more frequently in one category of church than another.

bombarded by the messages from many media and social sources: "Clergy political messages are more clearly received by members thoroughly networked socially within the church ... [And] when members are bombarded with information from the media, pulpit, and social networks, they will respond, but the offhand mention of an issue in a sermon is not likely to generate much attention or opinion movement" (72). We found that this possible mechanism for raising the salience of sermon message content equally plausible in both Pentecostal and Catholic congregations, given their similar organizations of small groups.

The one aspect of lay church experience that did differ somewhat across denominations was the witnessing of different modes of social service provision. Both types of congregations had women's, youth, and men's groups and programming geared at the needs of each type of member within the church. Both types of churches offered "emergency" relief to church members on a case-by-case basis and had some form of "care and encouragement groups" that visited members in need at their homes in order to provide prayers and support. Thus, in terms of social insurance and social welfare provision *to members* of their congregations, Pentecostal and Catholic churches were quite similar. Both types of churches also engaged in some regular form of outreach. Even the poorest congregations had some sort of social outreach component: a regular activity or program that involved church interaction with people in the larger community (nonmembers). But the nature of those outreach programs did differ somewhat between the Pentecostal and Catholic congregations we observed. Fewer of the Pentecostal churches than the Catholic churches we observed engaged in large-scale provision of material handouts. Every Catholic church ran either a regular nutrition program, orphanage, school, literacy program, or health clinic. The outreach activities of Pentecostal churches by contrast often centered instead on evangelism, on running conferences and seminars to help individuals find and strengthen their own faith, and on providing counseling and encouragement to people facing any kind of personal challenges (financial, familial, psychological). One of the Pentecostal churches we followed held Saturday feeding programs for children,[7] and one conducted a yearly clothing drive. Both of these churches expressed hopes of running health centers and vocational or secondary schools

---

7 The messaging during the children's feeding program was interestingly very similar to the Sunday sermon content we heard in that church. The leaders of the program spent the session telling children that they are each special in the eyes of God, that they are capable of enacting change in their own lives, and that they need to have a mindset that appreciates their own value and that connects to God.

TABLE 3.1 *Similarities in social organization and programming across denominations*

	Midweek worship	Social organization	Social service provision
Pentecostal	Morning prayers, evening prayers, Wednesday/ Thursday services.	"Home cells," "home fellowships," neighborhood or thematic, nonhierarchical; women's groups, youth groups.	Emergency and material support for members; regular outreach to nonmembers focused on evangelism, psychological and financial counseling.
Catholic	Morning prayers, evening prayers, Wednesday/ Thursday services.	*Jumuiyas*, "small Christian communities," neighborhood or thematic, nonhierarchical; women's groups, youth groups.	Emergency and material support for members; regular outreach to nonmembers focused on material handouts.

but were not yet doing so. In both Pentecostal and Catholic churches, clergy (including nuns, pastors-in-training) usually led and managed these different modes of outreach, with the occasional help of lay member volunteers. Thus, the existence of and level of lay participation in outreach programs were similar across denominations. But the content of those outreach programs differed. Catholic churches provided more in the way of handouts: health care, food, shelter, and so on. Pentecostal churches provided more in the way of psychological support. These differences in content are consistent with the thematic differences in sermon content that we describe in this chapter. Catholic sermons and church activities locate the source of earthly problems in factors external to the individual and address them accordingly, whereas Pentecostal sermons and church activities locate the source of earthly problems in the faith and psyche of the individual. Thus, to the extent that we found differences in lay church experience, those differences coincide with and complement differences in sermon content.

DOCUMENTING DIFFERENCES IN SERMON CONTENT

When we observed Sunday worship services and collected sermon texts, both in Nairobi and in other African cities, we found distinctive differences in sermon content between Pentecostal churches, on the one hand, and Mainline Pentecostal and Catholic churches, on the other. These differences did not revolve around explicitly political topics, even during election periods; they did not take different positions on specific policy issues, candidates, or political parties, nor did they give explicit calls to political action. Instead, the striking differences were in the ways sermons answered deep metaphysical questions about causal attribution and possibilities for change, and the differences were most striking between Pentecostal churches, on the one hand, and Catholic and Mainline Protestant churches, on the other. We did not expect in advance to find so much consistency *among* Pentecostal congregations, nor did we expect to find so many commonalities between Catholic and Mainline Protestant sermons. Those were the patterns that emerged.

Pentecostal sermons pointed consistently to factors within the individual when explaining earthly problems, and promised imminent material change in this world, as well as rewards in the next. The Pentecostal sermons pointed to weakness in individuals' internal faith, to their not having a strong enough relationship with God and to their not embodying strong faith as sources of earthly problems. Through transformation of mindset, through strong belief in God and living as if change has been realized, listeners can achieve the change they want to see for themselves and for society more generally. By contrast, both Mainline Protestant and Catholic sermons tended to diagnose earthly problems by pointing to factors outside of the individual, and made no promises of material change in this world, even as they pointed to rewards in heaven. The Mainline Protestant and Catholic sermons discussed poor relationships, cultural problems, and lack of structural fallbacks for people in need as sources of earthly problems. They encouraged listeners to act rightly and try to correct such issues, but they promised no high likelihood of success.

Other observers have called the Pentecostal message the "prosperity gospel" or the "health and wealth" gospel (Gifford, 1994, 2009; Freeman, 2012). These names are consistent with what we observed: Pentecostal sermons explicitly connected individual faith with material well-being. The sermons did not always focus explicitly on monetary wealth; they rarely offered "get-rich-quick" solutions. But they did focus on imminent material change and prosperity, very broadly defined. They encouraged listeners to think positively – "like a victor, not like a victim" – so as to overcome obstacles to their personal goals, whatever those might be. The messages were gospels of inner confidence, or gospels of success, as Gifford (2009) calls them, rather than gospels about money per se (Martin, 2002; Gifford, 2009).

We expected in advance to find more differences between Mainline Protestant and Catholic sermons than we did. Historically, scholars have paid much attention to the theological differences between these two denominational categories. Indeed, the differences between Catholics and Calvinists were the subject of Weber's seminal *Protestant Ethic*. Yet, in the time and places we observed, sermons in these two denominational categories did not differ much in how they answered deep metaphysical questions about causal attribution and the possibility for change. We should note that the connection contemporary Pentecostal sermons make between faith and material change differs from the principle of *sola fide* (by faith alone) espoused by Mainline Protestant churches during Reformation, particularly by Lutheran and Calvinist theologians of that time. The idea of "justification sola fide" is that people receive forgiveness for their sins and salvation on the basis of faith alone, not on the basis of their "works" – that is, not on the basis of what they have done. Mainline Protestant leaders proclaimed this principle in protest over the Catholic Church's practice of indulgences (money given to the church to receive temporary relief from punishment of sin), a practice that has largely been dropped by the Catholic Church today. In the era and context we study, both Mainline Protestant and Catholic sermons emphasized the importance of good works for achieving salvation (rewards in the next life). And their world view differs quite a bit from the emphasis in the Pentecostal sermons on the relationship between faith and concrete, material change in this life. The differences are not as much about the relationship between faith and salvation (as in the principle of sola fide).

We also expected in advance to find more variation in sermon content *among* Pentecostal congregations than we did. In their work on ideation and socialization in US churches, Djupe and Gilbert (2003) observed: "Denominations are [often] better conceptualized as loose confederations of affiliated congregations that evince considerable diversity within them" (77–80, paraphrased in Djupe and Gilbert 2009: 88). The Pentecostal and Charismatic category, which is a category whose definition and boundaries are the subject of considerable debate, seemed particularly likely to fit this notion of "loose confederation." Pentecostal churches encompass a wide variety of types of congregations (from small corrugated tin shacks to megachurches), are for the most part not under a centralized authority,[8]

---

[8] There are Pentecostal church bodies, e.g., the Pentecostal Assemblies of God, the Full Gospel Churches, and Deliverance Church, as well as collections of churches under one pastor or "bishop," but overall, Pentecostal churches are much less centralized certainly than the Catholic Church.

and do not involve consistent and centralized training of clerics. We thus oversampled Pentecostal churches in order to document differences in messaging *within* that category. Nevertheless, the striking differences that emerged were between Pentecostal churches and more mainstream (Catholic and Mainline Protestant) churches, rather than within the category of Pentecostalism.

AN ORIGINAL SURVEY OF SERMONS AND CHURCHES

We began our church observation and sermon collection efforts in Nairobi. Nairobi provided a useful place to start for a number of reasons. Typical of many major urban centers in anglophone sub-Saharan Africa, Nairobi is denominationally diverse, exhibiting significant shares of the population affiliated with Catholic and Mainline Protestant churches as well as growth rates of Pentecostalism typical of urban Africa more generally.[9] Apart from its religious landscape, it is also economically and demographically diverse, and Nairobi therefore, exhibits churches that cater to varying types of congregations, from very rich megachurches and cathedrals to small (ten-to-fifteen-person) congregations meeting in informal shacks and tents. It was important for us to work in a site that allowed us to explore whether religious leaders vary their messages by tailoring them to the economic and ethnic makeup of their congregations. Nairobi is a place where, along with research assistants, we could observe services from the most prominent Christian denominations in sub-Saharan Africa, both in rich and poor congregations (and in large congregations drawing from all economic strata), in suburbs and slums, and across a range of ethnic groups.

In other ways, too, Nairobi is an important place in which to examine the content of religious messages and their impact. Levels of religiosity

---

[9] Catholics make up 20–25 percent of the population of Kenya, while Pentecostals currently make up at least 15 percent, and the total number of Pentecostals continues to rise with an average growth rate of approximately 11 percent per year. The Pew survey conducted in Kenya in 2006 reports that the number of Pentecostal churches in Nairobi has more than doubled since the 1970s (Pew, 2006). Kenya is among the fourteen countries in the world with the highest absolute numbers of Pentecostals, according to the World Christian Database. (In order, starting with the highest number of Pentecostals in the country, the fourteen countries are Brazil, Nigeria, the United States, Indonesia, Ghana, Kenya, South Korea, the Democratic Republic of Congo, South Africa, Angola, India, Tanzania, Mozambique, and Burkina Faso.) Kenya also has a significant Muslim population (about 11 percent of the total population), and while this differentiates it from some sub-Saharan African countries where Pentecostalism is growing (e.g., South Africa, Zambia), it makes it more similar to others (e.g., Ghana, Nigeria).

in Nairobi, and throughout Kenya, are high and typical of the continent as a whole.[10] Nairobi thus serves as an appropriate place to investigate the role of religion in shaping political behavior even where practically everyone is religious. Kenya also has well-known, and well-researched, ethnic cleavages that are highly politically salient.[11] Nairobi and many other parts of the country experienced significant interethnic electoral violence in 2007–2008, and ethnic voting is robust and well documented (Bratton and Kimenyi, 2008; Dowd and Driessen, 2008, inter alia) in Kenya generally, and Nairobi specifically. Nairobi and the country in general thus offer the opportunity to study the influence of different types of religious messaging even where ethnicity (tribe, linguistic group), rather than religion, is a politicized and salient identity cleavage. Finally, Kenya's contested multiparty system means that there is some space for political engagement but also contestation over which forms of engagement and citizen–state interaction are appropriate, both during and between electoral periods. Furthermore, due to high levels of corruption, inequality, and distrust of the electoral system, political participation can be intimidating to the average citizen.[12] In this context, understanding whether and if religious messages shape citizen approaches to political participation is theoretically and practically important.

We focused on Sunday sermons, which are central vehicles for clergy–congregant communication among Christians both in Nairobi and throughout the world.[13] Some Nairobi Christians also watch Christian TV, listen to Christian radio, or subscribe to social media feeds and WhatsApp groups of churches. However, by and large, these sources replicate (in many cases literally rerun) sermons delivered in churches in

---

[10] In the 2011–2013 round of the Afrobarometer, 86 percent of all sub-Saharan African respondents said that religion is "very important" in their lives. In the 2011–2013 Afrobarometer, there is no statistically significant relationship between urban residency and saying that religion is personally very important among any Christians except those who identify as "other Christians" and not as Catholic, Mainline Protestant, or Pentecostal; even among "other Christians," the relationship is only marginally significant.

[11] Although see recent work by Berge et al. (2017) documenting low levels of prejudice across ethnic groups in 2014 in Nairobi, despite ethnic electoral violence there in 2007–2008.

[12] Kenyan citizens do not generally have high levels of trust in the government (Logan and Sentamu, 2007) and report middling levels of citizen engagement despite interest in politics (Gyimah-Boadi and Attoh, 2009).

[13] If we were to conduct the same research on Islam in Kenya, we would focus on Friday sermons, which are increasingly the subject of research on the influence of religious ideas on political activity (Mackay, 2011).

the city, and the experience of Sunday worship service is more consistently a part of each practicing Christian's life than these other sources.

To our knowledge, there is no existing repository of sermons in Kenya, and there is very limited data available on sermon content from sub-Saharan Africa in general.[14] There have been important and rich ethnographic studies of single Pentecostal churches (Marshall, 2009; Deacon and Lynch, 2013) but few survey and observe worship services across a number of churches (cf., using other methods, Martin, 2002; Miller and Yamamori, 2007; Gifford, 2009).[15] We therefore strove for as close to a random sample of these types of churches in Nairobi as possible.

In order to approximate a random sample of such churches, we generated two comprehensive lists of (1) Pentecostal churches[16] and (2) Catholic and Mainline Protestant churches[17] in Nairobi based on data from Google Maps. Because some churches are new, poor, or not officially registered, we did not work from government registration lists, nor did we rely on capturing information only from church websites. Instead, we sought a method that allowed us to capture information not

---

[14] Cf. Trinitapoli and Weinreb (2012), who collected some sermon observations in their study of religious discussions of HIV in Malawi and whose data we explore later in this chapter.

[15] Although some previous studies examine Pentecostal churches in a number of countries, few before this one have systematically gathered sermon and services observations, or examined variation within Pentecostalism.

[16] Following the Pew (2006) survey, we use the term Pentecostal to refer broadly to churches that are Pentecostal, Neo-Pentecostal, Charismatic, or Renewalist. Because the churches are not under one overarching authority, there is some debate about their definition and grouping (Freston, 2001; Ranger, 2008; Grossman, 2015). In our surveys of the clergy of Pentecostal churches in Nairobi and Johannesburg, we asked pastors to self-identify the denomination of the church to confirm that they would use the terms Pentecostal, Charismatic, or Renewalists. We did not end up with any Catholic or Anglican Charismatic churches in this sample.

[17] In Google Maps, we first generated a comprehensive list of possibly Pentecostal, Mainline, and Catholic churches in Nairobi, using the following search terms such as "church loc: nairobi, kenya," "pentecostal loc: nairobi, kenya," "catholic loc: nairobi, Kenya," "protestant loc: nairobi, Kenya," "anglican loc: nairobi, Kenya," "methodist loc: nairobi, Kenya," "presbyterian loc: nairobi, Kenya," "presbyterian loc: nairobi, Kenya," "lutheran loc: nairobi, Kenya," "charismatic loc: nairobi, kenya," "evangelical loc: nairobi, kenya," "revivalist loc: nairobi, kenya," "protestant loc: nairobi, kenya," "renewal loc: nairobi, kenya," "bible loc: nairobi, kenya." We then randomly sampled one hundred Pentecostal churches and fifty Mainline/Catholic churches (simple random sampling using a random number generator), expecting that there might be more variation among Pentecostal churches because they are not centralized, nor do they provide centralized training. More information on our procedure for surveying the Pentecostal churches is in McClendon and Riedl (2016).

just on high-profile, official, and internationally connected churches but also on smaller and more informal churches.[18] For the denominational lists we generated from Google Maps, we then randomly selected one hundred Pentecostal and fifty Catholic/Mainline churches for in-depth exploration. We selected a higher number of Pentecostal churches because there is less information about these churches' messages in existing scholarship and because, given their high level of decentralization, we expected more variation among Pentecostal churches than among churches of other denominations.

Research assistants and we attempted to locate and contact each of the churches in order to conduct a survey with a senior pastor or priest, and to obtain records of the church's sermons, if any were kept. Some churches provide video, audio, or written recordings of their sermons online, in which case we were often able to collect information on sermons going back a few weeks or a few months in time. Where no sermon records were provided, our research assistants or we attended a Sunday service and took copious notes. We found that taking notes during sermons was not particularly obtrusive. Pentecostal congregants often take notes during the sermons. It is relatively less common for Catholic and Mainline Protestant congregants to take copious notes, but we found that some still did and that our research assistants and we did not stand out much for doing so in any of the services. From the visited services, we have notes on the entire service as well as close-to-verbatim notes on the sermon. For churches with online or hardcopy recordings, we typically have only the content of the sermons to examine. Churches that could not be located at all were randomly replaced from the list generated from Google Maps.

Because less is known about the range and content of sermons in Pentecostal churches, we began with the survey of Pentecostal churches. During the period from 2013 through June 2014, research assistants and we started at the top of the randomly sorted list of churches in the sample and attempted to collect sermons from as many churches on the Pentecostal list as possible. In July–August 2016, research assistants and we then visited as many of the selected Mainline and Catholic churches from the

---

[18] Nevertheless, one downside of the method is that it is less likely to detect congregations that meet in the rooms of other buildings. That is, we were more likely to detect congregations that meet in their own structures (large or small, formal or less formally constructed) than those that use school auditoriums or the insides of stores to meet on Sundays. We advance the effort to capture the full range of congregations but more work could be done to complement and extend our efforts.

TABLE 3.2 *Comparing churches from which we have sermons with those we do not*

	Have sermons	Do not have sermons	
Km from Nairobi center	10.9	10.5	0.4
	(7.11)	(7.00)	(p = 0.75)
Has a website	0.49	0.55	0.05
	(0.50)	(0.50)	(p = 0.53)

Note: Standard deviations or p-values associated with a two-sided t-test of the difference in means in parentheses.

selected sample as possible.[19] We also revisited four Pentecostal churches for in-depth follow-up, including attending additional Sunday and week-day services during the July–August 2016 period, often in the same weeks as the Mainline and Catholic services were visited.

In the end, we collected sermon content from sixty of the one hundred selected Pentecostal churches and from twenty-four of the fifty selected Mainline and Catholic churches.[20] Because we attempted church visits in as random an order as possible and randomly replaced churches that could not be located at all, we think it unlikely that a certain type of church (and sermon) is systematically underrepresented in our set of sermons even though we did not visit or obtain a sermon text from every church in each sample. No church refused to let us observe a Sunday service or to collect a sermon text. We do not know much about the churches we were unable to visit. However, we know where they are located in Google Earth and, thus, how distant they are from the center of the city. We also are able to identify whether those churches have a web presence or not. On these characteristics, the churches from which we were able to observe a sermon are not detectably different from churches from which we were unable to observe a sermon. See Table 3.2, which compares churches in the random samples from which we collected at least one sermon with those from which we collected no sermons on these characteristics.

---

[19] In this first round of service visits, research assistants and we typically could not visit more than one service per Sunday each, because the church location had to be found and a correct service time confirmed, and because services were often multiple hours' long. When service times were incorrectly advertised or changed at the last minute, the church had to be visited again the subsequent Sunday.

[20] The difference in rates is not due to differences in our ability to find or receive permission from churches to attend services.

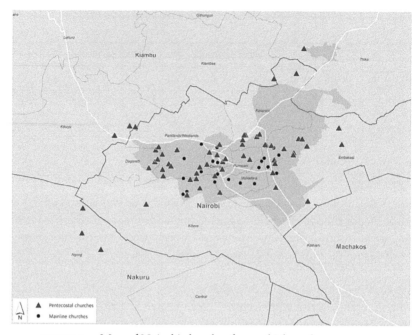

FIGURE 3.1   Map of Nairobi churches from which we have sermons.

Figure 3.1 shows a map of the Pentecostal and Mainline/Catholic churches from which we were able to collect sermons in Nairobi. Gray triangles show the Pentecostal churches; black circles show the Mainline and Catholic churches represented among the sermon texts.

Table 3.3 summarizes basic characteristics of the churches from which we have sermons. Using our sampling strategy, we collected information on a wide range of churches: from megachurches in the Nairobi suburbs and "in town" to corrugated tin churches in slum areas, from churches with their own YouTube channels to churches with no recording equipment. The characteristics summarized in Table 3.3 were measured through online information (church location and online presence), through researcher observations during services, and through clergy interviews in which the pastor, minister, or priest was asked to describe the socioeconomic, age, and ethnic makeup of the congregation, as well as to verify the language in which the church conducts services. We asked Kenyan research assistants also to make notes on the congregants' socioeconomic characteristics (poor or mixed income), based on whether congregants arrived in cars, dressed nicely, and had smartphones, or not. We also asked these researchers to note whether most people in

TABLE 3.3 *Nairobi church characteristics*

	Mean	SD	Range
Pentecostal churches (60)			
Informal settlement	0.47	0.50	0–1
Online presence	0.49	0.49	0–1
Ethnically mixed	0.62	0.49	0–1
Poor	0.36	0.49	0–1
Mixed income	0.51	0.50	0–1
Young	0.56	0.50	0–1
English or Swahilli	0.96	0.20	0–1
Mainline/Catholic churches (24)			
Informal settlement	0.29	0.46	0–1
Online presence	0.50	0.51	0–1
Ethnically mixed	0.66	0.48	0–1
Poor	0.21	0.41	0–1
Mixed income	0.42	0.50	0–1
Young	0.38	0.49	0-1
English or Swahilli	0.92	0.28	0–1

the congregation were young (under forty) or not, and to note whether they could identify one or two major ethnic groups that dominated the congregation or whether the congregation seemed mixed. In this study context, the research assistants judged ethnic makeup primarily on the basis of language use. They arrived early to services, stayed into coffee hour, and listened for different detectable languages used among congregants, as well as during the service itself by pastors, worship leaders, or other speakers. The research assistants who made these assessments were all Kenyans who felt equipped to judge the congregations for whether they exhibited one or two dominant ethnic groups or were more mixed. In no instance did we have major disagreement between the researcher's assessment and the clergy's assessments of socioeconomic and ethnic characteristics.

Pentecostal and Mainline/Catholic churches in this sample do differ on average in certain respects. A greater share of Pentecostal churches in our sample (47 percent) are in informal areas of the city, compared to 29 percent of the Mainline and Catholic churches from which we have sermons. A greater share of Pentecostal churches in our sample (56 percent) were observed to have congregations made up predominantly of people under the age of forty, compared to 38 percent of the Mainline and Catholic churches from which we have sermon observations. However, on other characteristics (e.g., whether the church has a website or Facebook page, whether the church conducts its services in English or Swahili rather than in a tribal language, whether the congregation in attendance exhibited a mix of ethnic groups or was dominated by one ethnic group), the two groups of churches were very similar. Note that both categories are dominated by congregations that are ethnically mixed, rather than by ones with an identifiable one or two groups dominating.

Strikingly, very few congregations in either category used local, ethnic languages in their main worship services. An overwhelming majority (96 percent in Pentecostal churches, 92 percent in Catholic and Mainline churches) used either English or Swahili, or a combination of the two. The need to move away from local ethnic languages is likely reflective of the prevalence of ethnically mixed congregations in both denominational categories as well as a product of city life. Rural areas are more ethnically and linguistically homogeneous to begin with and thus almost inevitably require the use of local languages for conversion strategies (Fernandes, 2009).

Our initial investigations of Pentecostal and Mainline/Catholic churches took place in nonelectoral years. We started the inquiry in 2013, after general elections had taken place in March of that year. In order to broaden our inquiry to electoral periods, in the eight weeks leading up to the 2017 Kenyan general elections (June–August), research assistants and we revisited the churches where we had previously collected sermons in order to observe any differences in sermon content in an election period.[21] The scheduled general elections took place on August 8, 2017, and included the presidential race as well as five other contests. The opposition subsequently contested the elections and, in a surprise ruling, the Supreme Court nullified the elections on September 1, 2017, and called for a new election, which ran later in the year. Our research design covered only the eight weeks leading up to the scheduled August 8 elections and did not capture church activity after the surprising Supreme Court ruling.

After these repeat visits to the churches (during a nonelectoral and an electoral period), we had a total of 179 Sunday sermon texts. We believe this is the most comprehensive dataset to date on Christian sermons and worship services in a major African city. Out of the 179 sermons,

---

[21] The process proceeded more quickly in the electoral period follow-up, both because we worked with a larger team of Kenyan research assistants and because we already knew the exact locations and service times for many congregations.

thirty-three were based on notes by an American researcher attending a Sunday service. The other 146 sermons came either from notes taken by a Kenyan research assistant (104) or from online recordings (forty-two). We could discern no difference in topics when a foreign (rather than Kenyan) researcher was present in a Sunday service (Cilliers, Dube, and Siddiqi, 2015).

SERMON CONTENT ANALYSIS: ATTRIBUTION AND POSSIBILITY

We employed two strategies to analyze the sermon texts we collected. As one strategy, we employed computer-assisted text analysis through the R-program Structured Topic Models (STM) (Roberts et al., 2014) – an unsupervised method for identifying the prevalence of topics in texts that incorporates metadata (in this case, congregation characteristics). As another strategy, we employed hand coding. The relatively small corpus of texts made human hand coding feasible, and hand coding allowed for a more nuanced reading of whether the sermons portrayed different relationships between the spiritual and physical worlds.

These two methods led to similar inferences about differences in sermon content. Using either method, we found that the differences in sermon content were starker between Pentecostal sermons, on the one hand, and Mainline Protestant and Catholic sermons, on the other, rather than within Pentecostal, Mainline, or Catholic categories. The differences were not in explicit political positions taken, or in issue areas raised, or even in the types of scriptures drawn on. Instead, the most vivid differences were in their attributions of responsibility for earthly problems and in their descriptions of the possibilities of earthly change.

The example of Job is illustrative. Both Pentecostal sermons and Mainline/Catholic sermons referred to the Book of Job in our sample, but the emphasis and interpretation of these same passages of scripture are strikingly different in the two categories. The Mainline Protestant and Catholic sermons used passages from the Book of Job to discuss earthly problems as something that can happen even to those with strong faith. Job is a righteous person, punished by Satan and tested by God. The responsibility for his earthly problems lies outside of himself. According to the Mainline Protestant and Catholic sermons, the story also illustrates the unlikelihood of completely thwarting suffering and injustice in this world. Human beings like Job cannot easily overcome challenges in this world, or create major change, even though they can sustain their faith in the face of it. In other words, the story of Job illustrates two common themes in the Mainline Protestant and Catholic sermons: earthly problems can be due to factors external to the individual, and efforts to change the world are not guaranteed to succeed. This interpretation of the Book of Job contrasts starkly with Pentecostal discussions of these same passages. The Pentecostal sermons tend to home in on a particular verse in Job, spoken by one of Job's friends: "You will also decree a thing, and it will be established for you. And light will shine on your ways" (Job 22:28). This verse underscores the power of positive thinking and prophetic prayer: have faith that something will happen, speak that it will happen, and God will make it happen, the passage says. The passage is spoken by Job's friend, who views Job's suffering as a product of his lack of faith. The verse locates responsibility for Job's earthly problems inside him – in his character and relationship with God. The verse also promises imminent change if Job strengthens his own faith and embodies that faith in his words and deeds. In other words, Pentecostal sermons use the Book of Job to illustrate two common themes in their world view: earthly problems are due to factors internal to the individual and his/her relationship with God, and efforts to change the world, if done through embodied faith, can meet with imminent success. Even when discussing the same scriptural text, the Pentecostal and the Mainline/Catholic answers to deep metaphysical questions about the sources of earthly problems and the possibilities for change are quite different.

Another illustrative example is how Pentecostal sermons and Mainline/Catholic sermons tend to interpret the story of David and Goliath differently. In the story, the young boy David, with only a staff and a few stones, stands up to the strong, powerful, and armored Goliath, whose Philistine army is fighting the Israelites. In Pentecostal sermons, this story is typically used to illustrate the ability of individuals with strong faith to overcome all odds and enact material change in this world by embodying their faith. One pastor put it thus:

David did the impossible and slayed Goliath. David had an ability that his brothers did not see. Ignore critics just the way David did. When God has decided, he has decided ... If you see yourself the way God sees you, you will conquer ... Start looking at yourself as successful ... All we have to do is believe in God and ourselves.

In this Pentecostal sermon, the story of David and Goliath is used to illustrate the power of individuals' internal characteristics and their relationships with God to enact material, earthly change, and to "conquer" earthly problems, against all odds. This perspective contrasts with how the story is typically interpreted in Mainline Protestant and Catholic sermons. In a Mainline Protestant sermon, this same story is used to illustrate how even people of strong faith suffer and encounter earthly problems, and how God helps people cope with (but not eliminate) the challenges they will inevitably face in life. "You remember David. David had an experience where someone asked him were you able to face Goliath ... [He said] the God who has helped me in the past with the lions and God who was with me during this is the same God who is going to help me face this Goliath. Sometimes we suffer because we are Christians and suffering here is also how we see that God uses it to teach us to help us to grow to maturity." In this Mainline Protestant sermon, standing up to Goliath does not represent the imminent possibility of earthly change through faith. Instead, in this sermon, Goliath represents the trials and problems that *even people of strong faith* inevitably encounter in this world. Earthly challenges are not due to lack of faith or individuals' internal characters: they are brought on by forces external to the individual, and there is no guarantee that they can be eliminated.

In other words, even when discussing the same passages of scripture, the world views presented by Pentecostal sermons, on the one hand, and Mainline Protestant and Catholic sermons, on the other, typically differed both in where they located the source of earthly problems and in the degree to which they indicated a possibility of change in this world. Both sets of sermons discussed heaven and offered rewards for faith in heaven as a motivator for action in this life. A big difference was that Mainline Protestant and Catholic sermons offered heavenly rewards but gave no additional guarantee of material change on earth. One Mainline Protestant sermon put it thus: "We are eternity conscious; we know that our lord is coming back; and we are prepared, that is always in the front of our minds ... We are looking forward towards that day and that influences the way we live. It influences the way we act, it influences the way we interact, how we relate with other people because we have the return of the lord to reckon with as believers." The possibility of change in this life is low, even as the promise of heavenly rewards is made salient. Pentecostal sermons, on the other hand, typically offered earthly triumph as well as heavenly rewards.

Computer-Assisted Text Analysis

Through the use of computer-assisted text analysis, we were interested in "uncovering" topics of communication from clergy to congregation, through an unsupervised approach (Grimmer and Stewart, 2013). These programs are typically used with a large number of texts when all documents cannot feasibly be coded by hand. Yet, even with a smaller corpus of texts, computer-assisted topic modeling programs can provide certain advantages, including that the analytic procedure is fairly transparent and, although researcher interpretation is required, "uncovering" surprising patterns is often more likely than when researchers are coding texts by hand. We used computer-assisted text analysis to take a first cut at analyzing the sermons in order to leave open the possibility that we would find unanticipated patterns. Among text analysis programs, the STM program allowed us to incorporate metadata on the sermon texts into our analysis, including whether the sermon came from a Pentecostal, Mainline Protestant, or Catholic church; whether the sermon was delivered during an electoral or nonelectoral period; and whether the congregation exhibited certain demographic characteristics.

We pooled all sermons together, identified common topics in the entire corpus of texts, and then estimated differences in mean prevalence of sermon topics across church categories. We prepared the text corpus by removing numbers and punctuation, converting all text to lower case, removing standard English stop words and stemming words. We chose the number of topics to ask the program for by running a selection model with different numbers of topics requested (from two to fifty) and then choosing the model producing topics that scored highest on both semantic coherence and exclusivity. In STM, semantic coherence indicates the degree to which the most frequent words in a topic cooccur.[22] Exclusivity means the extent to which words strongly associated with a given topic are weakly associated with others. We were looking to ask the program to identify a number of topics that would maximize scores on both indicators. Figure 3.2 summarizes the topics generated when requesting twelve topics,[23] and using indicators for Pentecostal (versus Mainline Protestant/Catholic), a predominantly young congregation, an English-speaking service, an ethnically mixed (rather than ethnically dominated) congregation, location in an informal settlement, and election (versus nonelection) period as covariates. Each topic appears in 6–12 percent of the texts in

---

[22] See Roberts et al. (2014) and Stewart, Roberts, and Tingley (2014)'s appendix for more detailed definitions.

[23] In some previous versions of the book, we requested as many as twenty-four topics but with further probing found these topics to be difficult to interpret as distinct, and an error in coding revealed that the frequency and exclusivity (FREX) score for twenty-four topics was lower than that for models generating fewer topics.

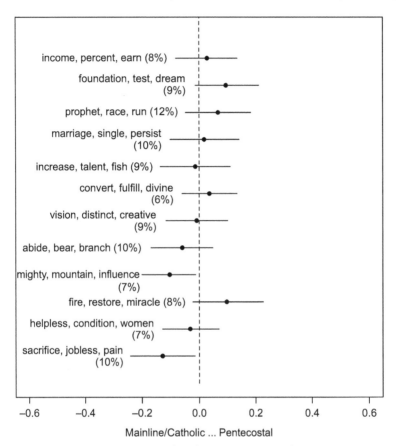

FIGURE 3.2 Sermon topics across church categories (Nairobi). Point estimates denote estimated differences in prevalence between the two church categories. Bars around point estimates denote 95 percent confidence intervals.

the corpus, as indicated in parentheses. The figure shows "best words" according to latent Dirichlet allocation (LDA) scoring.

Two aspects of Figure 3.2 are noteworthy. First, none of the topics is explicitly political. Instead, they revolve around such subjects as finances, dreams and plans, marriage and singleness, suffering, and miracles. Second, for the most part, Pentecostal and Mainline/Catholic sermons are discussing similar subjects. The topics for the most part are not detectably features only of Pentecostal or only of Mainline/Catholic sermons. All categories of churches are discussing money, the future, marriage and women, persistence and striving. However, a couple of the topics are statistically associated more with one church category than the other, and these are illustrative of our main arguments. For instance, an excerpt from a sermon associated with the topic of "fire, restore, miracle," which is slightly (though not statistically significantly) associated with Pentecostal sermons, comes from a Pentecostal sermon wherein the pastor preached, "We've been looking at understanding the miracle power of praise ... We praise God to make things happen. We don't just praise God for what has happened but we praise God to make things happen ... Many are devastated, stranded, destroyed simply because they lack an understanding or an insight into the miracle and mystery of praise." The message focuses on the connections between individuals' internal characteristics (their understanding of the power of praise) and material problems, and it emphasizes the imminent possibilities of change in this life ("We praise God to make things happen"). In contrast, an excerpt from a sermon associated with the topic of "mighty, mountain, influence" (which is statistically associated with Mainline Protestant and Catholics sermons), comes from a Lutheran church and speaks about the promise not of change in this life but of paradise in the next: "Eat and drink from the feast that is to come, the eternal feast, the feast on the mountain top, and the wonderful wine where God comes to dine with you swallowing not the earthly food but swallowing up death ... Let God's dream come true there ... a dream of you being treated as an equal by others and treating others as equals." The discussion in this sermon is of an end to earthly problems through right relationships between people, but that kind of change is possible in the next life ("the eternal feast") rather than in this one. An excerpt from a sermon associated with the topic demarcated by "sacrifice, jobless, pain" comes from a Catholic church, in which the priest encouraged listeners to remember the promise of eternal life as they mend their relationships with others: "The death in which we are suffering is like as Jesus was sacrificed. The sacrifice of Jesus was a generous death ... a death of love to mankind. When you are generous [with others], then you are partaking the candle you receive ... [and] will be rewarded in heaven." The message is one of repairing relationships between people, of honoring Jesus' sacrifice through right relationships, but the discussion is not about achieving an end to earthly problems in this life but rather about acting in this way in order to receive rewards in the next life.

Beyond these isolated examples of distinct topics, Pentecostal sermons and Mainline Protestant/Catholic sermons differed in how they discussed even the same subject matter. Figure 3.3 shows the words associated with a topic, grouped by whether the topic was discussed by a Pentecostal (to the right) or a Mainline Protestant/Catholic (to the left) sermon. The

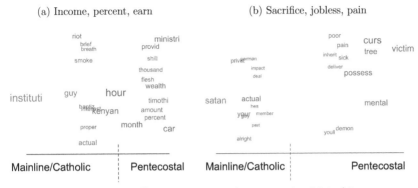

FIGURE 3.3 Difference in perspectives on topics (Nairobi).

larger the words, the more frequently they appeared. The further to the left or right the words are, the more strongly associated those words are with that category of church. On the subject of income and earnings (left), the Pentecostal sermons focus on individual wealth and ministry to cultivate personal transformation, whereas the Mainline Protestant and Catholic sermons focus on institutions, proper relationships, and violence as facilitators or obstacles to prosperity. On the subject of sacrifices and suffering (right) – a topic that appeared more frequently among Catholic and Mainline Protestant sermons – the Pentecostal sermons, when they discussed it, focused on a person's mental state, whether she had a "victim" mentality, was internally possessed by demons, or was denying curses on her faculties and character. In contrast, Mainline Protestant and Catholic sermons focused on whether individuals were "members" of cultural and social groupings that exhibited generosity and care for the less fortunate; they drew attention to factors outside of the individual – even to Satan – as causes of financial suffering and lack. Indeed, the discussions of demons and Satan are telling: in Pentecostal sermons, they tend to be about individual (internal) demons, whereas discussions of Satan in Mainline Protestant and Catholic sermons more often treat him as an external force.

But perhaps by differentiating by denomination, we are missing substantial variation within denominations across different types of congregations. To explore this possibility, we estimated models in which topic prevalence was allowed to vary by whether the church where the sermon was delivered was in a slum area of the city or not, by whether the congregation of the church was predominantly young (under forty) or not, by whether the service was delivered in English rather than in Swahili or another language, by whether the congregation was deemed ethnically mixed or not, and by whether the sermon was delivered in the months just before the general elections or not.

Sermon topics did not vary much across different types of congregations within denomination categories, even though the congregations we examined were socioeconomically diverse. Indeed, with only a few exceptions, the point estimates were very close to zero, meaning that even with uncertainty around the point estimates due to smaller sample sizes, we can be fairly confident that there was little difference in topic prevalence across congregations with young versus more mixed-age congregants, with Swahili or English services, with more ethnically homogeneous or mixed congregations, and so on.

We also estimated whether the prevalence of these topics changes between electoral and nonelectoral periods but detected no differences in topic prevalence between the two periods, and the point estimates of differences in topic prevalence were very close to zero. The one exception was that a slightly greater share of Pentecostal sermons in the 2017 election period discussed financial investment and the parable of the five talents than of Pentecostal sermons in the nonelectoral period. This is an interesting finding that might warrant future research on the consequences of religious communication on economic behavior during electoral cycles. But, by and large, topic prevalence is similar within church categories across the two time periods. With the exceptions of prayers for peace (which we discuss a bit more later in this chapter), preaching was remarkably consistent during both time periods.

Hand Coding Results

We did not have a large corpus of texts by machine learning standards, so we could feasibly also pursue a hand coding approach. There are additional advantages to hand coding. For instance, given the smaller number of texts, the computer program can estimate differences in topic prevalence but only with high levels of uncertainty. The STM program is also best for identifying groups of words that cooccur (topics) but not as adept at identifying different logics and arguments around similar topics (Benoit et al., 2016). Through a separate hand coding approach, we corroborated the findings from the STM program and looked for more nuance in the logics and arguments around sermon topics. Three coders, blind to whether the sermons came from Pentecostal, Mainline, or Catholic churches, read each text independently in order to summarize the main themes of each sermon and code them as individually empowering or dis-

TABLE 3.4 *Hand coding results (Nairobi sermons)*

	Pentecostal	Mainline/Catholic
Individually empowering	0.82	0.21
	(0.39)	(0.42)
Individual faith to earthly problems	0.87	0.16
	(0.34)	(0.37)
Mention of structural unfairness/injustice	0.06	0.52
	(0.24)	(0.51)

empowering as connecting individual faith/mindset to earthly problems or not, and as mentioning structural unfairness or systematic injustice or problems with institutions. There was very little disagreement across coders. Where disagreement occurred, we present the coding that cuts against our main findings (that is, that codes Pentecostal sermons as disempowering and as not connecting faith to earthly problems, or that codes Mainline/Catholic sermons as empowering and as connecting faith to earthly problems).

Table 3.4 summarizes results of this hand coding exercise. Each cell in Table 3.4 reports the share of sermons in that church category that were coded as consistent with a particular theme. Standard deviations are reported in parentheses. The results corroborated the findings from the computer-assisted analysis. The Pentecostal sermons came out much more likely to be interpreted as individually empowering; they were also more likely to argue that changes in strength of faith and mindset can directly make a material difference in people's lives or that individual faith is responsible for early problems. By contrast, Mainline and Catholic sermons were more likely to mention injustice, structural unfairness, or institutional (including cultural) flaws in connection with earthly problems. Even though hand coding can be noisy or subject to disagreement across coders, the differences here are large enough that noise and disagreement are unlikely to wipe them out. Of course, it is not the case that every single sermon in either church category discusses these themes explicitly, or that certain themes are never taken up by a church in a different category than the typical one. Nevertheless, certain themes *tend* to appear in Pentecostal rather than in Mainline Protestant/Catholic sermons, and vice versa.

These main themes and differences in service and sermon content were not explicitly political. Coders also noted whether sermons mentioned explicitly political topics: interethnic peace/violence; free and fair (credible) elections; specific politicians, candidates, or policies; political institutions; or political actions (e.g., encouraging listeners to register or to vote); but the sermons very rarely mentioned specific officeholders, candidates, policies, political institutions, or even ethnicity. Our first set of observations were from 2013 to 2014 and from July to August 2016, after the Presidential and National Assembly elections had taken place in January and February 2013. Five sermons delivered during this time mentioned concerns about "tribalism," but ethnic identity and conflict were not the principle topics even of these sermons.[24] During the preelection weeks in 2017 as well, sermons very rarely addressed explicit political topics. The exception was that, in the weeks leading up to the 2017 elections, religious leaders did take moments during the services to pray for peace.[25] Peace was rarely the principal topic of a sermon but it was frequently mentioned during services in the preelection period. The lack of explicit political endorsements and directions, coupled with the focus on peace, may be a product of religious leaders' hesitancy in Kenya to play any role in stirring interethnic violence following the 2007–2008 election violence (Deacon, 2015). Largely apolitical sermons and a focus on peace characterized all congregations, no matter the denomination or other differences in service content.

Table 3.5 summarizes the results of hand coding the sermons for mentions of peace, free and fair elections, specific candidates, officeholders or policies, specific government institutions, and specific calls to political action (e.g., to vote), and of dividing the sermons according to whether they were delivered during an election period or not. Table 3.6 shows the same, but dividing sermons according to the church category in which they were delivered. One can see that mentions of peace for the country and encouragements to vote are both more prevalent during the electoral period of 2017. However, during that election period, Pentecostal and Mainline/Catholic churches were praying for peace and calling for people to vote at similar rates. Mention of free and fair (as opposed to peaceful) elections, of specific candidates, parties, and policies, and of specific

---

[24] For instance, one sermon argued that "Christians should be categorical in the fight for reconciliation in this nation and not involve themselves in tribal politics." But the sermon mentioned this issue only in the first minute and then moved on to discuss God's work in business affairs. Another sermon argued that if congregants' tribal affiliation "has not been subdued by the Christian message, you are not a true Christian," but most of the sermon discusses the achievement that comes from focus and commitment ("if you're committed you will achieve whatever is your dream").

[25] In 2007–2008, Kenya experienced significant interethnic violence in the aftermath of contested and disputed elections. In the electoral periods since then, all organizations, including religious ones, have called for peace (Deacon, 2015).

TABLE 3.5 *Explicit politics in electoral and nonelectoral periods (Nairobi)*

	Electoral period (2017)	Nonelectoral period (late 2013–2016)	Difference
Prayed for peace in the country	0.29 (0.46)	0.03 (0.16)	0.26 (p = 0.000)
Mentioned election credibility	0.03 (0.18)	(0.02) (0.13)	0.01 (p = 0.52)
Mentioned specific candidates/policies	0.02 (0.13)	0.05 (0.22)	−0.03 (p = 0.28)
Mentioned govt offices or institutions*	0.10 (0.31)	0.09 (0.29)	0.01 (p = 0.85)
Encouraged voting	0.17 (0.38)	0.02 (0.13)	0.15 (p = 0.004)

* E.g., mentioned the office for the president, the parliament, or courts. Standard deviations or p-values associated with a two-sided t-test of the difference in means in parentheses.

government institutions remains low in both electoral and nonelectoral periods, and did not detectably increase during the preelection period. Furthermore, during the election period, Mainline/Catholic sermons were no more likely to contain such references than Pentecostal churches were.

Other political topics were addressed only infrequently as well. For instance, only three of the sermons in the entire set explicitly mentioned (and voiced opposition) to homosexuality, and those three sermons did so only briefly.[26] Two sermons briefly touched on abortion. We might not have expected variation in positions on these topics across church categories. In Kenya, Pentecostal, Mainline Protestant, and Catholic churches have all taken conservative stances on homosexuality and abortion.[27] Sunday worship services largely did not discuss these topics.

[26] Grossman (2015) marshals evidence to argue that the salience of homosexuality issues in sub-Saharan Africa is in part due to the growth of Pentecostal, Charismatic, and Renewalist churches. We do not argue here that adherents of Pentecostalism and Mainline Protestantism/Catholicism are tolerant of homosexuality; rather, we find that the Nairobi sermons we observed spent little time on this issue. Where we have notes on entire services, we also found that the issue was not a prominent part of other parts of worship in any denomination. This does not mean that antihomosexuality agendas are not mobilized in other ways in these churches.

[27] The Catholic Church, including in Kenya, has long taken an open conservative stance on restricting abortion. During the debates over the 2010 constitution, Pentecostal leaders joined with Mainline and Catholic leaders to opposed reforms that loosened restrictions on abortion and created personal and family law courts for Muslims, called Kadhi courts, as we discuss in Chapter 6.

TABLE 3.6 *Explicit politics during election period, by denomination (Nairobi sermons)*

	Pentecostal	Mainline/Catholic	Difference
Prayed for peace	0.29	0.25	0.04
	(0.46)	(0.46)	(p = 0.81)
Mentioned specific	0.02	0.00	0.02
candidates/policies	(0.14)	–	(p = 0.32)
Mentioned govt offices	0.09	0.12	−0.03
or institutions	(0.30)	(0.35)	(p = 0.84)
Encouraged voting	0.18	0.13	0.05
	(0.39)	(0.38)	(p = 0.71)

As we saw in the previous section, the striking sermonic themes (linking individual faith to material change, describing God's will, describing systematic injustice) did not diminish in electoral, rather than nonelectoral, periods, or vice versa. These sermonic themes were also not delivered in explicitly political terms. Certain political themes (peace, voter turnout) did take a more prominent place in sermons during the preelection period, but they did so in both Pentecostal and Catholic/Mainline churches. Other explicitly political topics (specific candidates, institutions, policies – including electoral reform, homosexuality laws, and abortion) were rarely the subject of sermons in either church category and in either time period.

SERMONS FROM ELSEWHERE IN SUB-SAHARAN AFRICA

In order to investigate whether these same sermon themes appear in other contexts across sub-Saharan Africa, we took two additional steps.[28] First, we conducted in-depth looks at sermons in two other contexts quite different from Nairobi's: one in rural Malawi and one in Johannesburg, South Africa. Second, we conducted a cursory examination of sermons from a set of African cities where Pentecostal churches have grown rampantly and gained international media attention: Accra, Lagos, and Kampala. We found that whether sermons draw a direct connection between internal faith and earthly problems and whether they promise imminent material change in this life or not are central differences in messaging between Pentecostal and Mainline/Catholic churches in these other contemporary contexts as well.

---

[28] As we discuss in the concluding chapter, the themes also likely extend well beyond sub-Saharan Africa.

First, we examined a small set of sermons collected from Pentecostal and Mainline churches in rural Malawi by Jenny Trinitapoli (Trinitapoli and Weinreb, 2012). Trinitapoli collected these sermons as part of a research project aimed at understanding religious organizations' teachings around HIV/AIDS, and generously shared the notes with us. Trinitapoli (2009) describes her methodology in collecting the sermons thus: "I located congregations to observe by conducting a census of religious organizations in the 60 sample villages from which survey respondents [for the Malawi Diffusion and Ideational Change Project (MDICP)] were drawn in two districts [Balaka and Rumphi] ... Over a period of two months [during the summer of 2004], each congregation was observed at least once during a main weekly service. Trained research assistants were instructed to observe and write reports on each congregation's service (with a particular focus on the message of each service)." The data thus cover all houses of worship in all villages within two rural districts of Malawi and collect information not just about how churches discuss HIV/AIDS in their sermons but also on all topics and messages discussed in worship services. By our count, Trinitapoli compiled notes from twenty Pentecostal churches and eighteen Mainline or Catholic churches during this time.[29] The churches were on average quite small, with typically somewhere between thirty to one hundred attendees. (One of the sermon notes for a Pentecostal church described attendance as in the thousands, but this church was by far the outlier.) The Mainline Protestant denominations included Anglican, Baptist, and Presbyterian. The notes varied from almost-verbatim transcripts to paraphrased summaries of the sermons. We read this small corpus of texts to assess whether similar themes, and differences in themes, appeared in the context of rural Malawi as had appeared in Nairobi.

Despite the very different context in which these sermons were collected, these rural churches exhibited similar thematic patterns in sermon content. As in Nairobi, Pentecostal sermons emphasized individual's internal (psychological) attributes and internal faith as the source of earthly problems and promised change in this life if individuals can strengthen their own faith and promote good internal character: "Only God can give you what you want"; "God promotes us for the good things we do

---

[29] We excluded churches for which the notes did not indicate a denomination clearly to us. Trinitapoli collected more than one sermon from some Mainline Protestant and Catholic churches, such that we had access to notes from twenty-seven services from these eighteen churches.

if we call on the Holy Spirit." Like the Nairobi sermons, the Malawi Pentecostal sermons promise material and social change in this life through a change in the mindsets and characters of individuals. The key to escaping disease, poverty, and hardship, according to many of these sermons, is to have "an established heart" and to live a faithful life. Like the Nairobi sermons, these sermons did not advocate enrichment as a primary goal. "Do not worship money," one sermon explicitly cautioned. Another sermon warned congregants not to count on magic or miracles for money but rather to focus on living a decent life as the ultimate goal.[30] Nevertheless, the sermons promised material improvement, broadly defined, in this life and located the source of earthly problems in people's mindsets and characters.

As in Nairobi, the Catholic and Mainline Protestant sermons in Malawi largely connected faith to rewards in the next life but not to change in this one. Almost all of the sermons (Pentecostal or mainstream) promised entry to heaven for action: "We will be judged according to our deeds. Ask yourself this question: when God comes, where will I stand?" But in the Catholic and Mainline Protestant sermons, there was no promise of material change or an end to suffering *in this life*, even though listeners were asked to leave the world a better place than they found it. One sermon asks, "How will you leave this world? What we are considering is not the method of our departure, such as disease, accident or violence. We will not have a choice about these things ... We are considering the spiritual condition in which we leave this world." The Catholic and Mainline sermons thus highlighted systemic earthly problems that are not due to individual character, choice, or relationship with God but rather due to factors external to the individual. These sermons advocated taking action to curb such systemic sin and suffering. As one sermon argued, "Today ... Christians just leave everything in the hands of the Lord. They want God to shield them from evil, disaster and anything that comes their way without taking any initiative firstly by themselves. But God does not work this way. As Christians we need to take an upper hand in our own survival either physically or spiritually ... We should also be able to assertively say 'no' to evil." But, even as these sermons advocated action against injustice, they did not promise that

---

[30] Indeed, the Malawi sermons took a more reserved position on proclaiming the radical possibilities of individual achievement than the urban Pentecostal sermons in Nairobi did, a pattern that may point to important differences in Pentecostal theologies between urban and rural settings. In rural settings, the idea of dramatic changes in wealth may be more removed.

such actions would be successful (as the Pentecostal sermons did). In these ways, the Malawi sermons exhibited patterns that were consistent with the Nairobi sermons.

We also conducted a systematic survey of sermons being delivered by Pentecostal, Mainline Protestant, and Catholic churches in Johannesburg. Johannesburg (and South Africa as a whole) offers one of the few instances in sub-Saharan Africa of a place where a significant portion of the population reports being *not* religious. Whereas in most countries no more than 2–3 percent of the population says that religion is not or not very important in their lives, in South Africa, close to 10 percent of the population says that religion is not or not very important to them. And in contrast to the 84 percent in the continent as a whole who say that religion is very important to them, in South Africa, only about 70 percent of the population agrees. Of course, this latter share is still high compared to more secular regions of the world (including the United States), but, among sub-Saharan African countries, South Africa stands out. Johannesburg is also a context in which Mainline and Catholic churches dominate Pentecostal churches numerically, and in which other world religions (Islam, Hinduism, Buddhism) are practiced by only tiny minorities of the population (unlike in Nairobi, where more than 10 percent of the population is Muslim). For all of these reasons, Johannesburg provides a place to test whether the same patterns of sermon content hold in a very different context.

In Johannesburg, one of the authors collaborated with Maria Frahm-Arp at the University of Johannesburg and a team of local student research assistants in order to collect sermon observations from Pentecostal, Mainline, and Catholic churches in the city. We discuss the resulting sermon observations briefly here.[31] The effort began in December of 2015 and finished in February 2017. The team divided up the lists equally and worked down their randomly sorted lists. Fifteen of the sermons were collected in May through July of 2016, just before the August 3, 2016, local elections in South Africa. We code these sermons as having been delivered during an electoral period.[32]

---

[31] Because the details of the Johannesburg sermons may be the subject of separate writing and research by Frahm-Arp, alone or in collaboration with the authors, we discuss these only briefly here in regard to the relevant questions about thematic content in this book. We do not discuss the content of the clergy interviews.

[32] National and local elections do not take place concurrently in South Africa. The August 2016 elections were for seats on local councils in all municipalities in the country, including for seats on the Johannesburg City Council. While the African National Congress (ANC) still holds a majority at the national level in South Africa, local elections

The team was able to collect sermon observations from and interview the pastors of eighty-two churches. Of the churches from which we were able to collect sermon texts and observations, fifty-five were self-identified Pentecostal churches and twenty-eight were Mainline Protestant or Catholic churches.[33] We used the same procedure to select the churches as in Nairobi – that is, we used search terms in Google Maps to generate a sampling frame and simple random sampled from resulting lists of Pentecostal and Catholic/Mainline congregations, oversampling from the Pentecostal church list in order to explore variation across these decentralized congregations. As we did in Nairobi, we asked clergy to verify the denomination of the church and asked them to describe the basic demographic features of the congregation. The response rates of Pentecostal and Catholic/Mainline churches were similar: we attempted to visit and conduct interviews with ninety-eight Pentecostal churches (success rate: 56 percent) and fifty-five Mainline and Catholic Churches (success rate: 51 percent). As in Nairobi, churches that could not be located were randomly replaced. Some churches did refuse interviews, usually claiming that the clergy were too busy, but no church refused a service visit or sermon text.

Figure 3.4 shows a map of the churches from which we have sermons in Johannesburg. The locations of the Pentecostal churches are indicated with triangles; the locations of the Mainline Protestant and Catholic churches from which we have sermons are indicated with circles. We were able to carry out service observations and clergy interviews in most areas of the city, yielding a sample of churches that covers megachurches; informal pop-up churches; richer and poorer congregations; and predominantly white, predominantly black, predominantly colored, and racially mixed churches.

We used the STM program to identify common topics in the sermons. As with the Nairobi sermons, we chose the number of topics we asked the program to identify by inputting different requests (from two topics to twenty) and choosing the number that provides the highest score on both exclusiveness and coherence of the topics. This process led us to ask

---

tend to be more competitive, and for the first time in the 2016 elections, the ANC lost control of the Johannesburg City Council to the opposition Democratic Alliance and the Economic Freedom Fighters. (The Democratic Alliance did not win an outright majority and so formed a coalition.)

33 We include the Dutch Reformed Church in the category of Mainline Protestant and Catholic churches. The Dutch Reformed Church was the principal church of the Afrikaaner population in South Africa under apartheid and is not present in Nairobi.

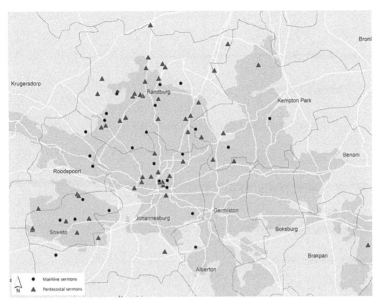

FIGURE 3.4 Map of Johannesburg churches from which we have sermons.

the program to identify nine topics across the eighty-two Johannesburg sermons. Figure 3.5 summarizes the topics generated when requesting nine topics and using Pentecostal (versus Mainline/Catholic) and election period as covariates. The figure shows highest probability words for each category and the percentage of texts in which each appears. The subject of grace and sin appears in over 20 percent of the sermon texts but is not more likely to appear in the sermons of one church category than another.

As in Nairobi, there is not much difference across church categories in the subject matters being discussed. Pentecostal sermons and Mainline Protestant, and Catholic sermons alike are discussing issues of money, women and the family, health and healing, wisdom, and sin. As mentioned earlier in the chapter, certain stories – like that of David and Goliath – appear across sermons of all church categories, though here discussions of sowing, reaping, and planting seeds are slightly (though not statistically) more prevalent among the Mainline Protestant and Catholic sermons than among Pentecostal ones.

But how these topics were discussed was telling. For instance, the topic "sow, reap, goliath" is also associated with a high incidence of the word "invest." But when Mainline Protestant and Catholic sermons discuss investment, sowing, and reaping, they are typically referring to investment

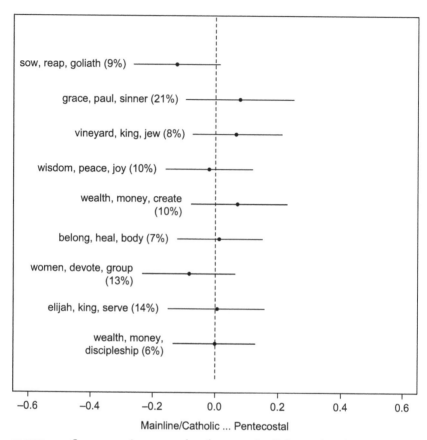

FIGURE 3.5 Sermon topics across church categories (Johannesburg). Point estimates denote estimated differences in prevalence between the two church categories. Bars around point estimates denote 95 percent confidence intervals.

in communities, in building institutions and investing in relationships. An excerpt from an Anglican sermon associated with this topic reads as follows: "[Let's engage] in activities that say the Kingdom of God is about more than just me, but also about the groups that we invest in, and the Kingdom of God is also about the hope for community in parts of the world where high walls can easily keep us apart. The hard stakes are currently stacked against us ... [but] we can act and put our heads in the game." The message is of investing in communities and relationships, even as the probability of change in this world is not high. By contrast, the Pentecostal sermon discussions of sowing, reaping, and investing typically focus on the imminent possibility of change in this world if individuals invest in personal transformation. An excerpt from a Pentecostal church associated with this topic urges listeners to invest in their own strength of faith, to cultivate it each day: "Sowing and reaping is both a law and a language. It's a language that God uses not just to construct history but to speak into our lives. It's a way for him to build our faith, to build our relationship with him … What you sow determines your harvest tomorrow … There is not gonna be a someday if you're not going to be willing to invest in today." The emphasis is on material rewards in this life and the next for investing, and in particular for investing in strengthening one's own faith, character, and relationship with God. Both types of sermons encourage generosity and giving – to the church, to others – as a sign of sowing and investing, but Mainline Protestant and Catholic sermons more often portray the route to change as low probability and as occurring through communities and institutions, whereas the Pentecostal sermons place a heavier emphasis on character and faith development and promise imminent results.

As in Nairobi, we found no evidence that these topics and perspectives differed between sermons collected outside of the 2016 preelection period and those collected during the three months leading up to the 2016 local elections in South Africa, although, given the small corpus of texts, the uncertainty around the estimated differences in mean prevalence is high. However, the point estimates are consistent with the patterns in Nairobi. Sermons stressing the material power of internal, individual characteristics (positive thinking, character, strong faith) were associated with Pentecostal churches in Johannesburg as well. Sermons stressing human limitations, suffering even for faithful people, and promising no rewards but those on judgment day were associated with Mainline Protestant and Catholic sermons. These differences did not detectably change or dissipate based on the electoral cycle.

We also took a cursory look at sermons in Accra, Lagos, and Kampala, three cities where Pentecostalism has grown dramatically and where much media attention has been paid to their particularities (Meyer, 1998; Asamoah-Gyadu, 2005; Marshall, 2009; Burgess, 2015).[34] In each of the three cities, we searched for Pentecostal, Mainline Protestant, and Catholic churches that appeared in Google Maps. We then collected any online sermons, recordings, or texts from the churches that had

---

[34] Pentecostal churches have received attention in Uganda in part due to high-profile Pentecostal preachers pushing for the criminalization of homosexuality there (Grossman, 2015).

websites, YouTube channels, or social media pages with sermon content. This method allowed us to examine the sermons of seven Pentecostal and seven Mainline/Catholic churches in Accra, eight Pentecostal and three Mainline/Catholic churches in Lagos, and three Pentecostal and two Mainline/Catholic churches in Kampala (for a total of thirty churches). Most churches had their most recent sermon, if any, available online, so the temporary coverage of these searches is limited to 2017. Of course, limiting our examination in these cities only to churches that make their sermons available online inevitably confines us to internationally oriented and/or wealthier churches that have the equipment and capacity to record and post sermons online. The expectations of these churches must be that current members, potential recruits, or possible donors have access to the Internet in order to access this content. Nevertheless, the exercise allows us to explore whether, at least among these types of churches, we still find evidence of the same thematic differences between Catholic and Pentecostal differences that we found in Nairobi, Johannesburg, and rural Malawi, where we looked at a broader set of congregations.

We find that the differences in metaphysical arguments between Pentecostal churches on the one hand and Mainline Protestant and Catholic sermons on the other also appear within this set of sermons. Pentecostal sermons in this set draw a blatant connection between individual mindset and material rewards, also often explicitly arguing that this connection between faith and material rewards is part of God's general way of working and ordering the world. A sermon from Agape House in Accra makes the connection between faith and material change explicit: "Mountain moving faith will not give up. It never quits. It keeps believing till the answer comes. What do you do in the storm? You don't give up ... Pray that the grace of God would be multiplied to you so that you will get ... a permanent, glorious and solid reward in your life." Fountain of Life Church in Lagos delivers a sermon arguing, "All things are possible to those who believe ... a faith declaration is a conviction from one's heart and it greatly determines the outcome of such a person in this life." Harvest International Ministries in Accra delivers sermons that are openly focused on promises of possessions and wealth as rewards for faith: "We want to move to a higher level, we don't just want to talk abundance, we want to live the abundant life ... let there be a revolution *in the heart* ... it's stewing in the spirit, this time next year you will have your own car!" (emphasis added). Pentecostal sermons mention rewards in heaven, too: Deeper Life Bible Church in Lagos focuses its entire sermon on the concept of salvation, but salvation includes both earthly and heavenly life.

The pastor exclaims, "He will do what he said he will do because he is God and there is nobody like him. Supernatural wonders is [sic] coming your way ... Supernatural wonders for all," and then explains that the wonders include not only salvation in heaven, but also cure from sickness and poverty in this life. The sermon promises, "Miracles everywhere. Comfort in every life." "One cannot enter the kingdom of God and ignore righteous living," argues a sermon from the Church of Pentecost. But the same sermon promises an end to earthly suffering for those who believe. In fact, the sermon also promises change in public life because God works through believers: we are "agents of His goodness so the wickedness in the world [will] not triumph ... If we put a lamp on a stand to shine, it dispels darkness." There is a sense in all of these sermons of the imminent possibilities for change in this life, through the transformation and conversion of individuals and God's reward of people's strengthening of faith. Indeed, Watoto Church (formerly Kampala Pentecostal Church) delivered a series of sermons arguing that "He who has faith will see the fruit of your harvest ... Change the way you think ... and you will see the fruit." What is required to succeed is a change in thinking, a change in faith. Little attention is paid to structures and institutions. In the Pentecostal sermons we collected from these cities, the themes connecting individuals' strength of faith and character with material change were apparent.

Likewise, the Catholic and Mainline Protestant sermons in this set exhibited the same themes that were apparent in Nairobi, Johannesburg, and rural Malawi. The Mainline and Catholic sermons made promises of rewards for faith and action but only with regard to heavenly salvation, not to success or well-being in this life. Indeed, St. Barnabas Catholic Church in Accra focused an entire sermon on the promise of Jesus' coming again to judge, arguing that this is the moment that will "restore us." The sermon from Our Lady Catholic Church in Kampala promises eternal rest and peace for those who work against injustice: "The rest offered is security and peace of following the path of goodness," but another sermon from the same church reminds listeners that "Judgment will be rendered only at the harvest, end time." However, these sermons typically do not hesitate to mention issues of injustices and call attention to structural and institutions sources of poverty and other earthly problems, although they tend to speak in general terms without naming specific people in power or policies. The sermon from St. Theresa Church in Accra argued that "God wants our lives to show forth His goodness and mercy ... to fill human society and culture with the justice and beauty they need to flourish," but the sermon promises no success from this effort, only that it might bring eternal peace when judgment comes. A sermon from Lady of Perpetual Help Catholic Church in Lagos describes at length the systemic problems the country faces (again without naming names or policies): "If the needy and the weak of the society who cry to us daily do not get a favourable answer are we not opening the door for distress to come upon us and our nation? We cannot pretend that they do not exist." But the sermon does not promise dramatic transformation in the material conditions of this life: "Our inability to find a solution to the problems that confront us take us from pillar to post and from sea to sea." Faith makes the burdens feel lighter, the sermon argued, but real change may come only with Judgment Day. The Mainline and Catholic sermons in these cities[35] combine portrayals of structural and systemic injustice that should be addressed with recognition of human beings' limitations. In general, the set of sermons we have from these cities exhibit similar thematic differences to those in the sermons from Nairobi, Malawi, and Johannesburg.

FOCUS GROUPS: CONGREGANTS' TAKEAWAYS FROM SERMONS

How did ordinary congregants recall and interpret the content of sermons? In the course of our research, we held small focus group discussions with members of several different churches in Nairobi. With two congregations (one Pentecostal and one Catholic), we held focus groups purposefully staggered and held either at the end of the week or just after Sunday services. These discussions shed some light on how long the influence of sermons persists during the week, and we describe these conver-

---

[35] Certainly, there are exceptions that combine message types. In particular, there are instances where Mainline Protestants seem to adopt elements of Pentecostal messaging. Tesano Baptist Church mixes messages, arguing both that there is injustice in the world and that "It is you God who brought us to a wealth place," and urging people to adopt a posture of thanksgiving and positive outlook in order to achieve material success: "You need faith to accomplish the goals. Faith is the rope that pulls expectations to you ... The faith you generate from the word of God will bring you what you desire." Although we classified this church as Mainline Protestant, its clergy communicates messages that are more closely tied to the sermons of Pentecostal churches in the connection it draws between individual faith and material rewards in this life. Not every Pentecostal or Mainline/Catholic sermon adheres to the messaging typical of its category, and some denominations will deliver sermons that sit at the border between sermonic themes; for subsequent analyses in this book, we require only that Pentecostal sermons are more likely to connect individual faith and material rewards than Mainline/Catholic sermons.

sations in Chapter 5. We also held nonstaggered focus groups with seven other sets of congregants (two sets from Catholic churches and five sets from Pentecostal churches). We went to churches whose messages were typical of the patterns we have described in this chapter: that is, typical of individual-focused, high-possibility sermons among the Pentecostal set, and of society-focused, low-possibility sermons among the Catholic set. The Pentecostal churches included two megachurches with a mix of poor, upwardly mobile, and rich congregants, and three Pentecostal churches based in informal settlements, with typically poorer congregations. One Catholic parish was largely middle class, and the other was based in an informal settlement.

In our focus group discussions, congregants spoke to us about their interpretations of the sermons they had recently heard. They also spoke about how they make sense of the struggles in their own lives. At the end of the discussions, we asked them for their views on the appropriate role of citizens in politics ("As a Christian, what do you think it means to be a good citizen?"). Asking this question meant that we could observe whether and how discussion group respondents applied ideas from sermons to their thinking about appropriate ways to participate in politics.

The Pentecostal congregants in our discussion groups consistently pointed to the sermons' focus on encouragement and self-mastery. They agreed that worship services were rarely explicitly political. As one congregant put it, "We are always encouraged to pray for the nation and for our leaders, but neutrally and with respect; we don't pray that a particular leader will be elected so that they can deliver." The congregants all circled around similar themes when recalling the sermons' messages. One congregant from a Pentecostal megachurch explained that the sermon's message was to "keep on challenging ourselves to make yourself better (sic). Everyone [should be] going to school, getting a masters or some training to develop yourself." That same congregant then commented on the role of the citizen by explaining that "the best thing is to pray to God to be in [the leaders'] heart, and guide them. And to choose a good person, God-fearing … We listen to politicians every day on the news. Then you get to know them, their character." She connected a commitment to change through internal transformation to a focus on the recruitment and selection of political leaders on the basis of character. Her view was that her role as a citizen is to select leaders based on their internal characteristics (good, God-fearing) and their relationships with God and then to guide them to maintain those internal characteristics and motivation. Having spoken about the self-affirming content of the sermons, she further remarked, "We are the leaders of tomorrow. *We* have to lead." Her approach to politics involves selecting leaders with intrinsic motivations to serve the public interest and perhaps even running for office herself. Another congregant from a different Pentecostal megachurch commented, "The word that resonates with me in this church is that ... you can be excellent like anyone in the world; anybody can be a winner." A fellow congregant agreed and elaborated that excellence comes through a strong relationship with God, which is something available to everyone but has to be developed. Therefore, his role as a citizen is to sort through leaders based on their character and relationship to God: "A [good] leader must understand that he is under somebody else. He is not all powerful. Only God is that." A congregant from an informal settlement-based Pentecostal church put it this way: "The sermon was on 'Never give up,' how to handle your problems ... As Christians we should not be calm and comfortable with our situations till we reach our intended glory. ... So [you must] look out for godly attributes and virtues, voting with your own wisdom. And then acceptance of those elected even though it might not be your choice." The congregant views the appropriate path to change in politics is through the selection of leaders with valued internal characteristics – with "godly attributes" – and then to allow those internally transformed individuals to carry change through, without additional external constraints or resistance from citizens. In each of the discussions, the congregants interpreted what they were hearing in church as encouragement to focus on individual self-mastery and on improving one's own life through internal transformation. The congregants' approach to politics was then to focus on recruiting and selecting internally transformed leaders – those with intrinsic incentives to work in citizens' interests.

The discussions with Catholic parishioners had a different bent. On the one hand, just like the Pentecostal congregants, the Catholic congregants agreed that messages and discussions in worship services were not explicitly political. A congregant from the informal settlement-based church observed, "Youth have a WhatsApp group within the church. Some use it for jobs, church activities. They are not posting about politics ... None of the churches encourage politics ... activism is a personal choice for each member." On the other hand, Catholic congregants described very different sermonic themes than Pentecostal congregants did, and they described a different orientation toward participation in politics as well. In describing sermons, Catholic congregants did not describe them as particularly uplifting or encouraging. Indeed, they often described themes of caution, coping, and managed expectations. "Not all problems have solutions," one commented. "I need to park it somewhere, leave it there." But when pressed to diagnose the problems of the world ("Whose responsibility is it then to address things like poverty?"), Catholic responses focused on structural factors rather than on individuals' internal attributes. For example, a congregant in the middle-class parish argued that when it comes to poverty, "The government has to deal with it because poverty has many dimensions. [At a high level], farmers in Kenya do not have the big markets as in Europe so the government must negotiate at that level to open up those markets against the restrictions that block us." The sources of poverty are structural and need institutional responses. Another congregant in that same church agreed: "The government must do something to eradicate poverty, get some money. Even us, we should do something, yes, but government is necessary." Each congregant drew attention to structural (rather than individual) sources of problems, and noted the difficulty of finding easy solutions. "I have to believe I will change something otherwise I'll go mad. But politics is so messed up ... The rut is so deep." The congregants were not opposed to taking political action, but they also did not exhibit the Pentecostals' expectations that such actions would necessarily meet with success. The Catholic congregants' political approaches were also not about selecting leaders with better characters but rather about holding existing public officials (whatever their internal characteristics) to account. "We should demand services from public officials, hold them in check," one congregant argued. "Vote on their manifesto and program; we hold them responsible," another argued. "Implement campaign finance law. That could change things because the strategies to convince voters would change," added a third. The congregants' focus was on responses and reforms that would affect the extrinsic incentives of public figures to serve citizens' interests – reforms that would sanction and check leaders' behavior once in office. Catholic parish discussions did not revolve primarily around the selection and recruitment of leaders with desirable internal characteristics.

These nonstaggered focus groups took place in the weeks leading up to the general elections. Although clergy did pray for peace during each of the proximate services, we did not observe otherwise explicitly political sermons in these churches during this time, which was in keeping with the discussion groups' insistence that church services are rarely explicitly about politics. The common refrain from participants across focus groups was that partisan discussion would divide the church membership and the pastor or priest would do best to stay away from it. A member of one of the informal settlement-based churches summed it up: "Our church is always neutral about politics and leaves this purely to individual church members but they usually encourage members to participate even in elective positions. People are given the same opportunities [within the church] irrespective of the party they are affiliated to." Another participant similarly commented, "We don't discuss policy, it is too divisive." The church recently had guest speakers from the electoral commission to educate the congregation on their right to vote and to explain the process, but the event was not partisan or focused on specific policies or candidates. The event provided the information about how to participate, and allowed the congregation the ability to "seek social justice and accountability" through the election, according to one member. The focus group participants corroborated that worship services focused on peace and voting and eschewed explicitly partisan discussions.

Yet when asked to express how they were thinking about citizenship, leadership, and facing challenges in the world around them, the focus group members often instead referred to the sermons they had most recently heard. A participant in a focus group in an informal-settlement-based Pentecostal church provides an illustration. When asked, "As a Christian, what do you think it means to be a good citizen?" she made no reference to an explicit political agenda of the church or to religious leaders' public statements. Instead, she said, "Being in the church is the best thing, because I get the word of God. Then I apply it every day. The Bible reminds me that he died and carried off anything that can oppress me ... The word of God is very powerful, it can change your circumstances. What I declare is what I possess, it becomes my fortune ... I appreciate myself as a citizen of Kenya. This is my divine purpose. I have to live it fully to accomplish this purpose." Her emphasis was on self-mastery and the possibilities of imminent change through declaring and embodying strong faith; she connected her approach to the words she had heard, to the ideas she is exposed to in worship service.

These discussions increased our confidence that our interpretations of the thematic differences in the sermons are close to the interpretations of ordinary congregants' themselves. They also suggested the plausibility of sermons' influence on different modes of political engagement. Catholics and Pentecostals alike were able to recall the specific theme of the prior weeks' sermons and relate it to their own strategies as citizens. And they think about their approach to citizenship and leadership through the lens of the message content they have heard in worship services.

SUMMARY

In this chapter, we have illustrated differences in religious message content across major categories of churches (Catholic, Mainline Protestant, and Pentecostal), both in Nairobi and in other areas of sub-Saharan Africa. The primary ways in which sermons differed were in how they attributed responsibility for earthly problems (to factors internal to the individual or external to the individual), and in how they portrayed the possibility of change in this world (as a high or a low possibility). These differences were stark across denominations, but, within denominations, the themes were very similar across congregations of very different demographic makeups. The patterns of Christian sermon content emerged in various parts of anglophone sub-Saharan Africa.

The sermons were rarely explicitly political, even during weeks immediately prior to a hotly contested general election in Kenya. Sunday worship services rarely, if ever, engaged in partisan politics or made mention of specific policies or candidates. In Kenya, this lack of political content may have been due to clergy's sensitivity at this particular point in time (2013–2017) to avoiding instigation of interethnic violence like that which had occurred in 2007–2008 (Deacon, 2015). Whatever the reason, in this particular point in time, we observed clergy of all denominations praying for peaceful elections and encouraging people to vote but not mobilizing people from the pulpit around explicit political issues, parties, or candidates. Nevertheless, even in contexts where sermons are not explicitly political, they may still be relevant to political behavior. Specifically, their metaphysical content may shape how ordinary congregants think about and respond to immediate political opportunities, as suggested in the focus group discussions. Religious teachings can shape people's notions of whether (and how) the physical and spiritual worlds are linked, and of what is possible in this life and the next, and, as such, they can influence how people approach political questions and problems. These effects are challenging to identify empirically, so in the next chapter we turn to the lab. There, we explicitly test the microfoundations of this argument using content from the real-world sermons we identified here.

4

Effects of Sermons on Citizens

Evidence from the Lab

The sermons described in the previous chapter draw on ideas about God and the spiritual world in order to paint different pictures of cause and effect in the physical world, and of the possibility for change. The Pentecostal sermons we observed point to factors internal to the self as causes of earthly problems meanwhile promising imminent material change. Weak faith, and acting without embodying strong faith – these are the things that create and sustain earthly problems; but strengthening one's faith, and embodying that strength of faith, can bring immediate material rewards. In contrast, Mainline Protestant and Catholic sermons turn to the quality of relationships among people, to institutions and culture – in short, to phenomena outside of the self – to explain earthly problems while at the same time promising no imminent material change. Earthly structures and institutions, culture the way people treat one another – these bear significant, even if not sole, responsibility for earthly problems. The Mainline Protestant and Catholic sermons encourage attention to these things. They promise no guaranteed success for actions aimed at changing them. The sermons differed in where they located the causes of earthly problems and in how they characterized the possibilities of change.

These differences in sermon content are evident in contemporary Nairobi as well as in many other parts of contemporary sub-Saharan Africa, but do they have an impact on listeners? Can they influence behavior in the political domain? Because the sermons were rarely explicitly political, one might be skeptical that exposure to these sermons would have any impact on political behavior. If one takes the view that links between religious world views and behavior are deep-seated, and likely to be fairly stable from childhood socialization and on, then it might seem unlikely that exposure to any one sermon, or even a set of sermons, would move people's ways of acting in the world in any significant way. At the same time, because the sermons tackle deep questions about cause and effect, and offer people ways to understand how the world works, they might shape citizens' diagnosis of worldly problems and their own agency, which might in turn influence whether or not they participate in politics. Does exposure to contemporary sermon content have an impact on political participation and, if so, how?

In this chapter, we take this question to the lab. Having collected and analyzed sermon texts in Nairobi, we created audio recordings drawn from real-world Pentecostal and Mainline/Catholic sermons delivered there. These audio recordings isolate differences in ideational content of the sermons while holding other aspects of sermon delivery (the voice, cadence, and rhetorical style of the preacher, and the environment and posture in which the listener hears the sermon) constant. We then invited Christians, of varying denominational affiliations, to participate in laboratory studies at the Busara Center for Behavioral Economics in Nairobi, where we randomly assigned each person to listen to one of the recordings on a headset. Across the three different studies, we measured different relevant outcomes: subjects' willingness to participate in realistic forms of political action, the content of that political action, their sense of self-efficacy, and their decisions in politician and citizen roles.

Exposure to sermon content did indeed influence listeners' political behaviors and attitudes around issues of political participation. The effects of message exposure were on both levels and types of political participation. Exposure to Pentecostal-like sermons increased levels of political participation: when we gave people the opportunity to voice their priorities and concerns to the government, study subjects who were exposed to Pentecostal teachings were most likely to take the initiative. Levels of participation were lower among people exposed to the Mainline Protestant and Catholic teachings. But the sermons also influenced *how* people participated, if they chose to participate. Exposure to the Pentecostal message generally oriented people around self-improvement and leadership concerns. Those exposed to the Pentecostal message often used the opportunity to participate in the text message campaign in order to offer themselves as political volunteers or to offer guiding comments to leaders. When we asked people to put themselves in the roles of politicians and citizens and to make decisions about spending (as politicians) and about reacting to politicians' behavior (as citizens), exposure to the

Pentecostal message moved subjects to focus on changing their *own behavior* as leaders,[1] but not to impose structural constraints on others. By contrast, those exposed to the Catholic/Mainline message took the text message opportunity to critique political institutions, laws, and the regime. When we asked them to act as politicians and citizens, exposure to the Mainline Protestant and Catholic message moved them not to improve their own behavior as leaders but instead to enact punishment on leaders who behaved badly – that is, to impose structural constraints on politicians. The Pentecostal message moved people to participate more and to focus on individual transformation as a way to improve governance. By contrast, the Mainline and Catholic message did little to boost participation but it did orient people to focus on institutional transformation as a way to improve governance.

The effects were in the same direction no matter the self-identified denomination of the subjects, but the effects were often strongest among listeners inclined to self-select into hearing those messages in their primary houses of worship. That is, the effect of exposure to a Pentecostal-like sermon was often strongest among self-identified Pentecostals. The effect of exposure to a Mainline Protestant/Catholic-like message was often strongest among self-identified Mainline Protestants and Catholics. These findings have important implications for the external validity of the findings. Because most sermon exposure is likely to come from regular church attendance, we might have been concerned that there are likely to be few real-world consequences of sermons, if people who self-identify with Pentecostalism, or with Mainline Protestantism/Catholicism, were to have been unaffected by the sermons associated with their primary houses of worship. We might have expected real-world consequences from incidental sermon exposure but not from regular attendance. Yet, instead we found that *sermons most strongly affect people who choose to hear them regularly*. That is, the main, real-world form of sermon exposure is politically consequential.

In addition, the short-term effects of sermon exposure tells us something important about the properties of religious influence.[2] They tell us that religious influence is not always a deeply-rooted source of political attitudes and behavior. Religious messages can also act as short-term

---

[1] Note that there is some evidence that the Catholic/Mainline Protestant message moved self-identified Pentecostals in this direction, toward acting as a good leader, as well.

[2] At least, they tell us something important about how religion works in the contemporary period and in relatively pluralist environments.

primes. Indeed, most houses of worship do not approach their work as if their influence is deep-seated and stops with early life socialization. Sermons are ideally delivered to congregants at least once a week, as well as during interim weekday services, in order to remind worshippers of important ways of seeing the world. As discussed in the next chapter, focus group participants from these churches expressed a felt need to return to church frequently to have their faith recharged. The *mechanisms of reinforcement* of religious world views are an important part of religion's role in the political world and should not be overlooked. We explore these insights further in subsequent chapters to show that divergences in political attitudes and behavior between people exposed to different religious teachings are evident observationally as well but only for a couple of days after exposure.

In subsequent chapters, we find patterns consistent with these lab results in survey data, focus groups, and case studies. People primarily affiliated with Pentecostal houses of worship report higher levels of political efficacy, make requests to and cultivate relationships with public officials, and seek change within existing institutions and structures, including by expressing interest in running for office. People primarily affiliated with Mainline Protestant and Catholic houses of worship are instead relatively more likely to express criticism of institutions and regimes and to protest and demand structural reform. In the lab, we can connect some of these aspects of political behavior directly to exposure to sermon content.

WHY AN EXPERIMENTAL APPROACH?

We used an experimental approach in order to take seriously the reasons for skepticism about religious messages outlined at the beginning of the book. If individuals choose to attend a religious service based at all on whether they find its message appealing, then the impact of exposure to religious messages on attitudes and behavior may be difficult to identify observationally. Differences in attitudes or behavior across people of different denominations might not mean that exposure to different theologies *causes* differences in attitudes and behavior. Instead, it could be that underlying preferences drive differences in church denominational affiliation, particularly when the barriers to switching are low. Laboratory experiments help with this problem. When people are randomly assigned to listen to different messages, as they were in the laboratory experiments we ran, we can be sure that any detected average differences in attitudes and behaviors after exposure are *due* to that exposure. At the same time, we can examine whether the treatment effects of exposure to a particular sermon are stronger or weaker among people who might otherwise have self-selected into listening to that sermon.

In the real world, it is also difficult to separate the effects of being exposed to particular religious ideas about how the world works from the possible effects of other parts of religious experience and identity. Religious practice is a bundle of things. When people hear a sermon, they are often also being exposed to a network of like-minded people as well as to the material benefits, organizational structures, hierarchies, and social practices of the church. Making claims about the effects specifically of exposure to sermon content can be difficult. In other parts of the book, we make the case that the churches we observed in Nairobi are quite similar in many of these other respects but quite different in their messaging. Indeed, we were surprised to find (as described in Chapter 3) that Pentecostal, Mainline Protestant, and Catholic churches in Nairobi and other parts of sub-Saharan Africa exhibit similar small group organizations within the church, display similar efforts at organizing midweek prayer services and outreach programming, and involve clergy in small group activities in similar roles. Nevertheless, in observational work we found it difficult to fully disentangle the content of religious teachings from other aspects of church experience.[3]

In the lab, we can more easily vary only the content of the message itself. We have control not just over random assignment of treatment but also over the content of the audio recordings and over the environment of the lab itself, which we can hold constant across treatment conditions. We can move much closer to isolating the effect of exposure to a given message by ensuring that the only thing that varies across participants' experiences in the lab is the type of message (the ideational content) to

---

[3] For instance, as mentioned in earlier chapters, it is difficult to fully separate churches' different approaches to social welfare provision from their differences in sermon content. In keeping with their message that earthly structures and how people care for one another are the source of earthly problems, Catholic churches especially often organized large-scale social welfare provision (hospitals, schools). Pentecostal churches, by contrast, in keeping with their message that earthly problems are linked to the internal life of the individual, organized psychological and spiritual training more often than large-scale social welfare provision. We found starker differences across these churches in their messaging than in their programming. Some Pentecostal churches are building schools and running medical camps even though their sermons are consistently focused on individual faith and imminent change. Some Catholic churches do little poverty relief, and most do not extensively involve the laity in social welfare provision. Nevertheless, the general relationship between messaging and programming remains.

which they were exposed. This level of control is available only in a lab setting. Among the empirical sections in this book, this chapter goes furthest in isolating exposure to sermon content from other aspects of religious experience and practice. Our study participants sat in cubicles in a laboratory and listened to the recordings on headsets. They did not engage in rituals, or listen to the messages communally; they did not receive social services that might otherwise be delivered in tandem with those messages. They were not encouraged to think about religious in- and out-groups. They had no relationship to the deliverer of the message, and even his tone, cadence, and identity were held constant. We come as close as we can to isolating the sermons' ideational content from other aspects of religious experience. One could argue that this provides a particularly tough test of the notion that sermons influence political behavior, because we have removed other aspects of the listening experience that might have amplified, or even driven, treatment effects.

EXPECTATIONS WHEN MOVING TO THE LAB

Because we viewed religious world views as possibly recharged through repeated exposure to elite messaging, rather than as necessarily deep-seated, we expected that once-off exposure to sermon content in the lab might alter individuals' attitudes and behavior. We also expected that exposure to sermons would influence the behavior of Christians from all denominations. People who regularly hear the same type of content in their primary house of worship might still be moved because the exposure serves to "recharge" that way of understanding the world. At the same time, because social boundaries between Christian denominations are relatively soft in Nairobi, and in many parts of sub-Saharan Africa, even people who do not regularly attend the houses of worship with which the sermons are associated might be open to their insights.

The specific religious teachings we bring into the lab provide no explicit political directions. But they do provide guidance about cause and effect and the possibility for change. We expected that, if people were shortly thereafter provided with opportunities for political action, their recent exposure to particular religious teachings would color their approach to those opportunities for political engagement. Participation in politics means, among other things, identifying what causes are worthy of support, contemplating whether one's own participation is likely to make a difference – things that should be shaped by how one understands cause and effect in this world, and things that the metaphysical discussions in sermons are aimed at addressing.

Our expectations about effects on particular forms of political behavior evolved during the project as we learned about the real-world observational patterns of political participation across denominations. When we initially conducted the first lab experiment described in this chapter, we expected that the focus in the uplifting Pentecostal sermons would increase a sense of internal self-efficacy and prompt a willingness to enter into intimidating arenas of life, including politics, especially relative to a message that offered no promise of immediate material change (McClendon and Riedl, 2015).[4] We further hypothesized that such a message would increase a sense of internal and external self-efficacy, and tested this in the second lab experiment. In the meantime, we learned more about anecdotal patterns of political behavior among Pentecostals and Mainline Protestants and Catholics in Kenya: for instance, Pentecostals often reported engaging in leadership training and engaging infrequently in protests, legislative campaigns, or demands for institutional reform, whereas Mainline Protestants and Catholics, if they participated, reported participating in forms of monitoring and sanctioning of politicians for patterns of poor governance. In particular, we learned more about these patterns of engagement from focus group participants. We then set up the third laboratory study to see if we would find evidence that some of these observational patterns were causal.

STUDY DESIGN

The laboratory studies we conducted all have certain things in common: their location, the subject pool from which they drew, and the religious treatments we use. We describe these common features first and then discuss each study and its results in turn.

We conducted all laboratory studies at the Busara Center for Behavioral Economics in Nairobi, the same city wherein we collected the sermon texts and conducted the focus groups described in the previous chapter. We are thus able to build our treatments around real-world content that we know is circulating in this same environment and to which our study participants could be realistically exposed in their everyday lives. We also know something already about how those sermons are interpreted and reacted to by laity.

The Busara Center is a standing laboratory that was started by researchers at the University of Nairobi, the Massachusetts Institute

---

[4] See our preanalysis plan for that study registered with EGAP: http://egap.org/registration/651.

of Technology, and Harvard in 2012 and that employs mostly Kenyan staff to help with the design and piloting of social science laboratory experiments and manage their implementation. The laboratory is situated close to Kibera, the largest informal settlement area in Nairobi, and it maintains a standing subject pool of adult residents who are interested in participating in research studies in exchange for time and transportation compensation. Our studies followed the lab's standard operating procedures. Participants were invited to participate by text message. They were not told the hypotheses in the studies in advance and told only that it would be a study of people's social, economic, and political preferences, which is a standard type of study at the Busara Center. Once they arrived at the laboratory, their identities were verified by fingerprint so as to link each participant to demographic characteristics collected at the time of initial recruitment into the sample. Sessions were each typically about an hour long. During all laboratory sessions, participants sat in separate cubicles, each with a touchscreen computer and an audio headset, which was used to play the treatment messages (described in more detail later in this chapter). Instructions for all tasks were delivered in kiSwahili by laboratory staff. The language on the computer screens was English. The Busara Center has found that this combination of English screens and Swahili oral instructions maximizes participant comprehension in the Nairobi lab.

Table 4.1 summarizes some basic characteristics of the studies, including their timing, recruitment strategies, types of treatments employed, various outcomes measured, size, and demographics. We do not claim these laboratory studies generate results that are representative of the adult population in Nairobi or of the national population. Instead, we look for consistency in nationally representative survey samples in other parts of the book. Nevertheless, for reference, the subject pools in our experiments had higher shares of women, of single people, and of people having completed secondary education compared to the Nairobi and Kenyan populations as a whole. In Study C, the latter difference was by design. In Study C, we recruited only people with higher levels of education so that it would be more likely that they would fully comprehend the politician–citizen ultimatum game in that experiment (more details are provided later in this chapter). The standing subject pool at the Busara Center lab underrepresents Kalenjins, which make up about 8.5 percent of Kenya's population and only 1–2 percent of the subject pool across our three studies. The set of participants in our Study C also overrepresented Luhyas, which make up about 14 percent of Kenya's population but 38 percent of the study pool in Study C. In total, we recruited 382, 141,

TABLE 4.1 *Laboratory studies details.*

	Study A	Study B	Study C
Dates	January 2014	July–Aug 2016	Aug–Nov 2016
Recruitment	Non-Nubians, Previous studies < 3	Non-Nubians, Novice participants	Non-Nubians, Education > Standard 8
Number of participants	382	141	556
Treatments	Pentecostal message, Mainline/Catholic message, Same messages w/ religious words removed	Pentecostal message, Mainline/Catholic message	Pentecostal message, Mainline/Catholic message, Control (Weather)
Outcome measures	Participation in text message campaign	Self-efficacy, affect	Politician– citizen interactions
Pentecostal	30%	29%	37%
Catholic	36%	30%	30%
Mainline Protestant	20%	19%	18%
Female	61%	62%	68%
Secondary education	58%	58%	78%
Age	34	31	35
Married	50%	45%	53%
No. children	2.1	2.2	2.3
Owns a TV	65%	68%	65%

and 556 Christian adult residents of Nairobi to participate in the three different studies. We should note that in our subject pool, as among many Kenyan Christians, ethnic (tribal) identity does *not* correlate tightly with denominational affiliation.

We sought to recruit only Christian adults to participate, because we expected Christians to be open to the different messages and also likely to be exposed to them, purposefully or incidentally, in the course of their daily lives. Exposure to religious messages is not completely mutable (Horowitz, 1985, 50), because the boundaries between major faith traditions can be quite strong (Barro, Hwang, and McCleary, 2010). In Nairobi, boundaries between major faith traditions (Islam versus Christianity) are strong, but the social boundaries between different Christian denominations are soft (Ngong, 2014). Churches certainly try to encourage loyalty from congregants and people tend to have a primary affiliation. Nevertheless, Christians have a fair amount of discretion over which houses of worship to seek out, and can switch between denominations from week to week. In this context, one can imagine a Christian being assigned to and open to any of the treatment conditions in their daily lives, even if they are most often exposed to a certain one.

The Busara Center collects information on various demographic characteristics (including sex, age, tribe, language, education level, and number of children) from individuals when they are recruited to the standing subject pool but does not collect information on religious affiliation. In order to strictly limit our study's recruitment to Christians, we would have had to first ask individuals about their religious affiliation before inviting them to the study, which the lab staff and we worried either would alert them to the hypotheses of the study (and perhaps influence their behavior in the laboratory)[5] or would encourage participation only from people highly interested in studies about religious identity or other religious topics. Thus, in order to avoid this problem while also maximizing the number of Christians in the study, we limited initial recruitment to non-Nubians because we knew this attribute in advance of the studies and because Nubians are more likely to be Muslim rather than Christian, whereas non-Nubians, who are the vast majority of the Kenyan population, are 80–90 percent Christian. Then, to again avoid the problem of priming study participants to the focus and hypotheses of the study, we asked participants for their religious affiliation (Christian versus non-Christian, and, if Christian, which denomination) at the very end of the laboratory sessions. This means that the measure of religious affiliation was taken after treatment was administered, and so caution about subgroup analyses is certainly appropriate. However, there are reasons to believe that answers to this question were not strongly influenced by treatment. Participants were asked for their primary religious affiliation, which has been argued to be a relatively sticky attribute even as people attend and expose themselves to content from other houses of worship (Olupona and Nyang, 1993; Ngong, 2014). Furthermore, before conducting analyses among only self-identified Christians and within subgroup analyses by denomination, we verified that treatment does not predict answers to the question about religious affiliation. For the analyses that follow, we drop non-Nubian non-Christians, because treatment assignment does not predict answers to questions about primary religious affiliation.

---

5 Experimenter-demand effects occur when subjects alter their behavior to try to conform to their understandings of the hypotheses of the study (of what the researcher is "looking for").

Treatments

Every participant in each study was randomly assigned an audio message to listen to. Individual computer screens during the audio recording were identical so as to minimize experimenter-demand effects. The lab staff could not identify treatment assignment for any participant by looking at her screen. Participants in the lab could not hear the audio messages other participants had been assigned to. In all studies, some participants were assigned to hear a recording of a message that drew on typical Pentecostal sermons in the city, and some participants were assigned to hear a recording of a message drawn from typical Mainline/Catholic sermons in the city. In Study A, we compared the behavior of people in these religious treatment conditions to the behavior of people randomly assigned to hear secular messages on similar topics (discussed later in this chapter). In Study C, we compare behavior of people in the religious treatment conditions to behavior of people assigned to hear an uplifting weather report, for reasons discussed later in this chapter. In each study, we afterward measured different attitudinal and behavioral outcomes to test whether exposure to these types of messages would have the effects proposed.

All audio messages were recorded by the same person in both English and kiSwahili. Participants could choose the language they preferred to hear. We found in our descriptive survey that churches in Nairobi regularly deliver sermons in kiSwahili or in English, or in a mix of both, and do not often deliver sermons in other local languages. Our use of English and kiSwahili thus also mimicked delivery of sermons in the real world. The speaker in all of the audio recordings is a male research assistant, who is educated and a lifelong resident of Nairobi. That research assistant was not present for any of the lab sessions so as to minimize experimenter-demand effects that might occur were subjects to recognize his voice. All audio messages were recorded with the same cadence and tone and were roughly the same length (about one minute, thirty seconds).

There are trade-offs in using treatments that draw on real-world content rather than those created for the purposes of research alone. An advantage is that real-world messages increase the external relevance of the experiments. These religious teachings are in fact being delivered in Nairobi, and we should want to understand their consequences in order to make sense of actual political behavior. Nairobians are also therefore likely to treat the messages seriously rather than as an artificial exercise. A downside of drawing on real-world messages is that we sacrificed conceptual purity to some degree, because real-world sermons are not conceptually pure. Real-world religious communication bundles concepts and logics, albeit into bundles that can be distinguished across sermons. We argue that the two sermon treatments we use differ primarily in their diagnoses of world problems and in their indications about the possibilities for change.[6] But even so, the treatments we use capture only one diagonal of the two-by-two theoretical scheme. As such, although the experiments are instructive about the effects of exposure to these different real-world sermons, which should be of substantive interest given real-world circulation, we have to leave to future research the task of testing the full two-by-two.[7]

The text of the two religious audio recordings appear in the following subsections. Both messages point to worldly problems. Both treatment messages portray a loving God who is concerned for the listeners, as do real sermons in Nairobi. However, the messages differ in where they locate primary responsibility for earthly problems. And they differ in the extent to which they underscore a real possibility of change in this world. The Pentecostal message locates the source of problems firmly *in the self*, in the internal life of the individual: "Financial problems are brought forth by lack of faith, by striving for wealth and power without faith in God." By contrast, the Mainline/Catholic message points right away to the behavior of others, and to the poor relationships *between people*: "Do you ever wonder at the arrogance, greed, or irresponsibility of some Kenyans with

---

[6] Prior to the first laboratory experiment, we had informants read the treatments in random order to identify where they thought they might hear the message and to recall aspects of the message they thought salient. Informants easily identified the sermons by denomination and as likely to be heard in church, and recalled optimism or fatalism about change, as well as whether the sermon talked about changing an individual mindset or changing society. We conducted a series of lab sessions in fall 2015 in which subjects were interviewed after hearing a randomly assigned audio recording, and found that subjects there were also able to identify the source and these thematic differences.

[7] Another argument for using real-world content is for ethical reasons. Few scholars have written about the ethical dilemmas of experimental research on religion. One exception, Nielsen (2015), argues that experiments intended to fundamentally change, rather than measure, people's religious beliefs can be unethical. He argues that people have a strong interest in forming their own beliefs about ultimate value in a nonmanipulative environment, and that any manipulation of such beliefs can therefore induce harm. Nevertheless, features of our experiment arguably do not raise the same concerns about experiments designed to change religious beliefs fundamentally. Rather than introducing new stimuli to try to fundamentally change people's religious beliefs, we are trying to estimate the change, if any, that occurs in people's daily lives when they are exposed to one or the other type of religious communication rather than another.

money? ... when and how [will they] wake up to the poverty around them?" Although it makes a reference to confronting problems "in the human heart," the primary emphasis is on other people's behavior and on relationships as the source of earthly problems. On the other dimension, the Pentecostal message promises imminent material change: "Those who seek the Lord shall not lack in any good thing ... Jesus will give you what you seek." The Pentecostal message tells listeners that material change in this world is quite possible, with the right mindset, with strength of faith, and with the right *embodying* of that faith (*make* money, *make* success). The Mainline/Catholic message makes no promises of earthly efficacy. The message calls on listeners to mend their relationships by caring for others but gives no indication that such actions will change their own material realities or change the world. In fact, the message asks people to adjust their expectations downward.

We shared the treatment texts with theologians and scholars of religion and politics and received feedback that the two religious texts were a fair reflection of Pentecostal and Mainstream Protestant/Catholic sermons in this context, which fits with our findings from the descriptive survey.

Text of the Pentecostal Treatment

Do you ever wonder at the difficulty of being financially successful like some other Kenyans with money? Do you wish you could end the years and years of trying to make ends meet, the years of trying to get by? Poverty, crime, violence, family breakdown, the myriad social economic and political problems people face are on the increase. Do you ever wonder whether, when and how you'll ever get the kind of lifestyle you deserve? God is concerned with the quality of your life, and you must know that He will reward the faithful with prosperity. Financial problems are brought forth by lack of faith, by striving for wealth and power without faith in God. But our Lord Jesus wants true Christians to be rich. Those who do not reconfigure their minds to what God has promised lack and suffer hunger, but those who seek the Lord shall not lack in any good thing. So let us be a friend to God, not forgetting that our efforts, our sacrifices to Him will be richly rewarded. You don't need to find money, make money. You don't need to find success, make success. We have not because we ask not. Jesus will give you what you seek if you give to Him and have faith.

Text of the Mainline/Catholic Treatment

Do you ever wonder at the arrogance, greed or irresponsibility of some Kenyans with money? Do you wish they wouldn't seem so unbothered by the plight of others? The world is moving away from godly morals and obedience to the teachings of the Bible. Poverty, crime, violence, family breakdown, myriad of social economic and political problems people face, corruption, exploitation of one by the other are on the increase. Do you ever wonder whether, when and how people with money will wake up to the poverty around them? God is concerned with the quality of human life, about the way we live, eat, speak, think, treat each other, and care for the world around us. We must work with and care for the poor, sick and suffering. Both the world's and Kenya's economic crises were brought forth by greed, un-godly greed for riches and power. But our Lord Jesus was compassionately touched by human physical needs. He healed the sick and fed the hungry. Let us be a friend to widows and widowers, not forgetting the less privileged. And for ourselves, we should become rich by making our wants few. Through Jesus, we must deal with greed and selfishness in the human heart.

The nonreligious messages used for comparison varied across studies. We could not employ a pure control condition in which participants did not listen to any audio message, because within any given laboratory session it would have been easy for both the lab staff and other participants to identify those not listening as people assigned to a different condition. As a control in Study A, we used secular messages with otherwise the same content. That is, we took the religious messages, removed any religious phrasing explicitly evoking God, Jesus, the Bible or the spiritual world, and then replaced it with nonreligious language in order to create comparable, secularly worded texts. Preexperiment, we had Nairobi informants read the English texts of all treatment messages in random order. Although the secular treatments were created as derivatives of the religious treatments, informants identified them as familiar types of secular messages: e.g., as excerpts of the secular self-help books prevalent in Nairobi that encourage positive thinking (England, 2005), or as excerpts from secular radio shows in the city emphasizing the arrogance of the Kenyan rich. Nevertheless, because religious messages are so ubiquitous in Nairobi, we viewed it as quite probable that the secular messages could be taken as having religious undertones. We thus expected that any comparisons of behavior in religious versus secular conditions would likely underestimate treatment effects of the religious content.

Text of the Secularized Pentecostal Message

Do you ever wonder at the difficulty of being financially successful like some other Kenyans with money? Do you wish you could end the years and years of trying to make ends meet, the years of trying to get by? Poverty, crime, violence, family breakdown, the myriad social economic and political problems people face are on the increase. Do you ever wonder whether, when and how you'll ever get the kind of lifestyle you deserve? *You are right to be* concerned with the quality of your life, and you must know that *people who succeed are those who believe in themselves.* Financial problems are brought forth *by lack of confidence and lack of self-discipline, by striving for wealth and power without believing in possibility for yourself.* Those who do not reconfigure their minds *to personal possibilities* lack and suffer hunger, but those who *reconfigure their mindset* shall not lack in any good thing. So let us be a friend *to ourselves*, not forgetting that our efforts, our sacrifices *will find success if we have the right mindset.* You don't need to find money, make money. You don't need to find success, make success. We have not because we *try* not. *You will get what you seek.* (Emphases indicate secular replacements for religious language in the Pentecostal message.)

Text of the Secularized Mainline/Catholic Message

Do you ever wonder at the arrogance, greed or irresponsibility of some Kenyans with money? Do you wish they wouldn't seem so unbothered by the plight of others? The world is moving away from *common decency and concern for others.* Poverty, crime, violence, family breakdown, myriad of social economic and political problems people face, corruption, exploitation of one by the other are on the increase. Do you ever wonder whether, when and how people with money will wake up to the poverty around them? *We should be* concerned with the quality of human life, about the way we live, eat, speak, think, treat each other, and care for the world around us. We must work with and care for the poor, sick and suffering. Both the world's and Kenya's economic crises were brought forth by greed, greed for riches and power. But *some people are* compassionately touched by human physical needs. *They heal* the sick and feed the hungry. Let us be a friend to widows and widowers, not forgetting the less privileged. And for ourselves, we should become rich by making our wants few. We must deal with greed and selfishness in the human heart. (Emphases indicate secular replacements for religious language in the Mainline/Catholic message.)

As a control in Study C, we employed a nonreligious message that Nairobians might realistically also be exposed to in everyday life: one mimicking weather reports about the ways in which weather improves as Nairobi moves from the wet and cold seasons in July, August, and September into the warmer, drier season in October, November, and December. Because the Pentecostal-like message is self-affirming (positive about the individual's capabilities and the possibility for change), we thought it might affect behavior differently than the other religious message simply by lifting respondents' moods and not because of a change in understanding of human agency and of the world order. Other studies in political science and economics have shown that messages about good weather, or about improvement in weather, can lift listeners' moods and thereby shape economic and political decision-making (Bassi and Williams, 2017). In addition to the realistic, secular contrast, this control message therefore provided a useful alternative contrast by controlling for affective change. For the purposes of increasing statistical power, we compared behavior only across the two religious conditions in Study B.

Text of the Weather (Control) Message

Do you dislike the colder temperatures in the winter months? Skies remain clear throughout September and temperatures rise into October. There are two dominant influences on the climate in Kenya: the onshore monsoon winds from the Indian Ocean, and altitude. Nairobi's high altitude means that the city's climate is more mild year-round. The winds determine the onset of Kenya's dry and rainy seasons, with the long rains finishing by early June, and the relatively cool season, from late-June to October, gets much less rain. Temperatures then start to rise, as the upcoming month of October is characterized by essentially constant daily high temperatures, with daily highs around 25°C throughout the month, exceeding 27°C or dropping below 24°C only one day in ten. Daily low temperatures are around 16°C. This season is one with dew points that are neither too dry nor too muggy. The dew point is a good measure of how comfortable a person will find the weather because it relates to whether perspiration will evaporate from the skin, thereby cooling the body. October and on is a comfortable and temperate season. It is also a season with only calm to moderate winds, rarely exceeding the speed of a fresh breeze. The wind during these months is most often out of the east and northeast. These months bring generally sunny, comfortable, warm days.

PARTICIPATION IN A POLITICAL TEXT MESSAGE CAMPAIGN

In Study A, we partnered with the Youth Agenda, a nonreligious, nonpartisan advocacy organization that promotes political participation: getting people involved in politics, promoting clean governance, and conducting civic engagement sessions.[8] During each experimental session, lab staff described the organization to study participants. The Youth Agenda was running a free, anonymous, open-ended short message service (SMS) campaign to encourage Nairobi residents to report their views on government performance and policy priorities. Participants in the experiment were told about this campaign during the session. At the end of the experiment, as staff confirmed M-Pesa payment information with each participant individually, they reminded the participant about the SMS campaign but then let the participant leave. So any actual texting to the Youth Agenda number was unsupervised. After the experiment, we collected data from the Youth Agenda on all mobile numbers from which it received SMSs in the weeks during and following the experiment. Over the course of those weeks, 34 percent of the participants in our experiment sent an SMS expressing their political views to the Youth Agenda.

---

[8] Youth is defined broadly as those under forty years old, and the organization involves older people interested in promoting these same issues. We partnered with this organization because they encourage a common but not-too-risky form of participation and one that is open-ended as to its level of criticism of the system.

Measuring this form of participation had several advantages. First, texting constitutes a type of political participation that is becoming increasingly common throughout the developing world. Other examples from sub-Saharan Africa include the uSpeak system in Uganda and Botswana Speaks, both of which have been instituted by governments to solicit feedback from citizens on government services (Grossman, Humphreys, and Sacramone-Lutz, 2014); Integrity Nigeria (Blair, Littman, and Paluck, 2019), an nongovernmental organization (NGO) project that collects citizen reports of corruption in Nigeria; and Text to Change, which has been implemented throughout Africa and Latin America. Second, it was an open-ended opportunity for participation. It offered participants a chance to articulate their views and priorities for government, but these could be of any bent: they could make personal requests, suggest personnel changes in government, offer to help with political activities, express criticism of institutions or of the regime, demand institutional or structural overhaul, or even express praise for the government. Later, we explore some of the content of the texts that were sent, in order to test expectations about the messages' effects on the bent of participation. Third, the measure was unsupervised, so results were less likely to be purely due to experimenter demand. Finally, although not capturing the full range of low- and high-risk political participation in which Kenyans might engage, it was an ethical measure of participation that did not have us inducing study subjects into participation that might put them at physical or financial risk.

We found that exposure to the Pentecostal message induced the highest levels of political participation in this campaign. In the lab study that used SMSs as a measure of political participation, we saw an uptick in participation from people exposed to the Pentecostal message, compared to other treatments, regardless of their denomination. Figure 4.1 shows rates of SMS participation across treatments. Together, 38 percent of individuals exposed to either of the Pentecostal/self-affirming messages (religious or secular) sent a text message articulating their priorities for the government, whereas only 29 percent of the individuals in the mainstream/fatalistic messages did so (diff = 9.0 p.p., p = 0.079). This difference remains robust to controlling for individual-level covariates, including number of previous experimental studies, sex, age, marital status, and household assets and ethnic identities.

We did not find that these effects on the binary measure of participation (versus no participation) varied much by denominational affiliation. That is, Pentecostals, Mainline Protestants, and Catholics were all moved

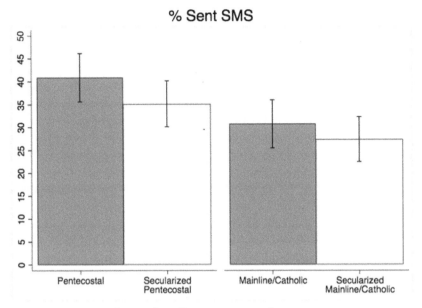

FIGURE 4.1 Rates of sending text message, by treatment group.

toward similar levels of participation in the text message campaign by the Pentecostal message, and compared to their levels of participation in other conditions. Perhaps the empowering aspects of Pentecostal messages are particularly effective on all listeners.

We also did not find detectable differences in rates of participation between the Pentecostal message and its secular equivalent (or between the Mainline Protestant/Catholic message and its secular equivalent). On the one hand, these null results between religious and secular treatment messages might reflect the weakness of a treatment-control comparison in a highly religious environment when the only difference between the treatments is the removal of a few religious words. On the other hand, the small (and statistically insignificant) differences across secular and religious conditions bolsters the general point that religious communication is a common form – but not a unique form – of metaphysical instruction. Religious messages are part of a family of messages that tackle deep questions about cause and effect and human agency. For instance, neoliberalism is a secular ideology that emphasizes individual responsibility. These secular messages are also likely to shape political participation by shaping how individuals attribute responsibility for earthly problems and conceive of their own political efficacy (Martin, 2018). In other words, many of the patterns we identify in this book may not be *unique* to religion. We expand on these points in the concluding chapter of the book.

Participation in the text message campaign, which was described as an opportunity to express views and priorities for the government, was fairly open-ended. Participants could write whatever they wanted, should they choose to send a text, and the content of the texts did vary. Some participants targeted criticism at the entire government or at entire sets of government institutions, writing views like, "We [have] a corrupt government," "I want to [complain about] the state government you have heard the rich alone," or "I want to inform the [government] not to do any rigging like last time." Others offered their own services and themselves as leaders ("I am [name] I want to be available to the government," "I would like to join the people of this group") or attempted to encourage public officials to follow Christian values and to provide forums in which citizens could provide guidance: "keep the going and God will help you," or, "Requesting forums on leadership in kibra constituency." Statements blatantly critical of institutions, laws, or the regime were in the minority of text messages sent. By our estimates, only 12 percent of all participants sent a text message criticizing institutions or political structures, so on the whole this task was taken up as one in which participants could become political active *within* the existing rules of the game, offering themselves as leaders or attempting to encourage and interact congenially with public officials, consistent with the Pentecostal message's having been the one to generate the highest participation. However, within the subgroup of Mainline Protestants and Catholics, exposure to the *Mainline/Catholic message* resulted in more texts that were critical of institutions and of the system, compared to the texts they sent in the Pentecostal message condition, though the differences are just shy of statistical significance in a small subgroup. Twelve percent of Mainlines and Catholics exposed to the Mainline/Catholic message sent a message directly critical of existing institutions, laws, or the regime. Four percent of Mainlines and Catholics exposed to the Pentecostal message sent a message critical of the political system ($p = 0.11$). In other words, exposure to the Pentecostal message boosted rates of participation across the board, but the resulting participation did not challenge existing institutions, structures, or rules. Among those inclined to select into Mainline/Catholic teachings, exposure to the Mainline/Catholic message led to less impressive rates of participation but seemingly to participation of a more structurally critical bent.

SELF-EFFICACY AND AFFECT

In Study B, we wanted to verify whether the two religious messages had differential implications for listeners' sense of self-efficacy, since we had interpreted the overall boost in political participation from exposure to the Pentecostal message in Study A to its likely effects on self-efficacy.[9] So, in Study B, after exposure to one or the other of the sermon messages, we gave participants a battery of questions meant to gauge a sense of hope, optimism, and self-efficacy. We used the Adult Hope Scale (Snyder et al., 1991) to measure a sense of efficacy. It is a scale that captures a "general sense of the efficacy of the self that undergirds a perception of adaptive adequacy."[10] We adapted the scale so that each item used a five-point Likert scale, because we found that it was too complicated to have people respond on a seven-point scale. It proved more straightforward for people to indicate that they "strongly agree," "agree," "neither agree nor disagree," "disagree," or "strongly disagree" with a particular statement. In addition, we used Watson, Clark, and Tellegen (1988)'s scales to measure positive and negative affect in order to explore the possibility that rather than changing participants' sense of efficacy as posited by the theory, the messages simply shifted affect. We used the items of both scales with some edits in order to facilitate translation into kiSwahili for the laboratory instructions.[11]

---

[9] In this study, we also limited participation to people who had never before participated in a Busara Center study, in case the results of our previous study were due to experienced participants' greater ability to guess the hypotheses of the study and tailor their behavior accordingly.

[10] In another part of the book, where we analyze observational survey data, we look at patterns of responses to a more standard political efficacy question and find consistent results. Here, we wanted to tap into a broader concept of self-efficacy beyond its articulation within politics, to see if that could plausibly be a mechanism linking Pentecostal message exposure to higher levels of political participation.

[11] The items for the Adult Hope Scale were as follows: "If I should find myself in a jam, I could think of many ways to get out of it"; "at the present time, I am working hard toward ~~energetically pursuing~~ my goals"; "there are lots of ways around any problem that I am facing now"; "right now I see myself as ~~being pretty~~ successful"; "I can think of many ways to reach my current goals"; "at this time, I am meeting the goals that I have set for myself." Strikethroughs indicate wording that we deleted or replaced in consultation with lab staff because of concerns about translating accurately into kiSwahili. The affect words in Watson, Clark, and Tellegen (1988)'s scale were *determined, upset, alert, proud, guilty, interested, ~~nervous~~, ashamed, distressed, ~~enthusiastic~~, strong, ~~irritable~~, scared, excited, ~~jittery~~, hostile, ~~inspired~~, active, ~~afraid~~, attentive*. For each word, participants were asked to indicate the extent to which they feel that way very slightly or not at all, a little, moderately, quite a bit, or extremely. Again, strikethroughs indicate wording that we

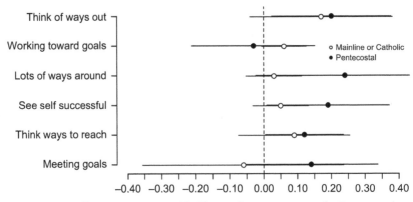

FIGURE 4.2 Differences in mean self-efficacy after exposure to the Pentecostal (rather than Mainline/Catholic) message.

Exposure to the Pentecostal message generally made people feel more efficacious, more confident, and more hopeful, relative to exposure to the Mainline/Catholic message (though the message had no effect on measures of positive/negative affect), regardless of denomination. After hearing the Pentecostal message rather than the Mainline/Catholic message, people were more likely to agree, for instance, that "If I should find myself in trouble, I could think of many ways to get out of it." See Figure 4.2, which shows movement on each of the scale items due to exposure to the Pentecostal message (rather than the Mainline/Catholic message).[12] Black dots show movement among Pentecostals; white dots show movement among Mainline Protestants and Catholics. Even where 90 percent confidence intervals around the point estimates include zero, almost all point estimates show an increase in agreement with the efficacious and hopeful statements in response to the Pentecostal message. The differences in means (which range from −0.03 to 0.20) on a five-point Likert scale are not huge but are in the expected direction. Among self-identifying Mainline Protestants and Catholics, the positive effects of the Pentecostal message on self-efficacy are clearly suggested by this graph, and the differences in the magnitudes of the effects between Pentecostals and Catholics/Mainlines are not statistically distinguishable.

The message's effects on behavior do not seem to be due to simple changes in affect. We observed no differences across treatment conditions

---

deleted or replaced in consultation with lab staff because of concerns about translating accurately into kiSwahili.

[12] Recall that there is no secular control in Study B.

in reported experience of either positive or negative emotions in the lab. Perhaps this lack of change in affect is due to the consistency in tone and cadence across the recorded messages, which was a feature of our experimental design as we sought to isolate the sermons' ideational content. In any case, we can be reasonably confident that the textual content of the Pentecostal message did not simply improve people's mood and thus move them to act. We further verify this contention in Study C when we compare exposure to the religious messages to a mood-lifting weather message.

PRIORITIZING INTRINSIC OR EXTRINSIC INCENTIVES FOR POLITICAL LEADERS

In Study C, we wanted to explore further the possibility that exposure to the two different religious messages would have an impact on the *bent* of political participation rather than on its level. We found in our observational studies in Kenya that Pentecostals tended to focus their efforts on working through the system, particularly on finding opportunities to hone their leadership skills and act benevolently as leaders. They seemed focused more on self-mastery, on being the best versions of themselves, rather than on reforming institutions, enforcing rules on elites, or creating structural incentives for leaders to work in citizens' interest. Mainline Protestants and Catholics, on the other hand, seemed more inclined (*if/when* they were active) to join in efforts to call for new legislation and institutions to ensure that leaders would work in the interest of citizens – that is, to demand sanctioning of poor governance and structural reform.

Within the confines of the lab, we endeavored to test for some of these patterns after random assignment to the Pentecostal and Mainline/Catholic audio messages.[13] We devised a politician–citizen task, designed to measure participants' willingness to reform their own behavior when in a leadership role absent any expectation of punishment and/or their willingness to create institutions to ensure that leaders work in the citizens' (rather than their own) interest.

[13] There are many other attitudinal and behavioral outcomes that are relevant to the main arguments. For instance, one could ask participants whether they think the system is unfair, or whether they would be willing to engage in protest for structural reform. We focus on revealed preferences in the lab but examine these other measures in observational survey data in other parts of the book.

The game was an ultimatum game with politician–voter labels and with efficiency losses (that is, an extra cost to the voter and the politician if the offer is rejected). Participants learned that they would be randomly and anonymously assigned into pairs, and that one member of each pair would be randomly selected as the politician, with the other player designated as the citizen. The politician started the game with an endowment of 500 Kenyan shillings (KES): 250 KES from his own salary and 250 KES from mandatory taxes from the voter. The citizen started the game with 250 KES, having already paid 250 KES in taxes. The politician then had to decide how much of the tax money, up to 250 KES, to spend back on the citizen. The citizen decided at what threshold of spending she would support the politician: if he spent no money on her, 50 KES, 100 KES, and so on, up to 250 KES. If the citizen did not support the politician, she had to pay a personal cost of 50 KES. And if the politician did not receive the citizen's support, he also paid a cost: 200 KES of his salary. If the voter chose to support the politician, then no additional costs were imposed on either player and the spending decision implemented by the politician stood. We asked each participant in the study to indicate how much she would spend as the politician and at what level of spending, if any, she would punish as the citizen. Subjects were then randomly assigned into pairs and roles, and their decisions were implemented accordingly (see Leight, Pande, and Ralston, 2016). Martin (2014) and Leight, Pande, and Ralston (2016) both used a similar task to measure accountability behaviors in Uganda and Nairobi, respectively. We thus felt confident that our participants would understand the incentives and significance of the game. To be sure, we limited participation in the study to participants who had completed Standard 8 (the last year of primary school) or more. All participants had to act as politicians and citizens (they could not opt out of the game), so we view Study C as helping us understanding more about modes rather than rates of participation.

Note that, even with the additional costs to punishment, no matter the amount spent by the politician, punishment is always the more costly option for the citizen (compared to accepting the politician's spending level). Even if the politician spends no tax money back on the citizen, she is better off accepting that spending level than punishing.[14] Anticipating

---

[14] In that scenario (in which the politician spends no money), if the citizen punishes, she pays 50 KES out of her existing endowment, and so walks away with 200 KES. If she had accepted politician's spending decision, she would have walked away with her initial endowment of 250 KES.

this, the politician is best off not spending any tax money on the citizen. The game is thus similar to a simple ultimatum game. In addition, it involves (and therefore makes salient) a punishment cost (and efficiency loss) and uses politician–citizen labels.

We conceptualize greater levels of politician spending as taking an opportunity to demonstrate good character – to act as a benevolent leader – as Pentecostals in our observational work indicated they were trying to do. Holding expectations about voter punishment constant, greater generosity as a leader should indicate an intrinsic willingness to behave more benevolently, which we take to be consistent with a posture focused on self-mastery and on the personal transformation of those in power, rather than consistent with attempts at altering their extrinsic incentives or creating institutions to constrain bad behavior.

By contrast, we conceptualize punishing politicians even under high levels of spending as an inclination to generate new incentives for elites to govern better, as Mainline Protestants and Catholics in our observational work indicated they were trying to do when they participate in politics. That is, holding expectations of politician spending constant, we view the decision to punish as trying to create institutions in which politicians face higher sanctions for bad behavior. That is, punishing more frequently indicates a focus on creating incentives for good behavior rather than relying on the character of leaders.

Subjects' expectations about the behavior of *others* did not change detectably with treatment. We asked participants, for instance, how much they expected others to spend in the politician role. We observe the fraction of the 250 KES in taxes that each participant expected their anonymous partner – if in the politician role – to spend back on them. Table 4.2 then shows results of regressing this fraction on treatment assignment, controlling for sex, marital status, education, and ethnic group.[15] The results indicate that treatment assignment did not predict people's expectations about how others would behave in the politician role. Assignment to the Catholic/Mainline message or to the Pentecostal message is not significantly associated with beliefs about the fraction of the tax money one's partner would spend. We also asked participants to report whether they believed that the choice they had made about spending as the politician would get them reelected or not. Treatment assignment did not influence answers to this question either. (Note, however, that 75 percent of people reported believing that they would be reelected, and answers to

---

[15] Results are substantively the same when excluding covariates.

TABLE 4.2 *Treatment effects on beliefs about others.*

	Amount believe others will spend (Pentecostals & Mainlines/ Catholics)	Amount believe others will spend (Pentecostals only)	Amount believe others will spend (Mainlines/ Catholics only)
Catholic message	−0.02	0.01	−0.05
	(0.04)	(0.06)	(0.05)
Pentecostal message	−0.00	0.06	−0.06
	(0.04)	(0.06)	(0.05)
Observations	470	203	267
R-squared	0.06	0.10	0.06
Control mean	0.63	0.62	0.64

Note: Included covariates: completed secondary education, female, married, Luhya, Kalenjin, Kikuyu, Kisii, Kamba, Luo (and "other" as reference ethnic category).

this question were not correlated with any demographic characteristics, so there may not have been enough variation on this question to assess treatment effects.)

However, we did find that exposure to the Pentecostal message influenced behavior most dramatically in the politician's role, relative to control, whereas exposure to the Mainline/Catholic message more robustly influenced behavior in the citizen's role, relative to control. Exposure to the Pentecostal message led to more generous behavior (higher spending) from the politician than in the control condition (see Table 4.3). Exposure to the Mainline/Catholic message led to more punishing behavior on the part of the citizen (see Table 4.4). All analyses are ordinary least squares (OLS) regressions (for fraction of the tax money spent or the fraction of the tax money demanded) or linear probability models (for binary dependent variables indicating whether as the politician a participant would spend *all* of the tax money or whether as a citizen she would demand all of the tax money). We also include pre-treatment covariates (education, sex, marital status, age, ethnic group) and cluster standard errors by lab session. Here, we detected heterogeneous treatment effects by primary religious affiliation. The highest levels of spending in the politician role came from the Pentecostals exposed to either religious message,[16] and

---

[16] Note that we cannot distinguish the effect of exposure to the Pentecostal message from the effect of exposure to the Mainline Protestant/Catholic message on fraction spent among Pentecostals, but we can distinguish the effects of the two messages on whether the politician spent *all* of the tax money on the voter among Pentecostals.

TABLE 4.3 *Treatment effects on politician decisions.*

	Fraction spent as politician (Pentecostals & Mainlines/ Catholics)	Fraction spent as politician (Pentecostals only)	Fraction spent as politician (Mainlines/ Catholics only)	Spent all as politician (Pentecostals & Mainlines/ Catholics)	Spent all as politician (Pentecostals only)	Spent all as politician (Mainlines/ Catholics only)
Catholic message	0.03	0.13**	−0.05	0.01	0.10	−0.07
	(0.04)	(0.06)	(0.05)	(0.05)	(0.08)	(0.06)
Pentecostal message	0.03	0.10*	−0.04	0.03	0.19**	−0.09
	(0.04)	(0.06)	(0.03)	(0.05)	(0.08)	(0.06)
Observation	460	199	261	460	199	261
R-squared	0.03	0.06	0.05	0.03	0.09	0.04
Control mean	0.51	0.46	0.54	0.22	0.17	0.26

Note: * $p < 0.10$, ** $p < 0.05$. Included covariates: completed secondary education, female, married, under thirty-five years old, Luhya, Kalenjin, Kikuyu, Kisii, Kamba, Luo (and "other" as reference ethnic category).

TABLE 4.4 *Treatment effects on voter decisions.*

	Frac demanded as voter (Pentecostals & Mainlines/ Catholics)	Frac demanded as voter (Pentecostals only)	Frac demanded as voter (Mainlines/ Catholics only)	Demanded all as voter (Pentecostals & Mainlines/ Catholics)	Demanded all as voter (Pentecostals only)	Demanded all as voter (Mainlines/ Catholics Only)
Catholic message	0.06*	0.07**	0.06	0.08**	0.08*	0.09*
	(0.03)	(0.03)	(0.05)	(0.04)	(0.04)	(0.05)
Pentecostal message	0.04	0.09	0.02	0.05	0.09	0.03
	(0.03)	(0.06)	(0.04)	(0.04)	(0.06)	(0.04)
Observation	438	192	246	438	192	246
R-squared	0.05	0.09	0.05	0.05	0.05	0.05
Control mean	0.37	0.32	0.41	0.09	0.07	0.10

Note: * $p < 0.10$, ** $p < 0.05$. Controls: completed secondary education, female, married, under thirty-five, Luhya, Kalenjin, Kikuyu, Kisii, Kamba, Luo (and "other" as reference ethnic category). Participants who did not understand the task and demanded an invalid spending amount excluded. Standard errors clustered by lab session.

the highest rate of spending *all* the money back on the voter came from Pentecostals exposed to the Pentecostal message. Thirty-seven percent of Pentecostals exposed to the Pentecostal message spent all of the tax money back on the citizens. As far as we can tell, in Table 4.3, Pentecostals responded to the religious messages, and to the Pentecostal message in particular, by dramatically changing their behavior when given an opportunity to act as a leader. By contrast, we do not observe any detectable treatment effects on politician behavior among Mainline Protestants and Catholics, relative to control. We view the results as plausible evidence (with caveats about small sample size) that those inclined to self-select into particular messages are most likely to be swayed by their suggested solutions to the problems of the world, consistent with other communications research (Leeper, 2016; Jo, 2017).

In the citizen role, the detectable effects relative to control are largely driven by exposure to the Mainline/Catholic message. Table 4.4 presents these results. We exclude thirty-two participants who did not understand the threshold task and chose an amount higher than the amount the politician in fact had in her possession to give (i.e., more than 250 KES). Among those who gave a plausible answer to the task, exposure to the Mainline and Catholic message increased their willingness to sanction politicians. Those exposed to the Mainline/Catholic message indicated a higher threshold of spending before they would support the politician, relative to control, even though punishment was costly to them. And a greater share of those exposed to the Mainline/Catholic message said that they would not support the politician unless he/she spent *all* of the tax money back on the citizen, relative to control. Among those who already identified as Mainline Protestants and Catholics, only the Catholic message moved them toward sanctioning the politician in order to induce him to work in the citizen's interest.

In other words, in Study C, we found patterns largely consistent with religious messages' orienting people around different modes of political engagement, when political action of some kind was compelled. Study C found that random assignment to the mindset-focused, empowering message did the most to increase generosity in leadership positions, particularly among those who already identified as Pentecostal, whereas random assignment to the less optimistic, externally focused message more consistently led to a focus on creating external incentives (rewards/punishment) for leaders to work in the public interest.

Let us make a quick note about these religious teachings and generosity. The results in Study C are not consistent with the notion that the primary difference between the two religious messages is that the Pentecostal message encourages no generosity toward others whereas the Catholic/Mainline message encourages generosity. Note that exposure to both messages results in generous behavior, just of different types. Exposure to the Pentecostal message results in more costly spending by the politician, exhibiting a willingness to give up some of one's own income for the citizen; exposure to the Mainline/Catholic message results in more costly punishment, exhibiting a willingness to give up some of one's own income to punish. The difference is not in selflessness per se but in whether the person takes the opportunity to be selfless when in a leadership position or when in a position to shape the extrinsic incentives of leaders.

At the very least, the results from these laboratory experiments together demonstrate that randomly assigned exposure to sermon content *can* alter people's psychological states as well as their political participation. The results are also largely consistent with our argument that religious teachings can influence both people's levels and their modes of political engagement, even when not explicitly political. In the concluding chapter of the book, we turn to questions about what these results tell us more generally about the consequences of Pentecostalism, one of the most remarkable global religious movements in recent times.

MOVING BEYOND THE LAB

In this chapter, we have taken an experimental approach to examining whether exposure to sermons influences political participation. Doing so allowed us to isolate the influence of sermon content from the influence of other aspects of religious practice and experience. It also allowed us to separate exposure to sermons from self-selection into those sermons. We found that one-shot exposure to Pentecostal and Mainline/Catholic sermon excerpts affected people's political participation, even though the sermon excerpts were not explicitly political. More specifically, we found evidence consistent with the notion that exposure to the Pentecostal message increased levels of participation relative to exposure to the Catholic/Mainline message. The Pentecostal message also oriented participation around self-improvement and personnel (leadership) change, whereas exposure to the Catholic/Mainline message if anything oriented people around institutional critiques, the extrinsic incentives facing leaders, and structural reform. These effects were in the same direction no matter the self-identified denomination of the study subjects, but the effects were often strongest among people who would have self-selected into hearing those sermons in the real world, suggesting that sermons strongly influence people who hear them regularly.

Notably, the effects we found were not unique to religiously worded messages. We found a similar contrast in behavior following exposure to a secular message emphasizing internal individual transformation and a secular message emphasizing the difficult work of addressing factors external to the individual. In other words, although the lab experiments demonstrated that sermon exposure can affect political behavior, these effects may be reflective of the power of exposure to metaphysical instruction (both secular and religious) more generally.

In the book, we combine multiple empirical approaches to probe these findings beyond the lab. Laboratory experiments have various limitations (Levitt and List, 2007). Among those limitations are that – due to laboratory space and staff constraints–laboratory experiments typically deal in relatively small sample sizes. As a consequence, there may be true treatment effects that went undetected in this chapter or just missed conventional standards of statistical significance (false negatives). Or the studies may have yielded false positives: rejections of true null hypotheses. Subgroup analyses should be treated with caution when trying to detect interactive effects, especially in contexts of small sample sizes. Last, the laboratory is a relatively artificial environment, so it is useful to know whether consistent patterns appear in other settings. So we would not want to stake our claims in this book on the results in this chapter alone.

Thus, having leveraged the advantages the laboratory provides for causal inference, in subsequent chapters, we employ various other methods in order to more fully probe the observable implications of the main arguments. These other methods do not share some of the strengths of the lab experiments (e.g., random assignment, the ability to isolate content from other features of religious experience), but they have strengths of their own: for instance, they collect measurements in less artificial settings, collect additionally relevant and rich outcome measures, bring to bear larger sample sizes, or examine participation at the levels of groups. For instance, we use observational survey data collected by Afrobarometer and Pew to examine whether different types of political participation and views of the government are observable across respondents affiliated with different Christian denominations across a range of sub-Saharan African countries. This effort allows us to test whether observational patterns outside of the laboratory are consistent with our experimental findings, and whether those patterns extend beyond Nairobi. Through controlled comparison case studies, we are able to ask across countries whether patterns of political participation by religious groups are different across denominations, despite differences in political context and church structures. Through these analyses, as well as through focus groups, we trace whether there have indeed been differences in approaches to political engagement across church congregations consistent with the world views being articulated in those churches.

We also use the focus groups and observational survey data in the next chapter to probe further whether the influence of sermon content is subject to decay and recharging over short periods of time. The findings in this chapter suggest that it might be: even people who self-identified as Pentecostal or as Mainline Protestant and Catholic were affected by exposure to the Pentecostal sermon or the Mainline/Catholic sermon, respectively, even though they had presumably heard a version of it many times before. This finding could be due to the influence of sermons decaying during the week, which would mean that even regular church attendees could still be influenced by reexposure to their churches' sermons in the lab session. In the next chapter, we take an explicit look at observational patterns of reported political attitudes and behavior as they vary across Pentecostal and Mainline Protestants and Catholics *during the week*. We find that Pentecostals exhibit different political attitudes and behavior than Mainline Protestants and Catholics *shortly after* Sunday services but then typically exhibit more similar attitudes and behaviors later on in the week. In other words, rather than being necessarily deep-seated and persistent, religious influence may also be an episodic form of priming, at least under some conditions. This finding has important implications for how we think about the timing of religiously motivated political behavior and for how political entrepreneurs might exploit religious ideas for the purposes of mobilization.

5

Recharging Sermon Influence

Evidence from Surveys and Focus Groups

> The distinctive worldviews that were originally linked with religious traditions have shaped the cultures of each nation in an enduring fashion; today, these distinctive values are transmitted to the citizens even if they never set foot in church, temple or mosque (Inglehart and Norris, 2011, 17).

In their seminal study of cultural change in the wake of economic development, Inglehart and Norris (2011) describe religious beliefs as some of the firmest constraints on political value change, as persistent and durable in the face of major economic shifts. Like many political scientists, they treat the connections between religious beliefs and politics as deep-seated and enduring. Similarly, in an overview of political science research on public opinion, Tesler (2015) characterizes religious beliefs as some of the strongest predispositions people bring into the political arena. Other scholars describe religious world views as potentially acquired at a young age, through family and community, and carried throughout the life cycle (Pearson-Merkowitz and Gimpel, 2017). In these views, religion's influence on political behavior, through beliefs, is persistent and pervasive, not necessarily requiring that people even attend church.

The book broadens and complicates that perspective. Religious world views may not always be deep-seated influences on political behavior,[1] but

---

[1] In this book, we focus on differences in sermons *within* large faith traditions, and find that the influences of different sermons recede and are recharged over short periods of time. We cannot rule out the possibility that differences in world views *across* large faith traditions (e.g., between Buddhists and Muslims) are more durable. In this sense, we amend the arguments about the deep-seatedness of religious world views offered in Inglehart and Norris (2011); we do not discard those arguments.

with repeated exposure to sermons, they can still be influential. Descriptions of the influence of religious world views as naturally deep-seated can sit uncomfortably with the ways that worshippers describe their own experiences. In focus groups we conducted with congregants, members of all denominations described needing frequent exposure to words from the pulpit. One respondent told us, "Missing services makes one lack of confidence in faith and a feeling of missing something." Others described feeling differently when they did not attend services frequently: feeling a lack of guidance, more at a loss for how to make sense of the problems they face in their everyday lives. "[My] problems become many, and even greater," said one congregant when describing weeks in which she did not attend church. By contrast, worshippers describe church as rebooting their ways of seeing the world: "The [Sunday] message renews; it renews our minds," one woman told us. Congregants recognize a need to recharge their own strength of faith.

Descriptions of religious world views as inherently deep-seated and enduring influences can also sit uncomfortably with the actual work that houses of worship and religious institutions do. Churches, mosques, and temples encourage their members to come repeatedly to worship services – not just once a week or month, but sometimes multiple times a week. Houses of worship encourage members to immerse themselves again and again in scriptures and teachings. Many churches in our sample organize midweek prayer and worship services; some record podcasts of sermons or have gift shops selling DVDs or audio recordings of sermons so that members can listen on their own throughout the week. Religious leaders do not take the word views of their members for granted. They treat those world views as needing support and reiteration. Each worship service serves a "recharging" function. Religious faith is in fact a practice. It entails work and reactivation.

From a psychological perspective, it seems reasonable that the links between religious world views and political decision-making might need to be frequently reactivated. Some cognitive psychologists have described religious world views as relatively "natural." Conceptualizing the divine is a task highly compatible with human cognitive infrastructure (Norenzayan, 2013; McCauley, 2015b). We can conceive of a separation between mind and body, so we have an ability to perceive differences between spiritual and physical worlds (Norenzayan, 2013). Our evolutionary need to discern threats in hostile natural environments means that anthropomorphic ideas are easy for us to adopt (McCauley, 2015b). But even if religious ideas are compatible with how our minds work, we may not be able to hold an understanding of the spiritual world at the forefront of our minds at all times. Ethnographic studies inside religious communities show how much work is required for congregants to develop a stable feeling of a relationship with God (Luhrmann, 2012). Mundane everyday tasks can easily consume most of our focus. Postures of awe, and of gratitude toward divine beings, are difficult to sustain without further priming. In pluralistic religious environments, this dynamic may be even more acute. When people leave a house of worship in a pluralistic environment, they are likely to come into contact with other, sometimes countervailing, religious world views – through elite messaging and everyday conversation – and the salience of the teachings from their own house of worship may fade without reactivation. Indeed, if religious teachings are anything like other forms of ideological and political communication, their influence is likely to ebb and flow depending on how many countervailing messages they encounter and depending on how often listeners are exposed to them. Discussing political messaging, Zaller (1996) argued that, "The longer it has been since a consideration or a related idea has been activated, the less likely it is to be accessible at the top of the head" (48). Thus, religious teachings may have a powerful effect on listeners' behavior directly after worship services but then need to be reactivated frequently in order for that effect to persist through iterated exposure.

And, indeed, in the previous chapter, we found effects of sermon exposure on political behavior in the lab. If people's religious world views were a chronic, deep-seated influence on their behavior, we would not expect them to be moved by hearing a short sermon recording in the laboratory. They would already be operating under the maximum level of influence of their own religious world views and so should not have been moved by the sermons coming from their own houses of worship. They should also have continued to bring their own religious world views to bear on their political decisions even when they had been exposed to sermons from other houses of worship. Instead, we observed a very different pattern in the lab. People were moved both by sermons from their own houses of worship and by sermons from other religious associations.

In this chapter, we further explore the consequences of religious recharging for patterns of citizens' political engagement in sub-Saharan Africa. We consider two types of evidence. First, we conducted a series of focus groups in Nairobi with members of different denominations at different points in the week. These conversations allowed ordinary congregants to speak in their own words both about their interpretations of sermons and about how religious teachings translate into their own political views. We conducted the discussions at different points during the week – sometimes at the end of the week before Sunday worship services had taken place, sometimes just after Sunday worship services – in order to examine how the content of these conversations varied depending on the length of time since congregants' last exposure to a sermon. Second, we analyzed three waves of observational surveys (two from the Afrobarometer and one from Pew) that were conducted across multiple sub-Saharan African countries. These surveys asked respondents for their denominational affiliation, frequency of practice, and political participation. Interviews for the surveys were conducted on different days of the week, allowing us to explore, controlling for correlates of interview day, whether respondents' answers varied depending on how soon after Sunday worship services they were interviewed.

Looking at survey and focus group evidence in this chapter allows us to explore the patterns of activation and reactivation of religious teachings' influences on political engagement. The forms of evidence also have other advantages, especially when considered in conjunction with other evidence offered in this book. Both sources of evidence allow us to probe whether findings in the previous chapter extend outside the artificial environment of the lab and beyond the lab's subject pool. The survey evidence in particular allows us to explore patterns of religious–political engagement well beyond Nairobi. The surveys also measure a wider range of individual-level forms of political engagement than we were able to collect in the lab. The focus groups delve more deeply into the thought process that connects message exposure to behavior. In all of these ways, the analyses in this chapter complement, and increase our confidence in, the findings in the previous chapter.

FOCUS GROUPS AT DIFFERENT POINTS IN THE WEEK

We held focus groups with worshippers in Nairobi at different times in the week in order to explore how they interpreted and experienced religious teachings when they had either just heard a sermon or recently spent several days outside of the church. We also used the focus groups as an opportunity to probe further whether and how congregants related religious teachings to their thoughts about political engagement, and whether particular themes of significance were reflected in their language.

We chose two congregations, one Pentecostal and one Catholic, from which to invite focus group participants.[2] We had already observed the sermons of these houses of worship and found that they typified the thematic differences described in Chapter 3. The two congregations were both modestly sized, in the same neighborhood in the city, and catered to similar types of congregations: working, middle-class, and mixed-age congregations. They thus shared many similar attributes but differed in the content of the messages delivered in their sermons.[3] With permissions from the pastor and the priest of these congregations, we approached congregants during coffee hour after a Sunday service to invite them to sign up if they were available on *both* a Friday evening *and* on a Sunday afternoon the following week. We compiled a list of interested participants from each congregation who could participate in either meeting time. We then randomly assigned each person on the lists to be invited to either a Friday evening discussion (i.e., a pre-weekly-sermon discussion) with others from their congregation or to a Sunday afternoon (i.e., a post-weekly-sermon discussion) with others from their congregation.

The discussions were casual and open-ended, involving small groups of fellow parishioners (between three and six people for each group).[4] The conversations lasted about forty-five minutes and all took place in a small hotel conference room in the neighborhood, which we selected because it was a convenient location for members of these churches no matter the day of the week, and because it provided a nonreligious setting in which we could host all focus group discussions, regardless of denomination. Participants were reimbursed for their transportation and

[2] The two congregations for this round of focus groups, in a nonelectoral period, were the Full Gospel Church of Kenya, Buru-Buru (Pentecostal) and the Blessed Sacrament Church (Catholic), also in Buru-Buru. Full Gospel Buru-Buru belongs to the larger Pentecostal Full Gospel Churches of Kenya body.

[3] We conducted interviews with pastors and congregants to verify that the social structures of the two churches were also very similar: both have regular worship and prayer services throughout the week, support groups for men and women and youth, and small prayer groups in which congregants regularly meet.

[4] We had seventeen participants in total from these two churches. Three individuals participated in each of the Friday discussions; five participated in the Sunday Pentecostal discussion and six participated in the Sunday Catholic discussion. Of course, there is inevitably self-selection into the discussions. That is, of the number of participants invited to participate on each day, only a fraction showed up. It was easier for church members to attend on a Sunday shortly after the service. However, we think it unlikely that there would have been differential self-selection by congregational affiliation on the two days. That is, we think it unlikely that the drivers of turnout varied systematically by denomination on the two days.

compensated (approximately three US dollars) for their time. We visited both churches again during the Sunday worship service between the Friday and Sunday focus groups so that we could observe the messages to which the congregants had been exposed. There was a high level of comfort within each focus group, because all members of the group were recruited from the same congregation, and they knew that they were part of the same church community, so the participants could speak openly.

There were palpable differences in tone and outlook between the Friday discussion groups and the Sunday discussion groups. When asked about the struggles in their daily lives, members of both churches expressed more anxiety and apathy during Friday discussions than on Sundays after church. Phrases like "I lack hope" were common on Fridays, especially among members of the Pentecostal church. Members of the Catholic church were also less sanguine on Friday than on Sunday, although the differences in whether they claimed they could overcome obstacles in their own lives were not as marked because in both Friday and Sunday groups members of the Catholic church were not confident that their own actions could bring about material change that was needed in either case. Responses suggesting that things are unlikely to change were also common among Catholics in discussion groups late in the week. They were cautious about predicting change, stressing that real change may not be possible.

After Sunday sermons, the themes of the two groups of congregants were strikingly different than they had been in the groups that met just days before. On Sundays, Catholics were quick to point out structural problems and injustices of the world following Sunday sermons, although they continued to express skepticism about the likelihood of change in this life. Sunday Catholic participants more often said they had to keep struggling against difficulties and injustices even in the face of defeat because their actions would ultimately be judged in the next life. "Sometimes these problems are tests," said one Sunday Catholic participant. "We have to pass to move to the next stage." Thus, while Sunday Catholic participants were not more optimistic about material change than Friday Catholic participants, they more frequently raised structural concerns and gave reasons to continue the struggle anyway.

Meanwhile, members of the Pentecostal church were almost wildly optimistic about the possibilities for change after Sunday worship. They were confident that any material challenge could be overcome through grace, through faith and positive thinking, and through embodying that positive outlook. Pentecostals in the Sunday discussion stressed that change could be realized through changing one's mindset and acting on that mindset, thereby strengthening their relationship with God. "Because God directs my life," argued one participant, "If you have a thought and do it diligently, then you will see the fruit." Pentecostal participants on Sundays frequently underscored their confidence that they could realize material change with the right relationship with God and with purposeful thinking and action.

These different outlooks translated in discussion into different ideas about how to interact with the state. We asked the participants in each discussion group, *What are the best strategies, in your mind, for fostering accountability in political leadership and in society at large?* In the Friday discussion groups, participants offered very few concrete ideas. A member of the Pentecostal church responded by saying that the business of politics is "too de-motivating" to do anything about. Members of the Catholic congregation sometimes made general references to joining together with others in the Friday discussions but did not rally around or get energized about forms of political engagement to any great extent. By contrast, in the Sunday discussions, participants from both congregations were much more specific and energized about political participation, even though the Sunday sermons they had heard had not been explicitly political. The particular forms of political participation raised in the two Sunday discussion groups varied across the two congregations. Members of the Pentecostal church raised forms of political participation that focused on leadership, including the idea that they themselves might run for office. They mentioned reaching out to leaders in collaborative formats: one participant thought it would be good to have "forums, when you can ask the leaders questions and they respond." Members of the Catholic church instead brainstormed ideas such as mobilizing people in the streets and on social media to raise demands for clean government and questions about how the government is handling issues like poverty and development. Both Catholics and Pentecostals showed more interest in discussing politics after the Sunday sermons and discussed specific, but different, forms of political engagement. We did not witness explicit references to these types of political engagement in either worship service that Sunday, but the congregants oriented their discussions quite differently in response to this open-ended question, depending on which worship service they had just attended.

All in all, the conversations were consistent with the following patterns: just after hearing a sermon in their house of worship, Pentecostals felt less overwhelmed by the difficulties and struggles of life that surrounded them than they had earlier in the week, more confident that through embodied faith and positive thinking they can make material change in this life, more interested in politics but also more positive about the status quo state of affairs. By contrast, just after hearing a sermon in their house of worship, Catholics were not particularly confident about making change in their own lives and in politics, but they were more cognizant of structural injustice. Whereas their attributions of responsibility for earthly problems on Fridays were fairly vague, just after Sunday services they pointedly focused on institutions and laws, and on elites corrupted by those institutions and rules. Among both sets of congregants, Sunday sermon exposure activated particular perceptions of the possibilities for change and attributions of responsibility for earthly problems that had waned during the week.

These results are not simply a product of people feeling more tired and run down on a Friday night than on a Sunday afternoon. We saw little difference in energy and optimism among Catholic participants depending on when during the week they were interviewed. The difference for them after a Sunday service was in their attribution of earthly problems, not in their dynamism. The difference for Pentecostals after a Sunday service was in a focus on individual faith and positive thinking and in a more fervent belief in the imminent possibility of change. We did not observe a consistent end-of-week versus end-of-weekend effect across all discussion group participants. Instead, congregants' outlooks diverged after Sunday services in ways consistent with denominational teachings but exhibited greater convergence toward the end of the week. This ebb and flow of religious teachings' influence is consistent with a story in which the influence of religious teachings is activated and reactivated through religious practice.

We also observed interesting differences across members based on their frequency of church attendance – specifically whether they attended throughout the week and not just on Sundays.[5] Frequent attendees – people who reported being at church and participating in church activities multiple times per week – always behaved like participants in Sunday afternoon discussions. They frequently referenced God, and sometimes referenced the main themes of the sermons they had heard, no matter whether they were in discussions on Friday evenings or Sunday

---

[5] All focus groups exhibited a mix of frequent and less frequent attendees. We were unable to hold discussions with only frequent attendees or with only less frequent attendees.

afternoons. Frequent Pentecostal attendees expressed no doubt that they could make material change in their own lives; they did not exhibit any dip in optimism, unlike the discussion participants who, on Friday evening, had not attended worship services since the previous Sunday. These observations complement patterns in the survey data, which we describe later in the chapter. Frequent attendees are constantly recharging. They exhibit less ebb and flow in the link between the religious teachings they have heard and their personal and political outlooks.

Within-group dynamics were striking as well. The goal of the focus group method is to exploit the synergies of group interaction as well as to observe individual differences during the conversation (Wilkinson, 1998). In these discussion groups, one frequent attendee could quickly reshape the direction, tone, and references of the conversation as a whole. This sequencing and take-up was particularly striking within the Pentecostal congregation Friday group. In this discussion group, most participants had not been to church since the previous Sunday. However, in the conversations with Pentecostal congregants on that Friday evening, one participant was a frequent service attendee who was also involved in volunteer and service roles within the church, and had been engaged in outreach prayers and worship services during the week. The conversation started out with the once-per-week attendees responding to questions about pressing problems they were facing, and what they think about how to address those problems. Usually, they did not reference God or the sermons in answering these questions. But the comments of the frequent attendee quickly changed the dynamic of the conversation.

Once-a-week attendee: Everyone has a challenge as an individual. My personal challenges are about education. To take your children to school, it increases poverty [is expensive]. You can't send your children to school as you would like, and get the things they need.

Frequent attendee: Well, as a Christian, one of the challenges is that we trust in God, but sometimes we forget and see challenges of human beings ... But if you search in his name, the Holy Spirit will direct you ... and that's the way for each and every Christian.

Once-a-week attendee: Well, it depends upon the background of each person. If your parents were not close, then you might engage with bad groups. Versus those who [had a better background], they are able to change their circumstances.

Frequent attendee: Each and every person feels his or her own challenges. It will depend on the relationship with God. If you don't have a relationship with God, the challenges will come.

Once-a-week attendee: Yes, the bible says we have to persevere because problems will be there, but through perseverance, we will become victors ... If you believe that you cannot make it, then you [be] come a beggar. Unless a person is cursed, you will stand strong and see problems, but do something with your own strength. And God is going to use you and expand you.

The Friday evening participant who had not been in church since the previous Sunday brought up challenges in his life but did not initially attribute to the strength of his internal faith or his personal relationship with God. The person who had just recently been to a worship service then reminded him to think in terms of his faith, saying, "It depends on the relationship with God. If you don't have a relationship with God, the challenges will come." After these reminders, the less frequent attendee then adopted this religious language as well. We should note that, although it is difficult to infer from the text alone, this participant began to speak enthusiastically in religious terms. We did not get the sense that he was doing so simply under the duress of social pressure, but rather that he felt encouraged by the other participants' words and reminders of the teachings she had recently heard. In keeping with Pentecostal teachings and the way the frequent attendee sees the world, the once-a-week attendee started relating his problems to his strength of faith and embodying of that faith. He switched to focus on self-mastery. Repeated exposure to the church's teachings – in this case, not just through the preacher but also through another speaker who has recently listened to a sermon – recharged his religious ideas. Here, as in the rest of the focus group discussions, we observed citizens' ideas about political engagement being influenced by recent sermon content in ways consistent with that content; and we also observed that influence dissipating and then being recharged by additional exposure.

SURVEYS ON DIFFERENT DAYS OF THE WEEK

To explore these patterns further, we analyzed two sets of surveys: the 2011–2013 and 2014–2015 rounds of the Afrobarometer, which were conducted in thirty and thirty-two countries in sub-Saharan Africa, respectively, and the 2008–2009 Pew Survey of ten sub-Saharan African countries, entitled "Tolerance and Tension: Islam and Christianity in Sub-Saharan Africa." Both sets of surveys measure whether or not respondents self-identify as Pentecostal, Mainline Protestant, or Catholic.

Based on our work in Chapter 3, we know something about the content of the sermons to which people affiliated with these different denominations were hearing during this time period. So we can use self-identified denomination as a proxy for exposure to those teachings. We assume only that self-identifying Pentecostals are *more likely* to have been recently exposed to a Pentecostal sermon than Catholics and Mainline Protestants are, not that they are never exposed to other types of sermons.[6] Both surveys measure a range of relevant attitudes and types of political participation: for instance, respondents' sense of political efficacy (Afrobarometer and Pew), their attitudes toward the state and institutions (Afrobarometer), and their willingness to participate in some forms of politics (Afrobarometer).

The surveys also provide the dates on which each respondent was interviewed. This information tells us whether a respondent was interviewed on the days just following a Sunday worship service, or whether the respondent was interviewed later in the week.[7] Controlling for observable correlates of identifying with a particular denomination and with being interviewed on a particular day of the week, we can examine whether differences in political attitudes and behavior between Pentecostals and Mainlines/Catholics are consistent with Pentecostals as *empowered players of the game* and Mainline Protestants and Catholics as *reluctant critiques* (as seen in the laboratory). We can also examine whether any differences in political attitudes and behavior between Pentecostals and Mainlines/Catholics are greater after recent exposure than at other times during the week.

Summary of Survey Findings

Table 5.1 summarizes the patterns that we found in the survey data. Across countries in sub-Saharan Africa in the current moment,

---

[6] Indeed, in an environment with somewhat fluid social boundaries across these denominations, people are likely to have been incidentally exposed to religious content from other denominations and even to have attended worship services in other denominations.

[7] Some respondents are interviewed on Sundays. Except for in the 2014–2015 Afrobarometer, we do not know the time of day at which respondents were interviewed, but many are likely to have been interviewed in the afternoon, after Sunday worship service. (In the 2014–2015 Afrobarometer, about half of Sunday respondents were interviewed in the afternoon, and when we drop those interviewed in Sunday morning, likely before they attend Sunday worship service, the patterns of divergence are often strengthened on Sundays.) We control for level of religiosity. In the Afrobarometer survey, 25 percent of respondents were interviewed on either Sunday or Monday. In the Pew Survey, 26 percent of respondents were interviewed on either Sunday or Monday. The modal day for being interviewed was Thursday.

TABLE 5.1 *Summary of survey findings.*

Empowered players		
System fair	Pentecostals early in week > everyone else	AB 2011
Internal/external pol efficacy	" "	AB 2011/Pew
Should avoid criticizing state	" "	AB 2014
Always make requests	" "	AB 2014
Would join to raise issue	" "	AB 2011
Reluctant reformers		Data source
System unfair	Mainlines/Catholics early in week > everyone else	AB 2011
Should *not* avoid criticizing state	" "	AB 2014
Would refuse taxes	" "	AB 2011, 2014
Among midweek worshippers	Evidence of reactivation	AB 2011, 2014
Other attitudes		
Trust in opposition	No differences	AB 2014
Prioritization of gender issues	No differences	AB 2014
Prioritization of poverty issues	No differences	AB 2014
Intended vote choice (Kenya)	No differences	AB 2011, 2014

Pentecostals, on the one hand, and Mainline Protestants and Catholics, on the other, orient themselves around relatively different forms of political participation and attitudes toward the state, and these differences are particularly stark *early in the week*, just after Sunday worship services. Mainline Protestants and Catholics were more inclined to judge institutions and systemic rules as unfair, to say that citizens should criticize the government as a whole, and to say that they might refuse to pay taxes. (They also report higher rates of having refused taxes in the past year.) Pentecostals, in contrast, reported a higher sense of self-efficacy but were more inclined to see institutions and the political system as fair, to say good citizens should avoid criticizing the government as a whole, and to say that good citizens should instead make requests of government officials and bring them their complaints.

The differences were in orientations toward particular modes of political engagement rather than differences in views over particular policy issues or in intended vote choice. We do not find that religion acts as a cross-cutting cleavage by, for instance, mitigating ethnic voting. Exposure to religious teachings did not seem to mobilize people to prioritize particular policy issues or to support particular parties. Regardless of which particular candidates respondents support, or which policies they prioritize, people's exposure to particular religious teachings correlates with *their general approach to politics*: whether through energetic engagement with individual leaders or through reluctant efforts to revise the system.

These differences across denominations appear most dramatically early on in the week – that is, just after most people are exposed to the content of Sunday worship services. Among respondents who report attending worship services midweek as well as on Sundays, some theoretically relevant divergences appear both right after Sunday services and right after midweek services (e.g., on Thursdays and Fridays). In other words, the influence of religious content on political attitudes and behaviors seems to be charged and recharged rather than act as a constant force.

Note that we do not present results for all measures of political participation, or attitudes about politics, that were collected in these surveys. One advantage of using available, large-scale survey data is that they offer attitudinal and behavioral measures beyond what we measured in the lab. A disadvantage, however, is that these surveys were not conducted with our research questions in mind, and so they did not set out to make clear distinctions between political participation that focuses on reforming institutions and political participation that focuses on improving individuals' characters. Better measures of this important distinction would be useful, and could be an aim of future research. In the meantime, we use measures from the surveys that approximate this distinction, such as whether respondents view institutions and laws as unfair, and whether they think that good citizens should criticize the government as a whole – both of which we think reflect institutionally focused forms of participation. Similarly, refusing to pay taxes is a form of systemic critique, rather than an act aimed at individuals. Other forms of participation investigated in the survey – such as joining a protest, or working for a campaign, or attending a rally – are not as easily interpreted as indicative of this distinction. People could participate in a protest against a specific leader whose character is in question, *or* to press for systemic reform. Likewise, a particular campaign could be focused on an institutionally minded platform, *or* be in service of a leader of strong character.

Correlates of Self-Identified Denomination and Interview Day

In the analyses in the rest of the chapter, we control for observable factors that differentiate self-identified Pentecostals from self-identified Mainline Protestants and Catholics, as well as for factors that correlate with the day of the week on which respondents were surveyed. Because country-level factors could differentially shape the relationships between religious teachings and political behavior, our analyses rely on differences within countries rather than across them by including country fixed effects.

There is quite a bit of variation in denominational affiliation among Christians surveyed by Afrobarometer and Pew. Of the sub-Saharan African respondents in Round 5 (2011–2013) of the Afrobarometer, 7 percent report being Pentecostal, 17 percent Mainline Protestant, 22 percent Catholic, and 23 percent report identifying only as Christian or with a church that doesn't neatly fall in one of these categories. Among Christians alone, 10 percent said they identify as Pentecostal, 25 percent Mainline Protestant, 31 percent Catholic, and 34 percent report identifying only as Christian or with a church that doesn't neatly fall in one of these categories. See Figure 5.1. The proportions in Round 6 (2014–2015) of the Afrobarometer were nearly identical. The Pew Survey provides slightly different response options, but the breakdown is very similar: among the 15,412 Christians in the survey, 15 percent of respondents identified as Pentecostal, 25 percent as Mainline Protestant, 37 percent as Catholic, and another 18 percent either gave no specific denomination (e.g., said they were "just Christian" or "just Protestant," said they had no denomination, or mentioned churches that do not fit into the other categories, such as Mormon). Another 5 percent refused to answer the question about denomination or church, or said they did not know. Respondents in the Pew Survey were also asked outright whether they would describe themselves as "Pentecostal Christian." Of the 14,532 respondents who answered this question, 24 percent said they would describe themselves as Pentecostal Christian. Figure 5.1 summarizes this variation in denominational affiliation.

As discussed in Chapter 2, there are many country-specific exceptions to these patterns but, on average, across countries, Pentecostals are more often urban residents, female, young, somewhat poorer, and less well educated than Mainline Protestants and Catholics.[8] Figure 5.2 presents

---

[8] Throughout, we exclude people who identify as "Other Christian" or "just Christian" because we cannot easily make assumptions about the content of the messages to which they are likely to have been exposed.

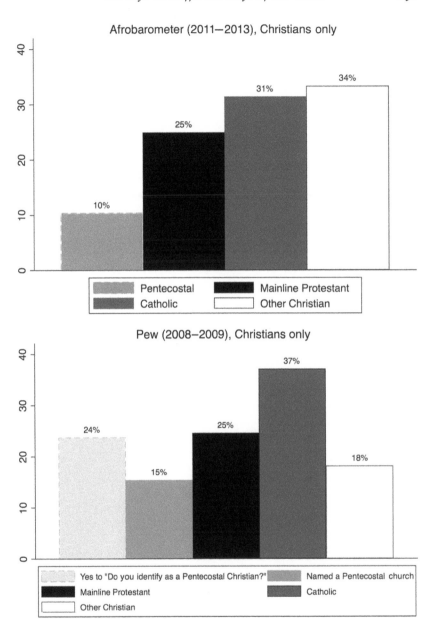

FIGURE 5.1 Distributions of self-identified denomination in the surveys.

results of linear probability models regressing denominational affiliation (Pentecostal v. Mainline, Mainline v. Catholic, and Pentecostal v. Catholic) on demographic variables: urban (rather than rural) residency, female, youth (thirty-five years or younger), experience of hunger in the last year,

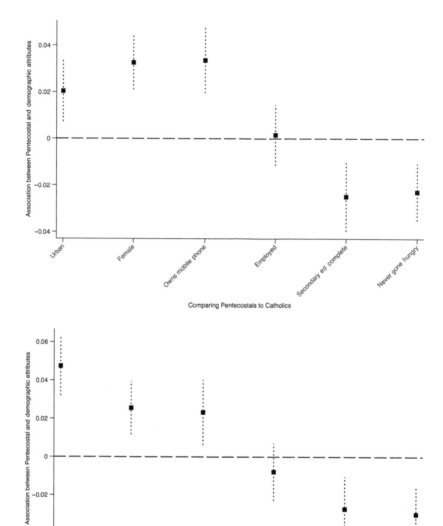

FIGURE 5.2 Attributes of self-identifying Pentecostals, compared to Catholics and Mainline Protestants (Afrobarometer 2011–2013).

mobile phone ownership, Internet usage, employment and education (whether the respondent has completed secondary education or not), including country fixed effects. Compared to Catholics and Mainline Protestants, Pentecostals are more often urban residents, more likely to say they have gone hungry in the last year, and less likely to have completed secondary education. The patterns are the same in the 2014–2015 round, with the exception that being young (under thirty-five) is a stronger differentiator than urban between Pentecostals and Catholics in that survey.

Figure 5.3 presents results from the Pew survey. The graphs show the coefficients from linear probability models regressing Pentecostal identification on a similar range of demographic characteristics as included in the Afrobarometer analyses. The bars around the point estimates are 95 percent confidence intervals. The conclusions here are similar: Pentecostals are more often young (under forty years old) than Catholics. They are also more often young than Mainline Protestants and with a slightly lower level of education. (Perhaps reflective of the Pentecostals' relative youth, they are somewhat more likely to own a mobile phone and less likely to use a computer.) Interestingly, unlike in the Nairobi church survey we did (discussed in Chapter 3), Pentecostals are slightly more often of higher than average income compared to Catholics in this survey.

These differences are far from stark or systematic, but to be sure that they are not driving the differences in attitudes and behavior we find later in this chapter, we control for these observable differences in subsequent analyses of these survey data.

We also leverage information on the days of the week on which respondents were interviewed. Figure 5.4 shows the distribution of members of each denomination interviewed on each day of the week in the Afrobarometer 2011–2013 round. Members of each denomination are evenly distributed across interview days. Among all survey respondents on each day, Catholics make up roughly 20–25 percent, Mainline Protestants about 15 percent or more, and Pentecostals between 5 percent and 10 percent. This distribution varies little by day.

There are not many observable correlates of interview day. Figure 5.5 presents the results of linear probability models that regress the incidence of being interviewed at some point early in the week (on Sunday, on Sunday or Monday, or in the first half of the week) on a series of demographic variables that might be thought to influence the days on which a person

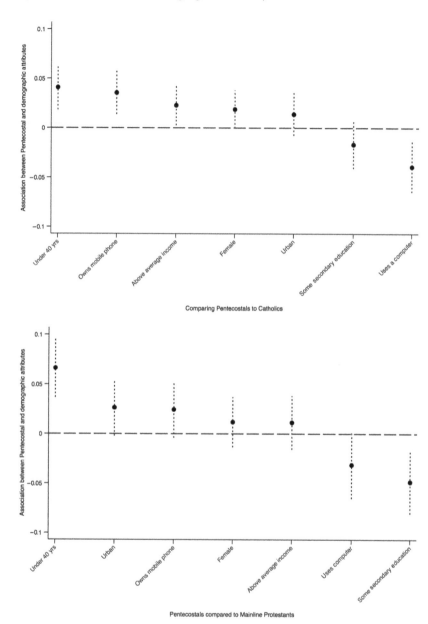

FIGURE 5.3 Attributes of self-identifying Pentecostals, compared to Mainline Protestants and Catholics (Pew 2008–2009).

would be free for an interview. The figure confirms that denomination is not correlated with being interviewed early rather than later in the week. (See the first two-point estimates in each graph.) Employed persons are interviewed more often on Sunday rather than on other days of the week,

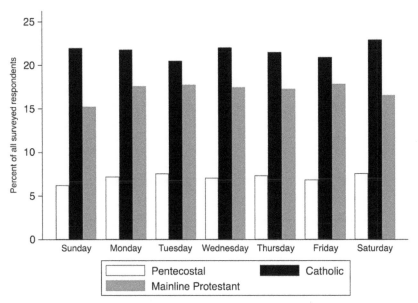

FIGURE 5.4 On each day, share of all survey respondents who are Pentecostals, Mainlines, and Catholics (Afrobarometer).

and urban respondents are somewhat less often interviewed on Sunday but are more often interviewed at some point in the first half of the week than rural respondents are. More religious individuals are no more or less likely to be interviewed on Sunday than during the rest of the week, but they are somewhat more likely to be interviewed in the middle of the week (e.g., on Wednesday). In light of these minor differences, we control for these observable factors in the analyses in this chapter.

In the Pew 2008–2009 survey, Pentecostals were somewhat less likely to be interviewed in the first half of the week than Catholics or Mainline Protestants. Urban residents were also less likely than rural residents to be interviewed early in the week. Otherwise, there was little observable difference between respondents interviewed earlier and later in the week. We control for observable traits in the subsequent analyses and draw inferences from comparing the attitudes of Pentecostals and Mainline Protestants/Catholics *on the same day* of the week. We also note that the weekly patterns of gathering respondents differs between the Afrobarometer and Pew surveys (that is, different observable traits correlate with day-of-the-week interviewed in each survey), and so, to the extent that we find similar patterns in both sets of surveys, we have more confidence that the patterns are general rather than features of specific survey designs.

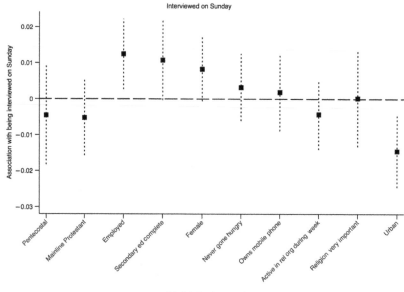

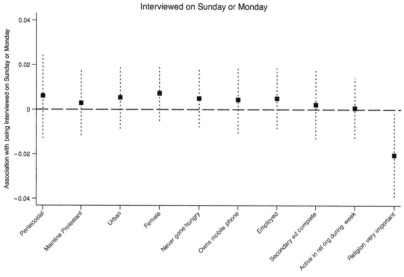

FIGURE 5.5 Correlates of being interviewed early in the week, Afrobarometer 2011–2013.

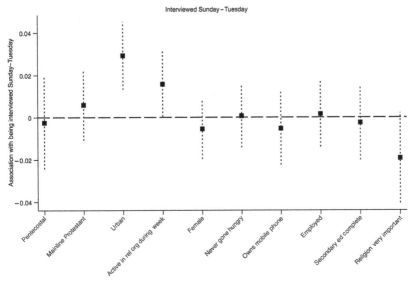

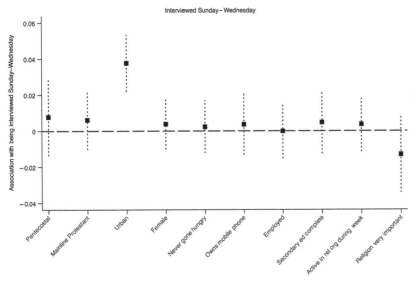

FIGURE 5.5 (cont.)

Orientations around Different Types of Political Engagement

When we look at theoretically relevant attitudes and behaviors in these surveys, we find that people affiliated with different denominations orient themselves toward different modes of political engagement but only *early on in the week*. On Sundays, we generally have to pool participants who were interviewed before Sunday services with those who were interviewed after, because we do not know the time of day when they were interviewed,[9] so it is difficult to interpret the comparisons of Pentecostals and Mainline Protestants/Catholics on Sundays. But we consistently find that the divergence in postures toward the government and in modes of public engagement between Pentecostals and Mainline Protestants/Catholics appears on Monday or Tuesday and then reconverges as the week goes on, no matter which wave or survey we examine.

In all of the subsequent analyses, we control for correlates of denominational affiliation (urban, female, cell phone ownership, secondary education, and income/experience of hunger); we also control for correlates of the day of the week interviewed (urban, employment). We often control for levels of reported religiosity so that we are estimating the effect of exposure to religious teachings (approximated by denominational affiliation) among respondents of similar levels of subjective religiosity and frequency of religious practice. In the Pew survey, about 38 percent of Christian respondents say that they attend once a week on Sundays, while 40 percent say they attend services during the week as well. Ten percent attend every couple of weeks to once a month. Less than 2 percent say they never attend church.[10] We include country fixed effects, and we control

---

[9] We have time of interview only for the 2014–2015, in which about half of Sunday respondents were interviewed in the afternoon rather than the morning. If we drop Sunday morning respondents in those analyses, we typically see more of a divergence in the expected direction on Sundays than if we do not drop those respondents who have likely not yet listened to Sunday sermons. However, here we report results with all Pentecostal, Catholic, and Mainline respondents.

[10] In the Pew survey, the questions that approximate religiosity are: "Aside from weddings and funerals, how often do you attend religious services, more than once a week, once a week, once or twice a month, a few times a year, seldom or never?" and "How important is religion in your life – very important, somewhat important, not too important, or not at all important?" The results that we report hold regardless of which measure we use to control for religiosity. The questions in the Afrobarometer do not always get at worship service attendance. Both waves as: "Tell me whether you are an official leader, an active member, an inactive member, or not a member of a religious group that meets outside of regular worship services" (2014–2015, 2011–2013), which allows us to look at the difference between people who participate in midweek worship service groups. Round

for whether each respondent is of the ethnic group as the chief executive of the country (president or prime minister). This latter control variable allows us to look at whether members of the same ethnic group within a given country nevertheless exhibit different orientations toward political engagement and different postures toward the state, depending on their denominational affiliation.

We observe divergences between Pentecostals and Mainline Protestants/Catholics in the view that the system is *unfair*. This divergence comes from Mainline Protestants' and Catholics' showing an *increase* in their view that institutions and rules are unjust and unfairly executed just after Sunday services, as well as from a slight *decrease* in the view of Pentecostals that institutions and rules are unjust. This outcome measure comes from the 2011–2013 Afrobarometer wave (Round 5). To generate a measure of general beliefs about the justness of the system, we created an index of the following items asked in the 2011–2013 wave of the Afrobarometer: "Are people treated unequally under the law?" "Are women treated unequally by traditional leaders?" "Are women treated unequally by the police and courts?" "Are women treated unequally by employers?" "Do officials who commit crimes go unpunished?" "Do ordinary people who break the law go unpunished?" and "Do people obtain household services, like water or electricity, without paying for them?" To each of these seven questions, respondents could answer "always"(3), "often" (2), "rarely"(1), or "never"(0). The 0–1 index weights each question equally and takes a value of 1 if individuals answered "always" to every item (indicating a strong perception of injustice) and a value of 0 if individuals answered "never" to every item (indicating a strong perception of justice). Higher values of the index are thus indicative of perceiving the system as more *un*fair or *un*just.

Figure 5.6 shows the results of regressing this unfairness index on indicators of denominational affiliation, day of the week, and the interaction between the two, controlling for individual-level demographics, coethnicity with the president (or head of government), and intensity of religious practice, and including country fixed effects. The results indicate that there is little difference between Catholics/Mainline and

6 also asks: "Aside from weddings and funerals, how often do you personally engage in religious practices like prayer, reading a religious book, or attending a religious service or a meeting of a religious group?" which encompasses both attendance and individual practice. Round 5 asks, "How important is religion in your life?" (2011–2013), which approximates subjective religiosity but does not ask about attendance.

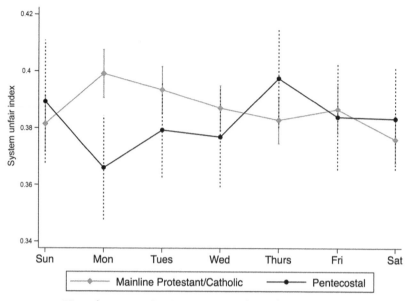

FIGURE 5.6 View that system/institutions are unfair, Afrobarometer 2011–2013.
Shows predictive margins on index (0–1) of beliefs about equal treatment/enforcement of laws by political institutions.
Controls: coethnic president, education, female, urban, owns mobile phone, age, country fixed effects.
Bars around point estimates mark 90 percent confidence intervals.

Pentecostals interviewed later in the week in their perceptions of system unfairness. But very early in the week, especially on Mondays,[11] Mainlines/Catholics exhibit heightened perceptions of unfairness compared to later in the week, whereas Pentecostals indicate slightly depressed perceptions of unfairness than they do later in the week. (These results do not change if we drop the items in the index having to do specifically with women.)

We next turn to ideas about what the "good citizen" should do. Questions about such views were asked in Round 6 (2014–2015) of the Afrobarometer. We found that, controlling for the aforementioned host of variables, including respondents' level of religiosity and whether they shared a coethnic connection with the head of government, Pentecostals more

---

[11] We do not know whether respondents interviewed on Sunday were interviewed before or after worship services.

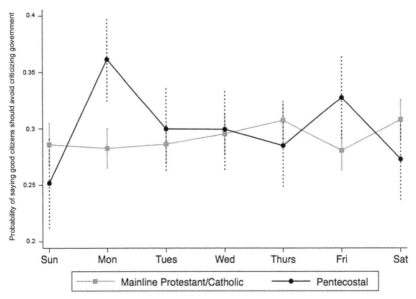

FIGURE 5.7 View that good citizens should avoid criticizing the government, Afrobarometer 2014–2015.

Shows predictive margins of agreeing or strongly agreeing that a good citizen should avoid criticizing the state.

Controls: coethnic president, education, female, urban, owns mobile phone, age, country fixed effects.

Bars around point estimates mark 90 percent confidence intervals.

often indicated that good citizens should avoid criticizing the government as whole, and should instead bring requests and complaints directly to government officials, than Mainline Protestants and Catholics. Figures 5.7 and 5.8 show the striking divergences on Mondays in views about what good citizens should do. Pentecostals show an increase on Mondays in the view that a good citizen should avoid criticizing the government as a whole, relative to Mainline Protestants and Catholics, but Pentecostals then return to the level held by Mainline Protestants and Catholics as the week proceeds (Figure 5.7). Similarly, they show an increase in the view that a good citizen should instead bring complaints directly to government officials (Figure 5.8).

Pentecostals also show a spike in political self-efficacy just after Sunday worship services. Figure 5.9 shows the divergence in reported political efficacy between Pentecostals and Mainline Protestants/Catholics in the Afrobarometer. The spike appears on Mondays before reconverging

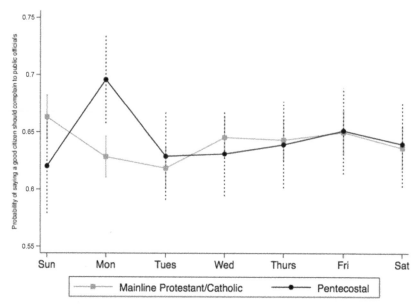

FIGURE 5.8 View that good citizens should bring complaints to government officials, Afrobarometer 2014–2015.

Shows predictive margins of agreeing or strongly agreeing that a good citizen should bring issues to public officials.

Controls: coethnic president, education, female, urban, owns mobile phone, age, country fixed effects.

Bars around point estimates mark 90 percent confidence intervals.

during the course of the week (with perhaps another boost later on in the week, which we discuss later when we look at midweek worshippers). The Afrobarometer survey, round 5 (2011–2013) contained a standard item measuring internal political efficacy: "Sometimes politics and government seem so complicated that a person like me can't really understand what's going on." Respondents were asked the extent to which they agreed or disagreed with that statement. The question is a standard measure from the American politics literature of internal political efficacy (Niemi, Craig, and Mattei, 1991; Morrell, 2005). Unfortunately, the survey did not contain other measures of political efficacy, e.g., of external political efficacy.[12] Figure 5.9 shows point estimates of the share

---

[12] Niemi, Craig, and Mattei (1991) distinguish external political efficacy – the ability to change political institutions and outcomes – from internal political efficacy – the ability to follow and participate in politics.

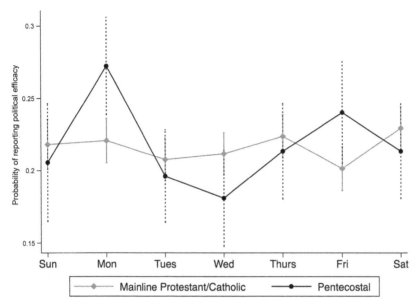

FIGURE 5.9 Reported level of political self-efficacy, Afrobarometer 2011–2013.
Shows predictive margins of disagreeing with "Sometimes politics and government seem so complicated that a person like me can't really understand."
Controls: education, female, urban, income, own mobile phone, use computer; includes country fixed effects.
Bars around point estimates mark 90 percent confidence intervals.

of respondents in each denominational category who disagree with the statement – that is, who report higher levels of political efficacy. Mainline Protestants and Catholics' reported sense of internal political efficacy remains fairly steady throughout the week, whereas Pentecostals show much more volatility, and are marked by a particularly dramatic increase early in the week, on Mondays, followed by a dip and return to levels very similar to Mainline Protestants' and Catholics'. The two categories of respondents are indistinguishable on Sundays, when we do not know the time of day (before or after services) at which they were interviewed.

The Pew survey (2008–2009) shows the same basic pattern. In the Pew survey, respondents were asked whether they agree or disagree with the statement, "People like me don't have any say about what the government does." The question thus taps a bit more into the concept of external political efficacy (the ability to affect political outcomes) than the question in the Afrobarometer did. Yet, the pattern in the Pew data is the same. Figure 5.10 shows the patterns of disagreement with the statement over

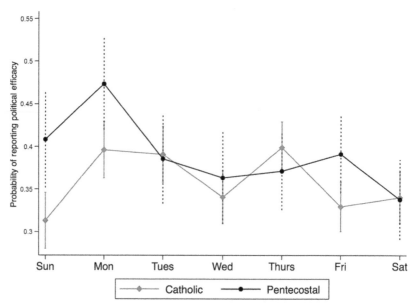

FIGURE 5.10 Reported level of political self-efficacy, Pew 2008–2009.

Shows predictive margins of disagreeing with "People like me don't have any say about what the government does."

Controls: urban, young, female, secondary education, owns mobile phone, above average income, religion very important, country fixed effects.

Bars around point estimates mark 90 percent confidence intervals.

the course of the week. Pentecostals and Catholics diverge early in the week, on Sundays and Mondays, and then reconverge as the week goes on and as Pentecostals descend from their initial boost in political self-efficacy just after Sunday services. The share of Pentecostals disagreeing that people like them don't have a say in what the government does is much higher early in the week (Sundays and Mondays) than it is later in the week (e.g., on Saturdays).

In other words, we see the following pattern: Pentecostals exhibit a boost in political efficacy early in the week, but a depressed view that the system is unfair and that the government as a whole should be criticized; among Catholics and Mainline Protestants, we see little evidence of a change in political efficacy but a heightened sense that the system is unfair.

These types of views translate into differences in inclinations toward political participation. The Afrobarometer 2011–2013 wave asked respondents whether, if they have not done so already, they would be

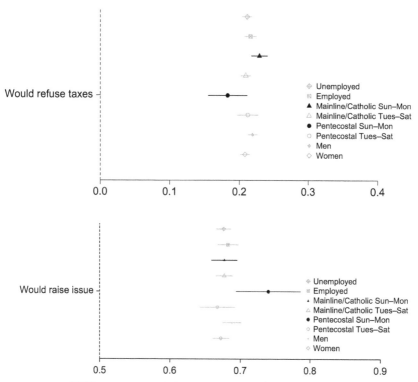

FIGURE 5.11 Willingness to participate, as it varies during the week, Afrobarometer 2011–2013.

Note: Point estimates are the share of respondents in that category saying they would be willing to engage in the relevant behavior (refusing taxes, or joining with others to raise an issue). Bars through the point estimates indicate 90 percent confidence intervals. Respondents identifying as Pentecostal, Mainline Protestant, and Catholic are included. Estimates are from linear regressions controlling for sex, employment status, mobile phone ownership, urban residency, religiosity, having gone hungry, and education and including country fixed effects.

willing to engage in various forms of political participation. One type, refusing to pay taxes, is an extreme form of personal action taken to challenge existing laws, policies, and structures. Another type, joining with others to raise an issue with public officials, aims to work through leaders rather than challenging the system as a whole. Figure 5.11 shows the differences in willingness to engage in these two actions, comparing Mainline Protestants and Catholics interviewed early in the week (on Sunday or Monday), Mainline Protestants and Catholics interviewed later in the week (Tuesday through Saturday), Pentecostals interviewed early in the week (on Sunday or Monday), and Pentecostals interviewed later in the week (Tuesday through Saturday). In terms of willingness to refuse to pay taxes (an institutional challenge), there is a clear divergence between Mainline Protestants and Catholics interviewed early in the week (who are *most* willing to refuse taxes) and Pentecostals interviewed early in the week (who are *least* willing to refuse taxes). Twenty-three percent of Mainline Protestants and Catholics interviewed early in the week say they would be willing to refuse to pay taxes, in contrast to 18 percent of Pentecostals interviewed early in the week. The inclinations of people in these two denominational categories are indistinguishable later in the week. In terms of raising issues with public officials (a leadership approach), there is again a clear divergence between Pentecostals interviewed early in the week (who are in this case the *most* willing to raise issues) and everyone else. Seventy-four percent of Pentecostals interviewed early in the week report being willing to join with others to raise issues, compared to an estimated 67 percent of respondents in other categories. Pentecostals interviewed later in the week give answers that are indistinguishable from Mainline Protestant and Catholic respondents.

These differences are substantively significant. Figure 5.11 compares the magnitude of these differences to differences across other common demographic correlates of political participation. Such differences (e.g., between men and women, between the employed and unemployed) are smaller than those across respondents of different denominations early in the week. Twenty-two percent of men say they would be willing to refuse taxes, compared to a very similar 21 percent of women. Twenty-one percent of unemployed respondents say they would be willing to refuse to pay taxes, compared to a similar 22 percent of employed respondents. Sixty-nine percent of men say they would be willing to raise issues, compared to a similar 67 percent of women. Sixty-eight percent of both employed and unemployed respondents say they would be willing to raise issues. None of these differences is statistically significant.

Unfortunately, none of these surveys asks about inclinations to run for office or to engage in leadership training, which would have provided more direct measures of the kinds of political participation we expect to be heightened among Pentecostals just after Sunday worship services. We heard evidence in favor of this expectation in our focus groups in Nairobi, and we use the case studies in the next chapter to look further for differences in focus on leadership training and politicians' character development.

Not about Issues or Vote Choice

The influence of religious teachings in this context is on citizens' general orientations toward fixing political problems and their general approaches to politics. It is on their sense of efficacy, their views about the justness of institutions, and their inclinations to participate through or against structures of government. The influence of religious teachings in this context is *not* about mobilization around particular parties, candidates, or issues.

The Afrobarometer asks questions about parties and political issues, too. We find no striking differences across religious denominations, and no divergence early in the week, with regard to these questions. For instance, the Afrobarometer 2014–2015 wave asked respondents, "How much do you trust, or haven't you heard enough to say, opposition political parties?" Cross-nationally, we use an answer to this question of "somewhat" or "a lot" as an indication of support for opposition rather than incumbent political parties. As Figure 5.12 shows, Pentecostals and

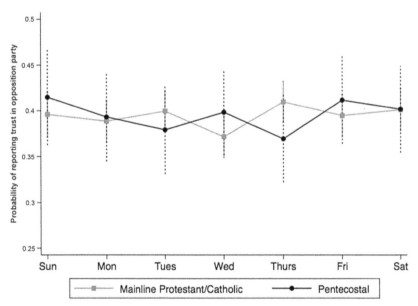

FIGURE 5.12 Trust in the opposition party, Afrobarometer 2014–2015.

Shows predictive margins of trusting opposition political parties somewhat or a lot.
Controls: coethnic president, education, female, urban, owns mobile phone, age, country fixed effects.
Bars around point estimates mark 95 percent confidence intervals.

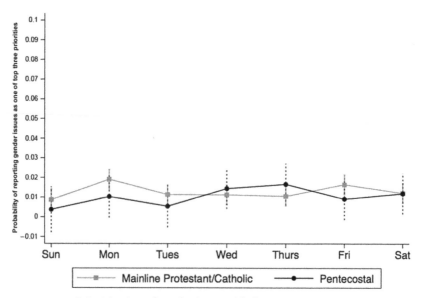

FIGURE 5.13 Prioritization of gender issues, Afrobarometer 2014–2015.
Shows predictive margins of placing gender issues in top three priorities.
Controls: coethnic president, education, female, urban, owns mobile phone, age, country fixed effects.
Bars around point estimates mark 95 percent confidence intervals.

Mainline/Catholics are not systematically more or less trusting of the opposition than one another, nor does their trust in opposition parties spike at a certain point in the week.

The Afrobarometer also asks respondents, "In your opinion, what are the most important problems facing this country that government should address?" One might suppose that religious denominations might be exerting political influence by mobilizing people to prioritize particular political issue areas, such as issues of homosexuality, conservative family values, or poverty alleviation (De La O, and Rodden, 2008; Grossman, 2015; McCauley, 2015a). Unfortunately, the coding of the question does not include LGBT issues or homosexuality. However, one set of answers is "gender issues," and another popular answer is "poverty/destitution." In Figures 5.13 and 5.14, we plot the predicted shares of respondents of different denominations who list gender issues (Figure 5.13) or poverty/destitution (Figure 5.14) as one of their top three priorities for the government to address. We see no differences across respondents of these denominational affiliations at any point in the week in how they answer

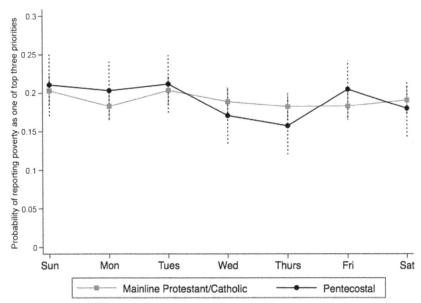

FIGURE 5.14 Prioritization of poverty issues, Afrobarometer 2014–2015.
Shows predictive margins of placing poverty and destitution in top three priorities.
Controls: coethnic president, education, female, urban, owns mobile phone, age, country fixed effects.
Bars around point estimates mark 95 percent confidence intervals.

these questions about political issue priorities. Indeed, Pentecostals and Mainline Protestants/Catholics show no detectable differences in how they answer any of these questions about political parties and political issues, no matter when in the week they were asked.

In most countries, the influence of religious denomination is also not about vote choice, which is often driven by other social identities, ones that are highly politicized. Almost everyone in Kenya will tell you that vote choice is about tribe, not about religion. In the 2014–2015 Afrobarometer round, which took place in Kenya just after the 2013 presidential elections, respondents were asked, "If presidential elections were held tomorrow, which party's candidate would you vote for?" Of the seven largest tribes in Kenya (which together make up close to 85 percent of the population), Luos most strongly supported the opposition ODM party, while Kikuyus and Merus were the strongest supporters of the recently elected president's National Alliance. Kalenjins were the strong supporters of the United Republican Party (URP), the party of the then-deputy president.

TABLE 5.2 *Ethnic membership by denomination in Kenya,*
Afrobarometer 2014–2015.

	% Catholic	% Pentecostal	% Mainline
Luo	27.0	15.2	15.6
Kikuyu	27.6	9.2	21.2
Luhya	17.2	33.1	22.8
Meru	15.1	11.6	27.4
Kalenjin	22.1	7.2	26.6

Each of these groups has members who identify as primarily Catholic, Pentecostal, or Mainline Protestant, as can be seen in Table 5.2.

However, respondents vote on the basis of tribe, no matter their religious denomination. Table 5.3 shows the associations between tribe and intention to vote for the incumbent president's party among Christians, first without accounting for denominational affiliation and then adding interactions between Catholic or Pentecostal affiliation and tribe. The first column shows strong evidence of voting on the basis of tribe. There is a strong association (positive or negative) between every tribal identity and intention to vote for the incumbent president's party, except among Kisiis. This pattern persists despite variation in religious affiliations across groups. Indeed, as the second and third columns show, including Catholic and Pentecostal affiliations adds very little to an account of vote intention. There is perhaps a slight increase in rejection of the incumbent party among Pentecostal Luos, but otherwise ethnic voting does not vary based on these religious affiliations. The third column reports results from a regression that includes other respondent attributes (sex, urban, education, employment status, religiosity, and so on) as controls, but these do not diminish the strong patterns of ethnic voting either. Notice that the r-squared term hardly changes across the regressions.

In Kenya, religion does not account for vote choice alongside or in place of tribe. In other countries, such as Nigeria and increasingly Tanzania, religious affiliation is a salient political cleavage that orients partisan affiliation. And in all places, the salient political cleavages are subject to change at certain moments in a country's history (Lipset and Rokkan, 1967; Laitin, 1986; Posner, 2005). Religion could, at some point, become a political cleavage that also plays a role in shaping vote choice.

However, even in places such as Kenya where religion is not the most salient political cleavage at this particular historical juncture, people's religious affiliations, and their resulting exposure to religious content, can still play a role in politics, specifically by shaping how people generally

TABLE 5.3 *Tribe, denomination, and vote intention among Kenyan Christians, Afrobarometer 2014–2015.*

Tribe/denomination	Vote TNA	Vote TNA	Vote TNA (with ind controls)
Luo	−0.40	−0.39	−0.38
	(0.07)	(0.08)	(0.08)
Luo*Pentecostal		−0.14	−0.15
		(0.08)	(0.08)
Luo*Catholic		0.05	0.04
		(0.07)	(0.07)
Luhya	−0.23	−0.22	−0.21
	(0.08)	(0.08)	(0.08)
Luhya*Pentecostal		−0.06	−0.07
		(0.10)	(0.10)
Kikuyu	0.49	0.49	0.50
	(0.07)	(0.08)	(0.08)
Kikuyu*Pentecostal		−0.07	−0.06
		(0.09)	(0.08)
Kikuyu*Catholic		0.03	0.04
		(0.06)	(0.06)
Kamba	−0.16	−0.17	−0.16
	(0.08)	(0.09)	(0.09)
Kamba*Pentecostal		0.11	0.08
		(0.16)	(0.17)
Kamba*Catholic		0.03	0.02
		(0.09)	(0.09)
Kalenjin	−0.26	−0.26	−0.26
	(0.08)	(0.08)	(0.08)
Kalenjin*Pentecostal		0.28	0.26
		(0.17)	(0.17)
Kalenjin*Catholic		−0.05	−0.04
		(0.08)	(0.08)
Kisii	−0.06	−0.08	−0.07
	(0.09)	(0.10)	(0.10)
Kisii*Pentecostal		−0.13	−0.14
		(0.15)	(0.13)
Kisii*Catholic		0.16	0.15
		(0.12)	(0.13)
Meru	0.43	0.43	0.46
	(0.08)	(0.08)	(0.08)
Meru*Pentecostal		−0.03	−0.07
		(0.11)	(0.11)
Meru*Catholic		−0.01	−0.03
		(0.11)	(0.11)
Pentecostal		0.06	0.06
		(0.08)	(0.08)
Catholic		−0.04	−0.05
		(0.05)	(0.05)
Obs	1,629	1,629	1,596
R-squared	0.48	0.49	0.50

TNA stands for "The National Alliance," which was the political party/alliance of the incumbent president during the 2014–2015 Afrobarometer wave. The main rival party during the previous (2013) elections was the Orange Democratic Movement (ODM). Robust standard errors in parentheses. Included as reference category: Masai, Mijikenda, Tita, Pokot, and Turkana. In the third column, control variables are female, urban, owns mobile phone, never used Internet, employed, secondary school completed, active member of a religious organization.

engage (or do not engage) with the state: whether through individual transformation or by pressing for structural and institutional reform. No matter who it is they want to see elected and who is in the government between elections, people exposed to religious teachings are influenced to approach politics through different world views.

Reactivation

But what about people who attend church multiple times a week? For these individuals, we would expect the patterns to be different, since they would be exposed repeatedly to religious teachings between one Sunday worship service and the next. The Afrobarometer 2014–2015 wave asked respondents, "Aside from weddings and funerals, how often do you personally engage in religious practices like prayer, reading a religious book, or attending a religious service or a meeting of a religious group?" This question is not perfect, because it asks about religious practice rather than church attendance, but since the Pew survey is the only one to ask about attendance specifically yet does not ask most political questions or ask about midweek rather than daily attendance, we use the Afrobarometer Round 6 question as a proxy. Fifty-three percent of Christians interviewed in that wave said that they engage in religious practice more frequently than once a week ("a few times a week, "about once a day," or "more than once a day"). Twenty-three percent of Christians interviewed in that wave said that they worship more frequently than once a week but not daily. It is among this latter set that we might expect to see more fluctuations in inclinations toward political engagement, as their religious world views are activated and reactivated at different points in this week.

If we look at those Afrobarometer respondents who report worshipping a few times a week – that is, more than once a week but not every day – we see some evidence consistent with two reactivations ("recharges") of distinct religious world views during the week. For instance, Figure 5.15 shows that, among Pentecostals who worship more than once a week but not every day, there are two boosts in the view that good citizens should avoid criticizing the government as a whole: once just after Sunday worship services, and once toward the end of the week, which is consistent with churches' having a Wednesday or Thursday midweek worship service. Likewise, Pentecostals who worship more than once a week but not every day show two "pump-ups" and subsequent dips in the view that good citizens should make requests of government officials. We see similar patterns in respondents' willingness to join with

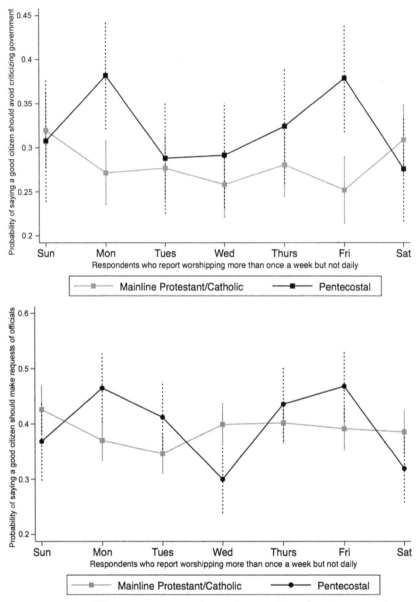

FIGURE 5.15 Views among respondents who worship a few times a week.

others to raise an issue, though the differences across days among Pentecostals are not statistically significant. Variables such as trust in the opposition, prioritization of poverty, and gender issues that showed no early week boost also showed no "two recharge" patterns among respondents who reported worshipping more than once a week but not every day.

Unfortunately, the Afrobarometer 2011–2013 wave and the Pew survey do not ask questions that allow respondents to distinguish among daily worship, midweek worship, and once-a-week worship. But the patterns in the Afrobarometer 2014–2015 wave suggest that, for those who worship midweek, additional exposure to religious teachings may reactivate views that would otherwise dissipate without additional exposure. The influence of religious content on political behavior may not inherently be deep-seated and persistent. But with repeated exposure, it can be charged and recharged.

IMPLICATIONS: REINFORCEMENT AND IMMEDIATE ACTION

If religious teachings sway people's political behavior only in the short term, how should we think about the aggregate impact of religious teachings on patterns of political engagement? The patterns here suggest that religious teachings' aggregate impact is likely to depend on the following factors: (1) how saturated a political context is with a particular set of religious teachings; and/or (2) whether political entrepreneurs provide opportunities for engagement in close proximity to the dissemination of religious teachings. Regarding the first factor, the patterns in this chapter suggest that the influence of religious teachings on political behavior can be activated and reactivated each time people are exposed to those teachings. If a political context is saturated with one particular set of religious teaching such that citizens are constantly inundated with that way of understanding the physical and spiritual world, we might expect stable modes of political engagement in accordance with those teachings throughout the week. If people are segregated into areas with only one type of religious teaching, and houses of worship invest heavily in encouraging repeated exposure to those teachings, we might expect consistent differences in modes of political engagement across members of different denominations throughout the week.

Regarding the second factor, even if an environment is not saturated or dominated by one set of religious teachings if political entrepreneurs attempt to mobilize people early in the week, we might nevertheless still expect to see certain modes of participation (e.g., demands for legislation on the one hand, leadership training on the other) dominated by members of a particular denomination, in keeping with the religious teachings to which they have been exposed. In the next chapter, we show descriptive evidence that the general divergences across individuals in this chapter

also apply to divergences in group-level political engagement by denomination, although the evidence does not let us tease out the implications of
the weekly duration patterns in this chapter. We encourage more research
to make these connections going forward.

SUMMARY

In this chapter, we have problematized the notion that the influence of
religious world views on political behavior is necessarily deep-seated and
chronic, and we have argued instead to conceptualize religion as possibly
involving activation and reactivation, recharging, and practice. This latter
view is more consistent with the work that houses of worship do when
they try to encourage congregants to expose themselves frequently to
religious teachings, not only during end-of-the-week worship services but
frequently during the week. This latter view is also more consistent with
how congregants themselves discuss their own experiences: congregants
in our focus groups described needing to "renew" their faith by hearing
words from the pulpit; they described difficulty in sustaining a focus on
God and in sustaining a particular view of the spiritual and physical
worlds if they had not listened to a sermon recently. In focus group discussions that took place either at the end of the week, before Sunday
services, or after Sunday services, we observed differences in how readily
congregants related their everyday challenges and political inclinations
to sermons, as well as in whether they spoke about political problems
in ways consistent with the content of the most recent sermon they had
heard. The link between sermons and political attitudes was more tenuous
the longer the temporal lapse since sermon exposure.

Across sub-Saharan Africa, Pentecostals diverged in their political
attitudes and types of political engagement from Mainline Protestants
and Catholics in ways consistent with the content of the teachings in their
respective houses of worship. The individual-level patterns described in
the previous chapter extend well outside of the laboratory and well
outside of Nairobi. We see the same differences in modes of political
participation and attitudes when looking widely across countries in
the Afrobarometer and Pew surveys and when listening to small group
conversations among congregants.

Yet, the divergence in political leanings across denominations was
most apparent *right after* Sunday worship services. As the week wore on,
patterns of political behavior and political attitudes across denominations
reconverged. Attention to the temporal dynamics of religious teachings'

influence tells us far more about the work that religious institutions actually do and offers important observable implications about the timing of religious-political mobilization. For instance, we should expect religious teachings' influence to seem particularly long-lasting where religious institutions are investing a lot in "recharging" the influence of their teachings throughout the week. And we should see the strongest potential for political entrepreneurs to mobilize particular groups of religious adherents early on in the week.

In other words, the links between religious world views and political participation are real but should not be taken for granted. Instead, we should pay attention to how religious world views are reinforced and recharged and to how and when political mobilization coincides with exposure to religious teachings.

6

Group-Level Political Engagement

Of what use are new laws if the good old laws are disregarded, not only for
new ones but also because of lack of values? With good values, many laws
would be unnecessary.

        – Kenya Twitter post

Empowering institutions rather than individuals is what will change the
face of Kenya.

        – Kenya Twitter post

Sermons in the modern age can shape how citizens see their own role
in society and politics, and how they categorize the types of problems
that need addressing and through what means. Even if the influence of
sermons is fleeting, and requires frequent reiteration, citizens who are
exposed to different types of religious messages are shaped by those ideas
to view themselves and their place in the world in specific ways. One of
the preceding Twitter quotes expresses the view that good governance
requires good personal values and that values and character may be more
important than laws. The other locates the focus of political change in
institutions. These quotes attribute responsibility for political problems to
different sources and, therefore, seek different types of political solutions.

  Throughout this book, we have demonstrated that religious teachings –
as expressed in sermons – can influence whether people engage in
these different forms of political participation, even where religious
teachings themselves are not explicitly political, where religious identities
are not highly politicized, and where practically everyone is religious.
Religious answers to deep metaphysical questions can affect how citizens
approach political problems and respond to opportunities for political
participation by shaping whether they feel efficacious, and how they

attribute responsibility for political problems (e.g., to people or to structures). In the religiously plural environments we have examined, the effects of sermons were strongest among individuals who seek out those religious teachings but were not limited to them. Thus, even when citizens encounter religious messages incidentally in their daily lives – such as on the radio or television in public spaces, in the newspapers, and in social conversations – such messages can shape their ways of understanding themselves and the political world. But the influence of sermons among those who seek them out, which is likely to be the most frequent form of sermon exposure, is equally strong or stronger. Such influence is activated and reactivated – with sermons exerting a strong influence in the short term, and then being recharged with additional exposure.

In this chapter, we extend our analysis to a broad range of political behaviors by groups affiliated with one denomination or the other, in order to determine whether the patterns we found experimentally, in focus groups and in surveys, are consistent with aggregate modes of participation in contemporary public life, across different time periods and different country contexts. We thus demonstrate further external validity to our arguments by showing that, across a number of countries and time periods, members of different religious denominations have been consistently engaging in different modes of political participation. These modes of political participation are important, at times entering at key moments into political debates or leading collective actions. Pentecostals[1] do indeed engage as *empowered players* – energized actors who seek stronger faith and better values in citizens and political leaders but do not seek to reform structures and institutions – while Mainline Protestants and Catholics engage as *reluctant reformers* – sometimes late to organize political action but consistently critical of existing institutions and structures of power.

We cast a broad net in this chapter by using a mix of historical and contemporary case comparisons in Zambia, Uganda, and Kenya, and a unique newspaper database of all anglophone countries, to demonstrate that patterns described in previous chapters extend outside of surveys, focus groups, and the laboratory. We move away from a sole focus on individual behavior and attempt to observe actions at the *group* level:

---

[1] Throughout the chapter, we often use the terms "Pentecostals," "Catholics," and "Mainline Protestants" as shorthand to refer to members of that church category broadly speaking – both laity and local leaders. As we note in this chapter, by moving to a group-level analysis and by observing these behaviors in the historical record, we often lose the clean distinction between lay worshippers and religious leaders.

e.g., lay members of a particular denomination working together to start a political movement or establish a leadership institute. However, the sources available to us (secondary and primary historical sources, newspaper reports) rarely make a distinction between lay and clergy behavior when reporting the political behavior of religious people. Thus, in this chapter we lose a neat separation between the religious clergy (those who compose and deliver sermons) and the laity (our focus in most of the book, as receivers of such messages). We gain observations of significant historical and contemporary political action and are able to show consistency in "Pentecostal" and "Mainline Protestant"/"Catholic" political engagement across political and social contexts. But these advantages come at the expense of being able to set aside the actors who formulate the sermons in the first place, and at the expense of always being able to identify a tight link between sermon exposure and resulting individual or group behavior.

The problem with not being able to delineate cleanly between clergy political engagement and lay political engagement is that clergy may be using their role as sermon writers to strategically push a particular political agenda, rather than being genuinely moved themselves by the metaphysical ideas in their sermons. Thus, the inclusion of clergy action in our descriptions of "Pentecostal" and "Mainline Protestant and Catholic" engagement does not cleanly illustrate the influence of sermonic ideas on political engagement, rather than the other way around. In much of the book, we have been able to bracket questions about where the sermons themselves come from and why they contain the metaphysical ideas they do, relying on particular methods to randomly assign sermons and to home in on individual reactions to sermons, whatever the sermons' origins. Here, we cannot sidestep these issues as easily.

A few features of this chapter mitigate the possibility that our group-level findings are driven *entirely* by clergy's own political agendas and their strategic formulation of metaphysical ideas in their sermons. We use a "most-different" case selection design to rule out some alternative explanations for patterns of political engagement. Specifically, we exploit variation in the organizational features of churches, in the historical and contemporary positioning of religious denominations vis-à-vis the state, in the churches' international ties, and in the churches' committment to social welfare provision, in order to rule out the possibility that these features of denominations (rather than the metaphysical ideas they communicate) are driving patterns of political engagement. We find that Pentecostals, on the one hand, and Mainline Protestants and Catholics, on the other hand, consistently engage as empowered players and as reluctant reformers, respectively, even as these other features of their organization, political positions, and service activities shift across time and across countries. These findings cast serious doubt on the possibility that these other features of church life are driving the differences in political engagement. The "most different" design also illustrates that clergy pursue these modes of political engagement in very different political-strategic contexts and under varying degrees of church hierarchy and resources – arguably even when it goes against the clergy's institutional, material, and career interests.[2] In some instances in the case studies, clergy demonstrably took the pulse of the laity before deciding to take a political stance outside of church. These examples suggest that, even if clergy formulate sermons in order to incline laity toward a particular form of political engagement, the reactions of the laity to those sermons in turn feed into whether the clergy take political action.[3] In other words, the influence of sermons on lay persons' behavior still plays a crucial role in accounting for patterns of political engagement if the laity have to be moved by the sermons in order for political action to proceed. Sermons may also have unintended consequences, resulting in clergy being pushed by their congregations to act in ways contrary to the clergy's own organizational and material interests.

Nevertheless, given the inability of the evidence in this chapter to zero in on lay actions alone or to identify a causal relationship between sermon exposure and political participation, we do not make strong causal claims on the basis of the evidence in this chapter. That is not the chapter's purpose. We offer the findings in this chapter in conjunction with the findings in other chapters of the book that do more causal identification work at the individual level. The switch in this chapter to group-level observations allows us to describe a broader view of actual types of real-world political engagement. These patterns are consistent with the micro-level insights established in the lab, focus groups, and survey data.

A MOST-DIFFERENT COMPARISON DESIGN

Once we move from analyses at the individual level to look at group-level patterns of political engagement across and within countries over time,

---

[2] For instance, as described in the case studies, Catholic and Mainline Protestant clergy often exert pressure for institutional and structural reform even when their churches have close ties to state power and are deeply embedded in existing political institutions.

[3] Religious "leaders may well add their personal voices ... once a sufficient groundswell has built up" (Haynes, 1996, 85).

one might hypothesize that any differences in political engagement across denominations could be due to differences in the political positions of those denominations vis-à-vis the state (Kalyvas, 1996; Warner, 2000; Philpott, 2007; Grzymała-Busse, 2015), to differences in the organizational features of those denominations (Hale, 2018), or to differences in the denominations' resources and support from abroad, rather than due to the content of the religious ideas and teachings to which their members are exposed. For instance, one might suppose that a denomination's proximity to state power would be a necessary, or even a sufficient, cause of its members' mode of political engagement. Leaders of a religious denomination that is well connected to the state might be unlikely to engage in actions that challenge existing institutions and structures, because they want to maintain the status quo in which they have resources and influence (Haynes, 1996; Grzymala-Busse, 2016). Members of more autonomous, independent churches that lack embedded church–state relations may be more willing to criticize the institutional and structural features of the state and more willing to engage in efforts to push for structural reform (Patterson and Kuperus, 2016, 321). Conversely, some scholars have argued that Pentecostals are more politically acquiescent because of their relative status as outsiders, as relative latecomers to the colonially established symbiotic link between Mainline Christianity and the state (Gifford, 1995). Lacking these channels of direct influence, Pentecostals might remain relatively uncritical of institutions in order to cozy up to (and not offend) political elites. In turn, elites might reward this less structurally critical posture with further support of the growth of Pentecostal churches (Sperber, 2016).

We might also expect that a particularly centralized or hierarchically organized religious denomination in a given country would be able to coordinate members and leaders to a greater degree, and therefore have greater capacity to coordinate and mobilize efforts to challenge and reform the system, leading perhaps to a greater incidence of protest behavior or forms of noncompliance. For instance, one might expect that the centralized nature of the Catholic Church provides the organizational foundation to mobilize structurally critical action to a greater degree than Pentecostal churches.

Similarly, international ties to outside authority and resources may give a particular denomination the leverage and autonomy to act in ways critical of institutions and regimes. Ties to the Vatican might make Catholic parishes more independent from the state and thus in a stronger position to criticize institutions. The support of international missionaries from the United States, Nigeria, or elsewhere might afford certain churches the space to challenge, rather than work within, the existing rules of the game.

Finally, one might expect that denominations with a greater reach and depth of social service provision could provide lay members with the opportunities to engage in public goods provision outside of Sunday worship services, which might in turn provide them the skills and social ties to engage effectively in systemically critical forms of collective action (Brady, Verba, and Schlozman, 1995; Campbell, 2004). They may be drawn into debates about institutions and rules of the game as they engage in alternative service provision and coordination through church-sponsored projects, schools, and clinics. Since Catholics are historically more deeply entrenched in social service provision, they may possess greater capacity and interest in systemic and regime critiques, whereas Pentecostal activities may be more focused on individual counseling and self-help, which may facilitate leadership development and minor requests of public officials but may not facilitate systemically critical collective action. The logic could also be inverse, if criticizing state institutions and the regime would risk service and missionary work.

To address these possibilities, we leverage a "most-different" design to assess whether we find consistent patterns in modes of political engagement across denominations despite varying configurations of these other variables. The most-different case comparison approach leverages cases that are different on a host of variables *other* than the key explanatory variable. It is a design that is best positioned to eliminate necessary causes of the outcome (Seawright and Gerring, 2008). It is sometimes considered a weaker case comparison method because it does not examine the counterfactual of, for instance, what Pentecostal political engagement would have looked like had Pentecostalism involved a different set of religious teachings (Gerring, 2006). We engage in that kind of counterfactual analysis in Chapters 4 and 5 at the individual level: showing that random assignment of religious teachings to listeners influences political participation in the lab, and showing that individuals who are otherwise very similar but different only in their denominational affiliations exhibit different modes of political engagement. Here, we set out to demonstrate that, across a wider stretch of time and place, patterns consistent with the individual-level findings also show up in group political action. We also set out to show that aspects of religious associations *other* than their teachings (their proximity to state power, organization features, external ties, service activities) are not a required part of the explanation

TABLE 6.1 *Alternative explanations ruled out by most-different design.*

Variable	Expected relationship	Findings from the case studies
Proximity to state power	Close –> empowered players (EP)	Catholics/Mainline Protestants are reluctant reformers even when close to state power; Pentecostals are empowered players even when distant from state power.
Centralization/ hierarchy	High –> reluctant reformers (RR)	Mainline Protestants are reluctant reformers even when exhibiting low centralization and hierarchy.
International ties	Strong –> reluctant reformers (RR)	Pentecostals are empowered players even when exhibiting moderately strong international ties; Mainline Protestants are reluctant reformers even when exhibiting weaker international ties.
Extent of service provision	Low –> empowered players (RR)	Pentecostals are empowered players when more heavily engaged in service provision; Mainline Protestants are reluctant reformers even when engaged in lower levels of service provision.

for these patterns.[4] For this latter purpose, a most-different design is advantageous.

Table 6.1 outlines various possible hypotheses involving these alternative variables as well as the findings from the case studies that cast doubt on their explanatory power. Tables 6.2 through 6.5 then summarize the country–regime–denomination cases and their values on these variables, to show why we selected these cases and what leverage they provide. Catholics, Mainline Protestants, and Pentecostals vary quite a bit across countries and within countries across time in how closely tied they have been to state power: e.g., in whether they share religious affiliations with the president and top leaders, in whether the state has actively sought

---

[4] We do not claim that ties to the state and churches' organizational features are unimportant for explaining variation in religious-political engagement (Kalyvas, 1996; Warner, 2000; Philpott, 2007; Grzymała-Busse, 2015; Hale, 2018). Rather, we argue that these factors are not the only explanations for religious-political engagement. Focusing *only* on these aspects of religion can leave important patterns unexplained.

to support them or to try to depress their growth and power, and in whether the state has encouraged religious competition and proliferation of denominations or not (Gill, 2001). We exploit differences in these factors across the cases of Kenya, Uganda, and Zambia, and also within those same countries over time. We do not include differences in individual characteristics of congregants by denomination, because we showed in Chapter 2 that the demographic attributes of Pentecostals, Mainline Protestants, and Catholics vary a lot across these three countries and cannot account for the consistent patterns of political engagement, across countries, by denomination.

Within each of the country case studies, we then make use of the variation in organizational structures, social welfare provision, and international ties *among Mainline Protestant churches* to show that those explanations are not necessary explanations for denominations' modes of political engagement. Pentecostal and Catholic churches differ starkly in their organizational characteristics (with the former more decentralized, and the latter more centralized) and in their international ties and service provision (with Pentecostals less often tied to global authorities than Catholic churches and less likely to be involved in large-scale social welfare provision). Mainline Protestant churches typically lie somewhere in between: they are typically more centralized than Pentecostal churches but more decentralized than the Catholic Church, often but not always tied to central church authorities abroad, and provide larger-scale social services than Pentecostal churches but are not always as invested in such activities as the Catholic Church. Furthermore, categories *within* Mainline Pentecostalism (Anglicans, Baptists, Methodists, Lutherans, Presbyterians, and so on) vary along each of these dimensions, with Anglicans closer to the Catholic end of the spectrum, and Baptists closer to the Pentecostal end of the spectrum. We thus exploit variation in the prevalence of these different Mainline Protestant churches to examine whether modes of political engagement persist across the Pentecostal versus Mainline Protestant/Catholic divide even when the Mainline Protestant churches share many other features of the Pentecostal churches.

In the next sections, we provide more details about how the country–denomination–regime cases score on values of the alternative explanatory variables: proximity to state power, church centralization and hierarchy, strength of international ties, and extent of service provision. We describe this variation variable by variable, in order to illustrate the most-different design. We then consider patterns of political engagement country-by-country, drawing on newspaper archives, scholarly secondary sources, and interviews. The interviews were conducted in four regions of Kenya and Uganda, with a concentration in Nairobi and Kampala, over a time period from 2012 to 2017. In order to get a sense of what congregations as a whole were doing, we interviewed religious leaders at many of the randomly selected Pentecostal, Mainline Protestant, and Catholic churches from which we collected sermons in Nairobi. Additionally, in both Nairobi and Kampala, we interviewed interreligious council representatives as well as religious leaders and administrative laity at religious organizations that carry out service and other projects on behalf of the denominations in order to get a sense of what the denominations as a whole were doing politically during this time. Even when not expected based on a denomination's proximity to state power, centralization, strength of international ties, and extent of service provision, Pentecostals tended to focus on leaders' characters, personal transformation, and leadership development, whereas Mainline Protestants and Catholics tended to focus on institutional, legislative, and structural reform.

Variation in Proximity to Power and Church–State Relations

Table 6.2 summarizes the variation in denominations' proximity to state power across seven country-regime cases. In Kenya, Catholics, Mainline Protestants, and Pentecostals have experienced varying degrees of exclusion, favoritism, and identity ties from and with the state across the two regimes listed in Table 6.2; yet their modes of political engagement have remained the same (as we detail in a later section). In colonial Kenya, the mission-based churches (particularly the Anglicans and Presbyterians) were largely aligned with the colonial state. The African Independent Churches instead played an important role in the preindependence period, fomenting nationalist sentiment and mobilizing against the colonial regime. Following independence, there was a general cooptation between Mainline churches and the state, a period of d'étente wherein the postcolonial state absorbed the institutional channels of influence of the major Christian denominations. The first president, Jomo Kenyatta, who practiced traditional Kikuyu religion (Kenyatta, 2015), allowed churches of all denominations to operate freely.

With the transition from Kenyatta to his handpicked and increasingly authoritarian successor Daniel Arap Moi, the Catholic Church as well as the Protestant Mainline churches found themselves increasingly excluded

TABLE 6.2 *Case studies: differences in proximity to state power.*

Country/regime period	Proximity to state power	Mode of political engagement
Kenya/Moi 1979–2002 (authoritarian)	Catholics: distant Mainline Protestants: distant Pentecostals: close	Catholics: RR Mainline Protestants: RR Pentecostals: EP
Kenya/Kibaki/ Kenyatta 2002–present (democracy)	Catholics: close Mainline Protestants: intermediate Pentecostals: distant	Catholics: RR Mainline Protestants: RR Pentecostals: EP
Uganda/Obote 1962–1971, 1980–85 (authoritarian)	Catholics: distant Mainline Protestants: close Pentecostals: few in number/banned	Catholics: RR Mainline Protestants: RR Pentecostals: –
Uganda/Museveni 1986–present (competitive authoritarian)	Catholics: intermediate Mainline Protestants: intermediate Pentecostals: close	Catholics: RR Mainline Protestants: RR Pentecostals: EP
Zambia/Kaunda 1964–1991 (elected, then single party)	Catholics: intermediate Mainline Protestants: intermediate Pentecostals: intermediate	Catholics: RR Mainline Protestants: RR Pentecostals: EP
Zambia/Chiluba 1991–2001 (multiparty democracy)	Catholics: distant Mainline Protestants: distant Pentecostals: close	Catholics: RR Mainline Protestants: RR Pentecostals: EP
Zambia/Mwanawasa/ Banda/Sata 2002–2014 (democracy)	Catholics: intermediate Mainline Protestants: intermediate/close Pentecostals: distant	Catholics: RR Mainline Protestants: RR Pentecostals: EP

Note: RR stands for reluctant reformers; EP stands for empowered players.

from the state (Knighton, 2009). Pentecostal and African Independent Churches by contrast were given certain privileges, including land and registration permissions. But the end of Moi's reign saw an electoral transition to Catholic President Kibaki and then Catholic President Uhuru Kenyatta. Kibaki was Uhuru's godfather, and played an important role in his religious upbringing as well as connecting him to the Catholic elite establishment (Kabukuru, 2013). Under these administrations, the Catholic Church no longer faced exclusion. President Kibaki was an advocate for the churches, acknowledging their role in locating the nation's conscience.[5] Under these administrations, Pentecostal churches could operate relatively freely, but registration for new churches became more restrictive through a policy seen as targeting the less well-established Pentecostal churches in particular (Githae, 2016).

In Uganda, Catholics have been in very different positions vis-à-vis the state under different regimes, and Pentecostals have been privileged by the state only more recently. In the early years of Ugandan independence, the Catholic and Anglican churches were both fully integrated into the political scene and given privileges by the state. Pentecostal churches were few in number. The Obote presidency (1962–1971) brought Anglicans close to the state and left Catholics as political outsiders (Carbone, 2003). The Catholics were the religious group most affected by Obote and military desecration and murder, including an attack on a mission station providing social services, including education and health, to the surrounding communities (Kasozi, 1994, 159–160). Then, during Idi Amin's brutal reign (1971–1979), all Christian denominations faced targeted violence. During Obote's brief return to power from 1980 to 1985, Catholic leaders faced the same structural constraints as outsiders. In the next political upheaval, however, Museveni's military victory consolidated the political arena to a single-party state and enacted a policy of broad-based religious incorporation across all Christian denominations and Muslim factions alike. Yet Pentecostals, who had now grown in number, enjoyed additional advantages through personal connections to the first family, as Museveni's wife and daughter attended, supported, and founded prominent churches.

In Zambia, too, Catholics, Mainline Protestants, and Pentecostals have been in very different positions vis-à-vis the state under different administrations. Pentecostals were highly favored in an earlier period, whereas Catholics have been increasingly courted more recently. When President Chiluba – a Pentecostal – was elected in 1991, he declared Zambia a Christian nation without consulting the established Mainline Protestant or Catholic Church leaders. He invited Pentecostal leaders to the State House for a ceremony, which culminated in his public

---

[5] While serving as a minister in the Kenyan African National Union (KANU) government under Moi, Kibaki addressed church leaders and said, "a modern church is expected to be outspoken because other groups must be cautious" (Sabar-Friedman 1997, 5, 434).

declaration of the new religious foundation of the country. Zambia's Catholics and Anglicans alike became outsiders during Chiluba's two terms. Following Chiluba's departure, a succession of Baptist, Anglican, and Catholic presidents have been in power. President Sata, a devout Catholic, explicitly sought to leverage Catholic voters' support and to make Catholic appointments to local governments in order to cultivate a closer relationship between the Catholic Church and the government (Cheyeka, Hinfelaar, and Udelhoven, 2014). At times he excluded Pentecostals from representation on government committees, seeming to favor Catholic appointees instead (Zimba, 2011). These three countries thus provide within-case variation in degrees of closeness between the Pentecostal, Mainline Protestant, and Catholic churches and the state.

Variation in Hierarchy and Centralization

Table 6.3 summarizes the variation in denominations' degree of centralization and hierarchy across seven country-regime cases. The Catholic Church is hierarchically structured and centralized, both in Africa and globally. Dioceses are overseen by bishops and further subdivided into parishes led by priests, with central authority vested in the Pope. Training for priests is standardized. This does not mean that the Church is without factionalism and power struggles. Local parishes vary in how closely they adhere to central directives.[6] Yet, despite some factionalism and local

---

[6] In Kenya, the roots of Catholic factionalism date back to separate Catholic missions, including the French Holy Ghost Fathers, the Italian Consolata Fathers, and the English-speaking Mill Hill Fathers, each competing for their own territorial and social converts (Sundkler and Steed, 2000, 560). Postindependence, the Catholic hierarchy was divided by ethnic and regional bases of power, with the Kikuyu Catholics and those from other regions maintaining some autonomy and competing factionalism. Kenya's Catholics also led postindependence reforms to become less "Western" and more "African," creating divisions within the Church hierarchy (Sundkler and Steed, 2000, 1027). Catholics continued to struggle with ethnic divisions throughout the Moi era; in the 1992 elections, the Catholic Church leadership supported the democratic opposition and was seemingly united behind Kibaki as an alternative to Moi, but by 1997 support had splintered across regions. The debates over the constitutional referendum in 2005 under President Kibaki left the Church divided internally along ethnic lines – divisions that continued into the national election in 2007 (Mwaura and Martinon, 2010). Following the 2007–2008 inter-ethnic electoral violence, the Catholic Church was then particularly loath to give the impression that it is involved in ethnic politics – a hesitancy shared by other churches as well. This may be one reason we do not observe explicit political directives in sermons in Nairobi in recent years.

TABLE 6.3 *Case studies: differences in hierarchy and centralization.*

Country/regime period	Centralization/ hierarchy	Mode of political engagement
Kenya/Moi 1979–2002 (authoritarian)	Catholics: moderate to high	Catholics: RR
	Mainline Protestants: moderate	Mainline Protestants: RR
	Pentecostals: low to moderate	Pentecostals: EP
Kenya/Kibaki/Kenyatta 2002–present (democracy)	Catholics: high	Catholics: RR
	Mainline Protestants: moderate	Mainline Protestants: RR
	Pentecostals: low to moderate	Pentecostals: EP
Uganda/Obote 1962–1971, 1980–1985 (authoritarian)	Catholics: high	Catholics: RR
	Mainline Protestants: moderate	Mainline Protestants: RR
	Pentecostals: few in number/banned	Pentecostals: –
Uganda/Museveni 1986–present (competitive authoritarian)	Catholics: high	Catholics: RR
	Mainline Protestants: moderate	Mainline Protestants: RR
	Pentecostals: low	Pentecostals: EP
Zambia/Kaunda 1964–1991 (elected, then single party)	Catholics: high	Catholics: RR
	Mainline Protestants: low to moderate	Mainline Protestants: RR
	Pentecostals: low	Pentecostals: EP
Zambia/Chiluba 1991–2001 (multiparty democracy)	Catholics: high	Catholics: RR
	Mainline Protestants: low to moderate	Mainline Protestants: RR
	Pentecostals: low	Pentecostals: EP
Zambia/Mwanawasa/Banda/ Sata 2002–2014 (democracy)	Catholics: moderate to high	Catholics: RR
	Mainline Protestants: moderate to high	Mainline Protestants: RR
	Pentecostals: low	Pentecostals: EP

Note: RR stands for reluctant reformers; EP stands for empowered players.

deviations from high-order directives, *relatively speaking* the Catholic Church is still the most organizationally coherent and vertically structured of the three denominations we consider in this chapter (Gifford, 1998).

Mainline Protestant churches exhibit middling levels of centralized organization on average, but their structures vary dramatically by country, and across Anglicans, Lutherans, Baptists, and the like, allowing us to leverage variation in degree of centralization and hierarchy. In Kenya, the Protestant missions came together at an early stage in the colonial period, despite their different denominations and cultural backgrounds, and formed the Protestant Alliance (Knighton, 2009, 3). Yet by the early postindependence years, the Mainline Protestants were highly diverse in practice and internal organization. The Anglicans were organizationally structured into synods and boards of service, whereas, on the other end of the spectrum, the Baptist churches operated more like federations. Like the centralized, hierarchical Catholic Church, the vertically organized Anglican diocese exhibited internal divisions, as evidenced by the decision in Kenya not to license the rising scholar and theologian David M. Gitari, who then took on leadership roles outside the organizational confines, such as the general secretary of the Bible Society of Kenya and chair of the Kenya Students' Christian Fellowship under the Kenyatta regime (1972–1975) (Knighton, 2009, 19). The National Council of Churches of Kenya (NCCK) has served as an umbrella body with a mission to promote fellowship and partnership, joint action by the membership, and build capacity to identify needs, acquire resources, and promote services. To this end, the NCCK has been public facing in advocacy and service delivery, and helps facilitate some coherence among Mainline Protestants (Ngunyi, 1995; Mwaura and Martinon, 2010; Karanja, 2008). Nevertheless, the centralization and hierarchy of Mainline Protestant churches in Kenya is on the whole low to middling.

In Uganda, Anglicans have dominated the Mainline Protestant scene, and they were organized hierarchically through provincial assemblies and consolidated formally into the Church of Uganda. Regional power centers maintained some autonomy: local Bugandan congregations challenged the Anglican hierarchy and the central state when the Church of Uganda did not select an archbishop from the Buganda region (Haynes, 1996). In the Museveni period, the Diocesean crisis in Busoga nearly tore apart the Anglican church in the 1990s (Ankrah, 1998; Gifford, 1998). Gifford (1998) argues that such pitfalls of leadership succession battles were due to the relatively weak organizational structure of the Church of Uganda, as a loose autonomous conglomeration of the Anglican Canterbury Church of England, whose autonomous relationship with its religious affiliations may have facilitated the internal divisions.

In Zambia, the set of Mainline Protestant churches is more diverse and differentially organized. Anglicans are smaller in number and organized more diffusely than in Uganda, with a council comprised of five dioceses as the umbrella organization. The Presbyterians in Zambia participate in the Church of Central African Presbyterian, with a Zambian Synod reflective of their pyramid structure, but authority is largely decentralized into representative councils of clergy and laity at the church level (Patheos, 2018). The Seventh Day Adventists are also more prominent in Zambia than in Uganda or Kenya, exhibiting a low level of centralization, split into northern and southern regions of the country with further subregional conferences. The Reformed Church and Baptists are also active in Zambia, with overarching conventions and member churches that connect their work but without a centralized authority. The United Church of Zambia (UCZ) is a remarkable ecumenical venture, largely unique due to its emergence in the Copperbelt among various Protestants migrating to the mines but with no church to receive them. The Reformed Church of Zambia is the daughter church of the Dutch Reformed Mission from South Africa. Together, the UCZ and the Anglicans are the most important members of the Christian Council of Zambia (CCZ) as an organizing body (Gifford, 1998).

Last, the Pentecostal churches are largely decentralized, with each church (or federation of churches) electing and training their own pastors and officers. The major variation by country is in the extent to which congregations belong to a globally organized fellowship, such as the Pentecostal Assemblies of God (PAG). The Kenya PAG was founded in 1967 by an American Pentecostal and joined with the American PAG in 1972. A survey in the early 1990s found the Assemblies of God to be Nairobi's fastest growing denomination, with an annual growth rate of 38 percent (Maxwell, 2000; Garrard, 2003). The PAG structure adds coordination through a centralized body within an international fellowship. The PAG is also present in Uganda with over 7,000 churches in 111 administrative districts, and to a lesser extent in Zambia. In Kenya, Pentecostals and some of the evangelicals have an ecumenical association, the Evangelical Fellowship of Kenya, to facilitate involvement in the public sphere, as a sort of parallel organization to the NCCK. Formed in 1976, they are estimated to have 10 million members, 308 denominations, and 38,000 congregations. Thus, on the whole, Pentecostal churches are the most decentralized and horizontally organized of the three church categories considered here. However, they share similarities with some Mainline Protestant categories: e.g., some operate as globally organized fellowships or federations, as some Mainline Protestant churches (e.g., Baptists) do, and they gather together under an umbrella fellowship similar in some ways to the NCCK.

Variation in International Ties

Table 6.4 summarizes the variation in denominations' international ties across seven country-regime cases. International ties vary by country and

TABLE 6.4 *Case studies: differences in international ties.*

Country/regime period	Strength of international ties	Mode of political engagement
Kenya/Moi 1979–2002 (authoritarian)	Catholics: strong Mainline Protestants: weak to moderate Pentecostals: moderate	Catholics: RR Mainline Protestants: RR Pentecostals: EP
Kenya/Kibaki/Kenyatta 2002–present (democracy)	Catholics: strong Mainline Protestants: weak to moderate Pentecostals: moderate	Catholics: RR Mainline Protestants: RR Pentecostals: EP
Uganda/Obote 1962–1971, 1980–1985 (authoritarian)	Catholics: strong Mainline Protestants: strong Pentecostals: Few in number/banned	Catholics: RR Mainline Protestants: RR Pentecostals: –
Uganda/Museveni 1986–present (competitive authoritarian)	Catholics: strong Mainline Protestants: strong to moderate Pentecostals: moderate	Catholics: RR Mainline Protestants: RR Pentecostals: EP
Zambia/Kaunda 1964–1991 (elected, then single party)	Catholics: strong Mainline Protestants: weak to moderate Pentecostals: moderate	Catholics: RR Mainline Protestants: RR Pentecostals: EP
Zambia/Chiluba 1991–2001 (multiparty democracy)	Catholics: strong Mainline Protestants: weak to moderate Pentecostals: moderate	Catholics: RR Mainline Protestants: RR Pentecostals: EP
Zambia/Mwanawasa/Banda/ Sata 2002–2014 (democracy)	Catholics: strong Mainline Protestants: weak to moderate Pentecostals: moderate	Catholics: RR Mainline Protestants: RR Pentecostals: EP

Note: RR stands for reluctant reformers; EP stands for empowered players.

denomination. The Catholic Church has strong international ties to the Vatican and the network of Catholic dioceses across countries and time periods. The international embeddedness of Catholic parishes means that on average they follow the liturgical calendar more strictly and have more resources for service provision in such areas as health and education. Mwaura and Martinon (2010) argue that the international ties of the Catholic Church lead the Church to avoid taking stances on national debates.[7] Nevertheless, as we have shown in other chapters, exposure to Catholic sermons increases lay inclinations to criticize and seek reform of national institutions and laws.

For Pentecostals, international links can be quite high for churches who are "planted" within a country by a foreign mission, for instance, from Nigeria, South Africa, the United States, Canada, Finland, or a neighboring East African country. The PAG of Zambia, for instance, was founded by the Canadian mission in 1955; Billy Graham's seven-day crusade was a powerful catalyst along the Copperbelt in the 1960s for Pentecostal ferment; and the British-sponsored Scripture Union movement established a legislative basis to introduce scriptural training and religious messaging in secondary schools (Cheyeka, Hinfelaar, and Udelhoven, 2014). Many of the early Pentecostal churches in Zambia were founded by Americans and South Africans, which have retained links and provide resources, and contribute to greater bureaucratic formalization (Kirsch, 2003). Throughout Kenya, Uganda, and Zambia, the Pentecostal missionaries have tended to focus on conversion, worship, and religious messaging, sometimes including leadership training. Pentecostal international linkages are thus often diffuse but central to the focus on international evangelization, in which prayers and ministries aim at swift conversion and integration of converts into the church fellowship. These churches see themselves as part of a global fellowship of believers who share an experience of being baptized in the Spirit (born again) (Cheyeka, Hinfelaar, and Udelhoven, 2014). The Pentecostal organizational fluidity also facilitates the prevalence of new "pop-up" or fully domestic churches, which have no formal international linkages but often are inspired and even instructed in messaging through globalized media technology, including radio, television, audio, and video recordings from abroad (Togarasei, 2011).

Mainline Protestants vary most dramatically in their degrees of international ties. The Anglican communion, under the Archbishop of

---

[7] This was particularly complex in states that had a large number of settlers, such as Kenya, where relationships were at times antagonistic between white settlers, Christian missionaries, and colonial authorities (Haynes, 1996, 25).

Canterbury, serves a supporting and organizational role for Anglican dioceses. Formally, it does not have an official legal existence or governing structure that might exercise authority over the member churches,[8] but it means that these churches do have international ties, resources, and support to a greater degree than some other Mainline Protestant churches. Baptist churches are largely autonomous federations, as are Presbyterians, with no one governing body internationally.[9] Methodists, Lutherans, Presbyterians, and Seventh Day Adventists participate in their respective world councils. The Lutheran church in Kenya is linked to the Lutheran World Federation, and this relationship is largely focused on support for aid and service provision. Churches are not required to adhere to the same practices.[10] The Methodist World Council provides more structure through standing committees to create official policy on issues such as education, evangelism, and social justice.[11] Thus, although the Catholic Church can be characterized as consistently exhibiting high levels of international ties, the Mainline Protestant churches exhibit more middling levels of international ties on average and vary quite a bit across church categories.

Variation in Social Service Provision

Table 6.5 summarizes the variation in denominations' involvement in social service provision across seven country-regime cases. Generally, churches are central providers of social services (health, education, nutrition) in sub-Saharan Africa. The Christian Health Association serves as the umbrella organization for health programs and services in many African countries, and estimates that Christian health networks contribute between 30 to 55 percent of health facilities in their respective countries (ACHAP, 2008). This maps on to a deep history of mission-established clinics and schools, where the Catholic Church in particular,

---

[8] For more information on the Anglican Communion, see www.anglicancommunion.org/structures.aspx.

[9] The degree of decentralization is evident even in Baptist global affiliations, which are represented by three organizations that have competing and antagonistic ideas about how baptism should be spread. Baptist churches do not have to join these organizations, but may do so for additional support. See www.bbfi.org/about-the-bbfi/.

[10] For more information on the Lutheran Federation, see www.lutheranworld.org/content/structure.

[11] For more information on the Methodist World Council, see worldmethodistcouncil.org/whatwedo/.

TABLE 6.5 *Case studies: differences in extent of service provisions*

Country/regime period	Extent of service provision	Mode of political engagement
Kenya/Moi 1979–2002 (authoritarian)	Catholics: high Mainline Protestants: low to moderate Pentecostals: low	Catholics: RR Mainline Protestants: RR Pentecostals: EP
Kenya/Kibaki/Kenyatta 2002–present (democracy)	Catholics: high Mainline Protestants: low to moderate Pentecostals: low to moderate	Catholics: RR Mainline Protestants: RR Pentecostals: EP
Uganda/Obote 1962–1971, 1980–1985 (authoritarian)	Catholics: high Mainline Protestants: low to moderate Pentecostals: few in number/banned	Catholics: RR Mainline Protestants: RR Pentecostals: –
Uganda/Museveni 1986–present (competitive authoritarian)	Catholics: high Mainline Protestants: low to moderate Pentecostals: low to moderate	Catholics: RR Mainline Protestants: RR Pentecostals: EP
Zambia/Kaunda 1964–1991 (elected, then single party)	Catholics: high Mainline Protestants: moderate to high Pentecostals: low to moderate	Catholics: RR Mainline Protestants: RR Pentecostals: EP
Zambia/Chiluba 1991–2001 (multiparty democracy)	Catholics: high Mainline Protestants: moderate to high Pentecostals: moderate	Catholics: RR Mainline Protestants: RR Pentecostals: EP
Zambia/Mwanawasa/Banda/ Sata 2002–2014 (democracy)	Catholics: high Mainline Protestants: moderate Pentecostals: moderate	Catholics: RR Mainline Protestants: RR Pentecostals: EP

Note: RR stands for reluctant reformers; EP stands for empowered players.

in addition to other Mainline Protestant churches, has long been heavily involved in service provision in education and health, and has increasingly been focused in development and relief (Haynes, 1996; Gifford, 1998). In the postindependence period, these services have often functioned as substitutes for state-provided services. Yet, as was true with institutional hierarchy, there is substantial variation in service provision across Mainline Protestant churches.

Among Christian religious organizations, Catholic churches consistently provide the highest levels of social services (Seay, 2013), though the staff involved in activities such as education, health, and relief provision are largely service professionals and not involved in the work of the parishes. In Zambia, Catholics provided an estimated 20 percent of the primary schools in the country, yet surrendered them to Kaunda's increasingly antagonistic government in 1973 (Carmody, 2002). A 2006 regional report assessing the country's response to the HIV/AIDS crisis summarized the historical foundations of the Catholic involvement: "The churches have always been involved in health and education ... the issue of HIV/AIDS seems to have increased the involvement of the churches in health. But right from the start, you see in the most remote rural areas, there are medical facilities provided by those early missionaries" (ARHAP, 2006). Estimates on the Catholic Church provision of HIV/AIDS care, including home-based care and support of orphans ranges from 25 to 40 percent across all of Africa (Benn, 2003; ARHAP, 2008). These services, supported partially by parishioner tithing (Kombo and Gogo, 2012), are often provided through various types of faith-based organizations in partnership with government, civil society, and international collaborations, which give each a distinct character. For example, Catholic Relief Services is a global organization focused on human development, with an agenda for peace, social justice, and dignity, that also itself partners with public and private affiliates within each country. Therefore, while the Catholic presence in service delivery is vast, it is also diffuse, multilayered, and permeated with many partners.

Mainline Protestant churches also engage in significant social service provision, although the extent to which they do so varies with the churches' degrees of centralization and access to international resources. In Kenya, the NCCK promoted rural development committees to support agricultural and health practices during the Moi era (Sundkler and Steed, 2000, 1003–5), and Anglicans in particular were engaged in running mission-established schools and health clinics. The Protestant ecumenical alliance fostered the elite Alliance high school in Nairobi in 1926. The Lutheran service provision is linked to the global Lutheran World Federation, and focused in particular in Kenya on assisting refugees, sustainable livelihoods, and education. In the post-Moi era, Methodists sponsored approximately 200 schools, a hospital, and dispensaries, as well as agricultural training institutes and vocational programs. Baptists remain at the low end of the spectrum, with a few schools, again paralleling the decentralized and autonomous organizational patterns. Similarly in Uganda, the Anglicans are the most centralized and historically rooted, and they have fostered rural development programs in 1979 (Sundkler and Steed, 2000, 1011), and operate centralized directorates for education, health, and financial planning. Presbyterians are limited, with small community projects. The Methodists supply a limited amount of medical, food, and training resources, but this is limited to eastern Uganda. The Adventists operate four schools and one hospital, and Baptists organize a limited number of schools. In Zambia, most Protestant churches surrendered their mission-based primary schools in the mid-twentieth century, and cooperate with the Catholics in health provision through the Churches Health Association in Zambia (CHAZ), together accounting for more than 50 percent of formal health care in rural areas and roughly 35 percent of health care nationally.[12] The Zambian Anglican Council is a separate body that coordinates the church's economic development work, overseeing a network of diocesan health care workers, education programs, income generation, and food security projects.

Pentecostals remain only weakly involved in service provision, with most initiatives coming from individual churches, as described in more detail in our survey of churches in Nairobi in Chapter 3. However, there are exceptions. In Zambia, the faith-based organization Jubilee Centre started working through community organizing as a response to poverty and violence, partnering with local churches to address social responsibility and create hospitals and schools to improve community quality of life (Burgess, 2015). There are also nascent faith-based community schools and training programs offered through individual churches in Zambia (Cheyeka, Hinfelaar, and Udelhoven, 2014). Further, international linkages allow for partnerships with the Evangelical Christian humanitarian aid organization World Vision, which focuses on development and child well-being in Kenya, Uganda, and Zambia.

* * *

With the preceding sources of variation in mind, we now show that modes of political engagement among Pentecostals, on the one hand, and

---

[12] For more information, see www.chaz.org.zm/?q=about_us.

among Mainline Protestants and Catholics, on the other, are consistent across these country-regime cases, in keeping with the denominations' teachings' differences in world views. Even when not expected based on a denomination's proximity to state power, centralization, strength of international ties, and extent of service provision, Pentecostals tend to focus on leaders' characters, personal transformation, and leadership development, whereas Mainline Protestants and Catholics tend to focus on institutional, legislative, and structural reform. These cases provide the observations that inform the coding of the patterns of political engagement by country-regime period in the tables shown earlier in this chapter, and follow the same rules as the newspaper analysis of the broader set of cases that we describe later. Reluctant Reformer includes actions or statements where the laity or the clergy engage in criticism of institutions and structures; pressures for legislative, electoral, or other institutional reform; mobilizing or protesting around a set of policy issues; and/or pushing for mechanisms of monitoring or sanctioning. These actions provide extrinsic incentives to shape political behavior for all members of the political community. Empowered Player includes any actions or statements that focus on requests to public officials for personal assistance or services; plans to organize or partake in political leadership training; assessment of the character of political officials; commentary on desirable leadership traits; and/or actions preparing to become a political leader oneself or campaign for a particular leader based on his or her personal traits. These actions are based on intrinsic incentives to change one's own behavior, because that behavior is internally rewarding, and evaluate others in the political realm by a similar set of criteria.

Forms of Political Engagement in Kenya

Kenya is a case of dramatic variation in power relations between the authoritarian era of President Moi's single-party domination privileging independent and Pentecostal churches, and his successors Kibaki and Kenyatta, who operated in contexts of contentious and fragmented multiparty competition and were aligned with established church interests. Throughout these periods, the state retained hegemonic control over the ultimate ability of churches to operate within the country. Thus, to a significant degree, all religious organizations shared pressure to maintain the status quo (Haynes, 1996, 80–83). And yet at certain points, religious laity and local leaders among the Mainline Protestants and Catholic denominations nevertheless challenged the government and engaged in institutional and regime critiques. In contrast, even where Pentecostals were closest to power under the Moi regime or restricted by it in the current Kenyatta period, and even when Pentecostals exhibited a significant degree of collective organization through the umbrella organization Evangelical Fellowship and the strength of Pentecostal Assemblies of God network, Pentecostals continued as empowered players of the game, seeking leadership and political change through individual transformation.

Despite over-time variation in the relationships of the churches to power, members of the Pentecostal churches have continued to act distinctly from those in other Christian denominations (Gifford, 2009; Throup, 2015). Starting with the social mobilization among the laity and Anglican bishops against Moi's increasing state repression (Sundkler and Steed, 2000; Knighton, 2009), localized Catholic priests and the Protestant umbrella organization NCCK increasingly became at the head of a political opposition centered on demands for human rights, democracy, and the rule of law (Throup, 2015). Catholics and Anglicans spoke out in opposition to Moi's proposal to implement queue voting, which would signal the end of the secret ballot, in the KANU single-party primaries. They mobilized collectively through "generating and sustaining a public discourse on democracy and change in Kenya as well as organizational grass-roots political activities" (Sabar-Friedman, 1997, 25). In the period of anti-Moi, prodemocracy mobilization in Kenya in the late 1990s and up to the 2002 election, Mainline Protestant leaders issued pastoral letters with a direct critique of the regime, arguing for the need to "arise when God-given rights and liberties are violated ... the Church ought to be a voice for the voiceless" (Bishop Alexander Muge, in Sabar-Friedman 1997, 32). Over the decades, the state mounted a vigorous campaign against churches in retribution for these positions. Anglican bishop Muge was killed in a car crash assumed to be politically orchestrated by the Moi regime because of his vociferous opposition (Haynes, 1996; Knighton, 2009). Meanwhile, Pentecostal churches left the NCCK and created the Evangelical Fellowship (EKF) as an alternative organizing body to better represent their distinctive approach (Phiri, 1997, 258). They used their new EFK organization and networks within independent churches to create new or deepened individual linkages to political elites and "served as clients of the regime and presented a theological apology for the state whenever it was attacked" (Ngunyi, 1995, 136). They, along with the African Independent Churches, became increasingly embedded with the regime and sought out the perquisites of power (Throup, 2015).

Following the ruling party KANU's defeat in 2002 and the transition to more pluralistic competition, Kenya's politics became much more fragmented but, relatively speaking, Catholics and Mainline Protestants continued their focus on systemic critiques and structural change. The churches, too, became more fragmented, sometimes along ethnic and political lines (Throup, 2015). The Catholic Church as an organization had strong support for President Kibaki, who was one of their prominent members; Kikuyu areas have a strong Catholic presence, though Kikuyus are not exclusively Catholic (Maupeu, 2007). But with ongoing debates over constitutional reforms, the extent of decentralization, and the possibility of Kadhi (Muslim) courts, Catholic religious leaders were very divided in their political stance vis-à-vis the administration, largely along Kikuyu/pro-Kibaki versus non-Kikuyu regions. With some exceptions, the Catholic churches generally took a step back from regime opposition and developed more specific areas of engagement around governance, family law, and public service provision. Yet despite the organizational interest of the Catholic Church to support Kibaki and further their proximity to power, some Catholic leaders spoke out against the government on issues of decentralization in the failed 2005 referendum, and added to the "oscillating, ambiguous disposition" that at times offered a significant critique (Mwaura and Martinon, 2010). Catholic bishops criticized interparty squabbling that led to a failed 2005 constitutional reform, and called for various factions to cooperate to find collective solutions (Mathangani, 2003). After the disputed 2007 elections and electoral violence, Catholic leaders were involved in significant humanitarian responses and peace mediation, and some local bishops courageously denounced those involved in conflict in dioceses affected by the violence (Mwaura and Martinon, 2010). However, lay members also took their own initiative. "The lay faithful sought to be pro-active in providing assistance to affected populations," and sought to "reach various political leaders to communicate that the country would not realize stable peace without justice. All these activities and actions are a reflection of genuine willingness to stand in solidarity and address the suffering in Kenya" (Mwaura and Martinon, 2010, 42). Mainline Protestants were also divided between organizational interests and their role as a critic during the Kibaki term. However, in the wake of the 2007 postelection violence, the laity also organized toward a humanitarian response and reconciliation among communities caught in the conflict, and called for renewed focus on justice and serving the needs of the poor (Mwaura and Martinon, 2010, 45). In this time period, the laity took the lead in formulating a political response.

Indeed, with church leadership more fragmented and withdrawn after the 2002 democratic transition, often it was the Catholic laity to take up issues of social justice and activism. Father Patrick Devine, the director of the Shalom Center for Conflict Resolution and Reconciliation,[13] described Catholic political engagement as institution- and structure-focused because laity interpreted the Church's "social message" as pushing for this type of agenda:

Our membership expects engagement in the sense of proclamation on the issues that are affecting the people, as distinct from engaging directly in the political process, taking on leadership as president, prime minister, ministers, or in Parliament. More along issue lines than for party or candidates. The Catholic Church proclaims its moral, ethical, and social message, and the expression of that social message, of course, in some way, people are guided by that and are influenced (Author Interview, Patrick Devine, 2013).

Father Patrick views Catholic laity as being influenced by the Church's message and as interpreting that message to not be about seeking leadership, or pushing for particular candidates. Rather, he views the message as compelling them to reach out in certain domains of social justice issues. For these initiatives, there is a bottom-up demand among the laity based on their interpretation of the Church's message, rather than simply a top-down supply among religious leaders who issue the critique and, in doing so, set the agenda for engagement (Author Interview with Reverend Eustace K. Kabui, Presbyterian Council of East Africa Mission Board, 2013). The result has commonly been a "commitment to participative development activities and a heightened concern with questions of justice" (Ngunyi, 1995, 152). Catholic laity attend meetings with local officials to plan for a new church-sponsored school; they focus on release "from degradation and poverty, which includes conscientisation" (understanding and overcoming the conditions which negate humanity via broadening one's social and political participation).

To address these core issues of poverty and government quality, Catholics and Mainline Protestants in Kenya took an approach that focused on critiquing the system: policies, structures, and institutions

---

[13] The Shalom Center is a nondenominational organization focused on root causes of violence in East Africa, partnering with civil society and led by an international missionary.

(Rhodes, 2015, 234, 244). Catholics put pressure on government public service projects to advance their own work in education, health care, and relief work as collective solutions to structural inequalities (Rhodes, 2015, 237). Catholics also called for the government to address institutionalized corruption and respect Christian doctrines in legislation (Rhodes, 2015, 261). Catholic and Mainline Protestant leaders also attempted to develop partnerships with the government to improve economic and social conditions in the country (Catholic Information Service for Africa, February 2009). In general, throughout the 2000s, Catholics and Mainline Protestants pushed for systemic reforms.

Catholic and Mainline Protestant laity have also engaged in the political realm to bring together local people to provide local solutions to problems. Notably, they have done so in ways that are disconnected from the institutional and organizational elements of the church itself, but that instead build separate organizations for social justice within civil society. In our interviews with some of these activists, they specifically referenced teachings and experiences in the church in their past as the material they draw upon to mobilize their movement going forward. For example, the coordinator at a leading social justice civic organization in Nairobi explained how his past Catholic practice taught him a great deal about injustices in the world and inspired him to build a justice and action-oriented movement (Author Interview, activist, 2017). Although the organization is secular, he explained,

Catholics preach values. Jesus is for the poor. If not for those values, I wouldn't have survived in civil society. I would have been corrupted by mainstream civil society who do nothing. That's how I started in [a particular initiative – a multisectoral form of inter-faith communities, the private sector, labor unions, and civil society to dialogue and prepare the country for reforms], welcoming the bishops. They shaped my consciousness. The church was progressive at that time: not just about political reforms, it was also about economic reforms and social justice ... The Catholic Church also recently started speaking out about development. This instigated a new discussion, how to shape the next generation? How do we build alliances, revisit alliances that were there in the past to amplify our impact? (Author Interview, 2017).

These conversations reveal a disposition toward both identifying the structural problems in the world and pressuring the government on these issues. The activist's comments also suggested a critical skepticism of power and power-seekers, rather than deference to leadership. His view on Pentecostals during the same period reflected this: "Which voices are you going to respect? Wanjiru and the other Pentecostals seeking office, they didn't have a message to increase social justice, so they are not doing anything. They promise people heaven [on earth] even if they live here in [the informal settlements]. Evangelicals are not oriented in the same way [as the Catholics]"(Author Interview, 2017). In this citizen's view, the Pentecostal focus on leadership is self-serving and casts issues of systemic injustices to the wayside.

We conducted another interview with a social activist who focuses on tax justice. She intimated a similar skepticism of Pentecostal activities and motivations, saying they have a limited platform upon which to preach social justice because they were "identifying with candidates who[m] they helped to win and then who engaged in political looting … so they lost relevance" to preach to the people on structural issues (Author Interview, 2017). She said that the mainstream churches play a role in generating activism by talking about human rights and institutional justice, going back to their push for multiparty democracy in the 1990s, though these days they often discuss such subjects in nonpolitical terms.

This same activist reported that the Mainline Protestant and Catholic youth are often engaged in programs addressing the structural challenges of their generation, such as rehabilitation for incarcerated youth, and concrete political action surrounding the structural sources of poverty, improving service delivery, and infrastructure for the community (Author Interview, 2017). This engagement provides way for lay members to connect the world view of the sermons to concrete political action.

Laity following Mainline Protestant and Catholic churches on Twitter in contemporary Kenya[14] also express their views in ways that are consistent with a reluctant reformist approach, identifying the challenges and major reforms necessary to make progress.

One recent tweet focused on legislative action, putting the responsibility for good governance on having good laws in place:

Societies everywhere are guided by laws and laws are made by legislature. Kenya in particular needs new and effective laws based on good values from our young legislature just like we need oxygen.

And many individual laity focus on institutions, policy, and process as the route to reform:

Uhuru Kenyatta's government needs to intensify diversification of energy sources to actualise its big four agenda.

---

[14] Religious affiliation is not easily gauged on Twitter unless the user explicitly states it in his or her profile. Here, we provide some anecdotal observations of tweets posted by users who locate themselves in Kenya and follow at least one Mainline Protestant or Catholic church account and who do not also follow a Pentecostal church account.

Catholic and Mainline Protestant followers on Twitter identified structural challenges, sometimes with little possibility to spur action:

Insecurity is a major challenge to the youth participating in competitive politics in @KAS_Kenya #DemocracyKE.

Others focus on specific reforms or public works being undertaken, while calling on official institutions to be accountable:

After FredMatiani is done with the matatu people please remove the motorbikes from the footpaths in town. The one next to Uhuru Park along Kenyatta Avenue is a mess @InteriorKE.

Engaging institutionally with policy making, such as around a referendum or specific legislative agendas, is where the reluctance could pivot to actual mobilization for reform. These messages reinforce the idea that the Catholic and Mainline Protestant religious messages simultaneously articulate two ideas that without spiritual connection may be hard to reconcile: individuals alone have little ability to transform the world around them, and yet the faithful should be oriented around a concern for the challenges in the world around them and will receive rewards in heaven or at judgment day for doing so.

The Mainline Protestant/Catholic approach differed from Pentecostal modes of engagement during this post-2002 period, with an approach of cultivating leaders and relationships within the existing system. Pentecostal leaders and laity were "concerned with central moral commandments, meeting individual material needs and individual personal choices to behave righteously. Individuals, not the state or the church, [were viewed as] thus responsible for their own personal situations" (Ngunyi, 1995, 152). Through the mid-1990s, Pentecostal individual engagement differentiated itself by this focus on personal responsibility. Rather than providing social welfare, they focused on communicating the power of divine grace as their mode of outreach, and also used it as a way to evaluate leadership (Ngunyi, 1995, 176). According to a member of the Pentecostal laity and the founder of a leadership training organization whose mission is "to equip the Leader in the Family, Church, and Marketplace to impact their area of influence for national transformation *through Personal Change*" (emphasis added), this philosophy of personal transformation affecting individual and public circumstances is at the core of Pentecostal approaches to politics. The lay Pentecostal member described his own engagement and initiatives through this light:

I ran for politics myself, [and] I began to think, okay, I could run and be one leader – but what if I could prepare many more leaders? So for my master's, I did leadership, and for my thesis, I did a training curriculum for political leaders for Africa ... At [my organization], that's part of what we do – preparing those who want to run, asking them the right questions – why do they want to run? And especially those from the faith. And I'm taking them through a course, just preparing them on how to be an agent of change in politics.

Also being able to take up political issues and engage with the politicians – with most of them, I'm able to relate because of where I was [as a candidate]. So I'm able to talk to sitting MPs, some leaders in government, ... [and I can engage other politicians, they] give me some respect, in that way, because they know I'm part of them – I could reason from their field, and I could also reason from these other fields. So I think that gave me some inroads into political leadership (Author Interview, 2013).

In this description, the Pentecostal follower describes a focus on individual candidates and leadership development rather than on institutional or structural reform. He describes an approach that is empowered but works directly within the rules of the game, through nurturing persuasive relationships with politicians and through pursuing leadership positions for Christians.

Other Pentecostal efforts to run for leadership positions in Kenya exemplify this approach. The MP Margaret Wanjiru is the leader of Jesus Is Alive Ministries, one of Nairobi's largest Pentecostal churches. Wanjiru ran for office as an Orange Democratic Movement (ODM) candidate in a strong Party of National Unity (PNU) constituency against a popular incumbent with a strong grass-roots network of support in 2007. She campaigned on her personal story of psychological and material transformation, born again through her conversion from witchcraft beliefs, and raised out of poverty despite being a single mother (Kavulla, 2008). She attributed her rise and victory to divine grace, and was anointed by an American evangelical pastor who told Wanjiru's congregation that "God had marked her for government"(Kavulla, 2008). Wanjiru herself announced her candidacy to her pulpit and asked the crowd to vote for her, saying,

When the righteous are in authority, people rejoice. When the wicked rule, people suffer. (Proverbs 29:2) God has called me because I am clean. Kenya needs clean people to tackle corruption in this country (quoted in Parsitau, 2014, 195).

Wanjiru's candidacy bears similarity to others in Kenya, such as Bishop Pius Muiru's and Teresia Wairimu's. Pentecostals' response to political problems is to become political leaders, believing that "because they are saved and uncorrupt, they are well-positioned to lead the country to alleviate people's suffering" (Parsitau, 2014, 195).

Pentecostal support for particular political leaders has also focused on key themes of emphasis: integrity, accountability of leaders to act morally and generously, transformation of their nations, participation, and inculcation of civic and leadership skills (Burgess, 2014). In the Moi era, Bishop Arthur Kitonga of the Redeemed Gospel Church articulated his ardent support for the regime, as did Samson Gaitho of the African Independent Pentecostal Church of Africa, despite the trenchant critiques of many Mainline Protestants (Cooke, 2015). Participating in the electoral process and selecting "godly" candidates, or running for office themselves, is a key strategy for African Pentecostals to influence society (Burgess, 2014), demonstrating their role as empowered players in varied contexts where they are first highly supported by the regime and, later, restricted by it.

Laity who follow a Pentecostal church on Twitter[15] also express similar political logics, focusing on leadership change and individual characters:

the problem is our leadership.. we won't develop kenya unless we think of Kenya and not politics and sentiments

... Power_Breakfast Track Record: Bsp DR Margaret Wanjiru has a track record of tangible development. She has the face of a Senator!

Your world view affects your values then behavior. Deal with the inside not outside.

These posts focus on the characters and identities of leaders as the main source of social and political problems. The focus is not on institutional change but on selecting and keeping good leaders who will work in citizens' interests, and also on how God works through individuals.

The debates surrounding the 2010 constitutional reforms are also instructive because they demonstrate that religious leaders may at times respond to the pulse of the laity when taking political action outside of church. Although the leadership of many churches from all major denominations pushed for "no" votes on the constitutional referenda because of their concerns about specific provisions reducing restrictions on abortion and supporting Islamic courts, many ordinary citizens saw the reforms as a way to devolve power closer to local communities,

---

[15] Again, because religious affiliation is not universally reported or easily gauged on Twitter, here we report anecdotal examples of tweets from users who follow at least one Pentecostal church account and not Mainline Protestant or Catholic Church accounts.

with the possibility of minimizing further electoral violence after the intense violence after the 2007 election. Primarily Mainline Protestant and Catholic laity – focused on the need for institutional reforms in this regard – spoke out against the church leaders on the public stances they were taking in favor of a "no" vote. For example, Anglican church member Muthoni Wanyeki and public voice of Kenyan human rights groups used her weekly column in the *East African* to ask "how institutions once at the fore of the movement for democracy, human rights and the rule of law have sunk so low"(Wanyeki, 2010). Some Mainline Protestant and Catholic clergy responded by supporting the proposed institutional reforms (Branch, 2010).[16] Timothy Njoya of the Presbyterian Church became an active campaigner in the referendum mobilization on behalf of a consortium of civil society groups called Katiba Sasa (Constitution Now). Again, clergy political action may further mobilize denominational political engagement, but it is not always the first mover in this regard and often responds to the political inclinations of the laity, which are shaped by their views of how the physical and spiritual worlds work.

We also looked at the activities of the Pentecostal and Catholic public-facing bodies – the Catholic Peace and Justice Commission and the Evangelical Alliance of Kenya – in order to capture a snapshot in time of their activities in the run-up to the highly competitive and tense August 2017 elections. A representative of the Catholic Peace and Justice Commission (CPJC) explained their programming as focused largely on governance and democracy. As part of that effort, the CPJC was highly involved in devolved governance to support regional Catholic offices to engage with the county governments and support citizen monitoring of county priorities and budgeting. This Citizen Oversight Forum (COF) was to partner with civil society organizations and submit memos on the policy issues facing the county government. Despite low capacity, the CJPC supported the COF's with technical assistance and citizen education programs, to help citizens engage with a better understanding of the local political reality (Author Interview, 2017, CPJC). In these activities, the Catholics focus on enabling citizens to create institutions and extrinsic incentives for leaders to engage in good governance.

The Evangelical Alliance of Kenya (EAK) has a similar goal of engaging on national political issues, but its modes of engagement are quite

---

[16] E.g., Reverend Timothy Njoya (Presbyterian), Archbishop David Gitari (Anglican), and Father Ambrose Kimutai (Catholic).

different. A representative of the EAK explained to us that the organization's main project areas around good governance follow from a top-down perspective on leadership and encouraging leaders to hold themselves accountable to be generous and transformative. As the director explained, "Leadership is God-given, we need to respect the leadership that is there. Whether it is good or bad, it is there for a purpose. It's God-given, and that means we must support, and that support should speak to the truth of what is going on. In that manner, the EAK seeks to engage with leadership by using what God has given each person to weed out the limitations to speak out, to have constructive comments to shape the government itself"(Author Interview, 2017, EAK). The EAK also works with county governments but does so to build the capacity of social leaders to reach out congenially to county officials to discuss services and benefits the county officials could be in position to provide (Author Interview, EAK, 2017). Within the Interreligious Council, the EAK acknowledged that it often focuses on the spiritual issues that affect the church, such as the Islamic Khadi courts in the 2010 constitutions (the EAK opposed special prerogative of religious legal and justice system for Muslims) and church registration, whereas Catholics are most focused on social justice and on service provision (Author Interview, EAK, 2017). The EAK director has even run for office[17] and is seeking to expand the EAK's capacity to support new political candidates: to "get them into elite political leadership. We haven't yet defined how to articulate sermons that can contribute to that, but we need to ... raise members within the church who could run"(Author Interview, EAK 2017). The director acknowledged this raises challenges in the political arena, given that the EAK and specific member churches also need to cooperate with incumbents to fundraise for church expansions, and to limit regulations on church registration, etc. But a major goal moving forward for the EAK is to continue to refine "how we engage in politics, how we get candidates into established leadership and government positions and major parties so that they can raise our standing and influence"(Author Interview, EAK,

---

[17] She ran as a candidate for Parliament, driven by her foundation as a Christian with a vision and an agenda to implement. Even though she is a reserved person, she felt a "call to politics, which dropped in my heart"(Interview, EAK, 2017). While she did not win, and she wondered what God had asked of her, she felt that by being "obedient to the call" a lot of good ultimately came out of it because God used that to open other doors for her, to make the greatest difference, and to know that she has touched other people's lives by her current leadership position.

2017). These sentiments reflect a Pentecostal vision of change through leadership rather than through institutional reform.

Across historical regime periods and shifting political contexts, and among both laity and religious leaders, the modes of political participation of Pentecostals in Kenya have remained distinct from those generally pursued by Catholics and Mainline Protestants. These modes of political engagement have been consistent regardless of how each denomination is positioned vis-à-vis the state and ruling party. And Catholics and Mainline Protestants have engaged similarly, despite the great variation among Mainline Protestants in organization and international ties. Even when Catholics or Mainline Protestants as church bodies have taken less reformist positions, groups of individuals have spoken out in favor of institutional reform. Pentecostals have remained engaged and sought to advance their vision of personal empowerment and transformation.

Forms of Political Engagement in Uganda

Uganda is a case in which the Mainline denominations historically enjoyed different positions vis-à-vis the state. The Pentecostals were historically much less prominent numerically in Uganda than in Kenya or Zambia, and their growth in the country is relatively recent. Yet under the more recent Museveni regime, they have enjoyed a close relationship to power through preferential links to the first family. Throughout the periods of authoritarian rule, all churches have incentives to seek incorporation and refrain from criticism. Despite these shared regime strategies at the institutional level, religious leaders and laity among the Catholics and Mainline Protestants have served at key moments as reluctant reformers, and Pentecostals have sought out positions and contact with the government to shape leadership and access services.

In the early years of Ugandan independence, the Catholic and Anglican churches were both active in building political parties. Interestingly, the Catholic-affiliated party, the Democratic Party (DP), was not built by religious elites to mobilize lay Catholics in support of their political control. Rather, "lay elites and activists were the central actors in the formation and expansion of the party. Church officials were certainly allies of the laity, but never controlled the party" (Kassimir, 1998, 62). The ascendancy of the Anglican Party in the 1962 independence elections and the Obote presidency (1962–1971) left Catholics as political outsiders, and largely disempowered (Carbone, 2003). When the Pope made a historic first visit to Africa in 1969, he pledged Ugandan Catholics' staunch loyalty to the country, further proclaiming: "The Church in no way desires to inject herself into the government of the earthly city. She claims no other authority than that of ministering to men, with the help of God, in a spirit of charity and faithful service (Ad Gentes, No. 12). By spreading the light of Revelation, the message of Love, she promotes the dignity of man, training hearts and minds in the virtues of a just and brotherly social life, for the cultural, moral, and social progress of the people, in peace, and a common awareness of the good of all." The Catholics were to focus on service and social justice in their time in the wilderness, and despite Obote's increasingly violent reign, the Catholics remained on the sidelines of explicit political interventions. The Catholics were the most affected religious group by Obote's military desecration and murder, including an attack on a mission station providing social services, including education and health care, to the surrounding communities (Kasozi, 1994, 159–160).

During Idi Amin's brutal reign (1971–1979), all Christian denominations faced targeted violence. "The churches found themselves dragged, against their will, into becoming a foci of [criticism and] opposition," because of the destruction of other protections for society (Pirouet, 1980, 15). Although the Catholic Church originally hailed Amin as a liberator, because he had overthrown the Anglican Obote and his "socialism," the main strategy for the Christian organizations was to lay low against his arbitrary and anarchical oppression (Gifford, 1998). Individual lay members and local priests opposed Amin, and the Church of Uganda Archbishop played a significant mediating role by addressing Muslim–Christian violence instigated by the Amin's apparent Islamization drive, and these meetings amounted to a wide-ranging denunciation of the regime (Gifford, 1998). Prominent Anglican Bishop Luwum was murdered by Amin after speaking out against injustice, evidence of both the regime's anti-Christian repression and the reformist stance the Mainline/Catholics took in this era.

During Obote's brief return to power from 1980–1985, Catholic leaders faced the same structural constraints as outsiders, but their role as the last resort of opposition began to peak. Catholic leaders began to issue a series of scathing commentaries on the ills of Uganda politics, echoing Exodus in claiming to "hear the cries of our people" and speaking out forcefully against the abuses of the security services (Carney, 2017, 84). Pentecostals were few in number in Uganda during this time, but Catholics exemplified a critical posture toward the state, under difficult and threatening circumstances. The Anglicans, favored under Obote, were also strongly centralized in the Church of Uganda (although in reality factionalized by regional disputes), and institutionally the Church had a weak prophetic voice due to its proximity to power (Pirouet, 1980, 139; Gifford, 1998). Yet lay members emerged to play leading roles in public and political affairs in their commitment to justice, reconciliation, and holding corrupt leaders accountable (Gakuru, 2016).

The current, dominant party, competitive authoritarian regime under Museveni then presents an important and difficult case to observe differences in macro-level outcomes between religious denominations. President Museveni and the ruling party National Resistance Movement (NRM) employ a combination of broad-based cooptation through patronage and state largesse to the religious orders, as well as tight security control and coercion for those outspoken against the regime. The broad-based cooptation signals that the regime is not simply providing preferential access to some religious groups, but is instead willing to dispense "brown envelopes" full of cash to religious leaders of all types, provide SUVs to newly ordained religious leaders, and give land titles and construction permits for churches and mosques alike (Author Interviews, 2013; Downie, 2015; Alava and Ssentongo, 2016). The regime also uses coercion to limit the public space for critical religious engagement, by silencing legitimate political resistance and jailing leading opposition figures, deploying security forces during and after elections in the name of ensuring peace, and threatening the loss of state support if religious clerics are too outspoken about politics. Alava and Ssentongo (2016) report that Ugandan religious leaders believe that their sermons are listened to, and that they would be reported to security officers if they cross the political line; others believed NRM cadres were spying from within the congregation; and many fear that they could lose their operating licenses, tax reductions, electricity, or personal safety should they be too outspoken on politics. These circumstances help explain why sermons are not explicitly political in this context.

Although in these current circumstances the strategic incentives facing Pentecostal and Catholic or Mainline Protestant religious elites are quite similar and limiting, their modes of political engagement continue to differ. Catholics and Mainline Protestants are not exactly outright democracy activists, but they focus on addressing structural causes of poverty and underdevelopment, whereas Pentecostals demonstrate an approach to striving for change through personal transformation and leadership. The Ugandan bishops' 2005 statement "Towards a Democratic and Peaceful Uganda Based on the Common Good" focused on the structural problems of past army impunity and destruction, and called for political reform, transition, and increased transparency to move forward (UEC, 2005, 13–14). In contrast, one of Kampala's leading Pentecostals, Pastor

Kayanja, instead focused on the personal sin of poverty and urged his followers to change their mindsets: "Demand first class ... See yourself as first class." He encouraged them to catch what was theirs in order to fulfill their potential and serve their personal goals (Lloyd, 2008).

Although Catholics and Anglicans have often been reticent to engage in direct criticism of Museveni and the ruling party, they have focused on issues of social justice and public welfare, often following clear pushes from lay members. At times this has brought them into key political debates, as reluctant reformers, when their social justice mission directly confronted the political arena. The Uganda Joint Christian Council (UJCC), made up primarily of the Catholic Church and the Anglican Church of Uganda, has made collective critiques at certain moments of Museveni's rule, in particular surrounding the third term debate and the abolition of presidential term limits in 2005 (Citizens Action, 2012). In a constitutional amendment, Museveni simultaneously allowed for a return of multiparty politics for the 2007 elections and abolished the term limits that would have prevented him from running. Protestant and Catholic leaders came out strongly against the term limit amendment, and Archbishop of Kampala Emmanuel Cardinal Wamala openly criticized the move (Dowd, 2015, 112). The Catholic leadership acknowledges they have been pushed by the demands of their membership on this front, suggesting that they spoke out against the constitutional reform in part because the "people told the Bishops that they should stand against the abolition of term limits. And they have been looking for the recognition of their rights through the Church ... it is the only place of redress. It is only the church which has a role of authority, to really speak and say no, enough is enough"(Author Interview, Father Centurio Olaboro, Uganda Catholic Secretariat, 2011). In other examples, the Ugandan Episcopal Conference themes of 2010 and 2012 were "Building a Peaceful, United and Prosperous Uganda through Free and Fair Elections: Consolidating Electoral Democracy in Uganda" and, in 2012, emphasizing the church's "Good Samaritan" contributions to sociopolitical development and social harmony, the church's role as the "conscience of society," and the church's hopes to collaborate with the state to foster the common good of all Ugandans (UEC, 2012, 20).

The Uganda Joint Christian Council (UJCC) has also been highly engaged in election monitoring and drew upon their own reports in the 2016 elections to level critiques concerning the belated opening of polling stations, missing ballots, and declaration of results without tallying in certain constituencies. The UJCC also raised concerns over opposition leader Kizza Besigye's detainment, saying "it constitute[d] impunity on the part of the State," and that the harsh security measures had "robbed the presidential election ... of a level playing field, its key elements being freedom of movement, of assembly, of expression and the right to equal protection of the law"(Alava and Ssentongo 2016). These are critiques of the system – of the rules of the game – not of specific leaders or leadership traits. Anglican Bishop Kisembo recently called upon President Museveni to respect the constitution's original age limit provisions and hand over power peacefully (Atuhair, Ashaba, and Basiime, 2018). Catholic Bishop Akiiki in Fort Portal joined his Anglican counterpart in advising the president to respect the oath he made to uphold and defend the constitution (Atuhair, Ashaba, and Basiime, 2018). As usual, these pronouncements drew harassment from government officials, telling the religious leaders it was not their role to comment on political affairs.

By contrast, Pentecostals in Uganda, as in Kenya, have focused on leadership development and personnel change. Pentecostals have been active at the local level in the 2016 elections engaging with candidates. Whereas the large nongovernmental organization (NGO)-type UJCC was not present at the local level and made its national statements through the media, Pentecostals were seen to be actively meeting and cultivating relationships with candidates. They have been critical of more structural critiques and forms of political participation that challenge policies and the regime. A Pentecostal pastor in Acholi, speaking in advance of the 2016 elections, criticized the "Walk to Work" campaign that protested the high cost of living, specifically the increased cost of transport and rapid inflation: "There is something about our nation: we have a spirit of rebellion. We have a really big problem with authority! The [government leaders] say 'let's have buses', you say, 'no problem, we will walk to work!'" (Alava and Ssentongo, 2016, 685) The pastor went on to encourage citizens to focus on choosing good leaders and then to let those leaders do their work.

The Pentecostal engagement and focus on leadership has also been evident in Uganda through the power of political persuasion of individual members, such as the First Lady and former Member of Parliament Janet Museveni, a prominent Pentecostal, and other key members of Parliament. Church members are encouraged to utilize this network with the first family and other powerful people to advocate for policy decisions that are informed by "Christian values." In general, the Pentecostals are seen as being more proleadership (New Vision, 2016). Common activities include ceremonies of national forgiveness for leaders whose conduct has fallen short of Christian principles, putting forward the idea of divinely inspired leadership and grace for those in positions of authority. President Museveni took up this theme of grace and forgiveness in his national jubilee commemorations in 2012, when he repented for his sins and the sins of Uganda (NewVision, 2012):

I stand here on my own behalf and on behalf of my predecessors to repent. We ask for your forgiveness. We confess these sins, which have greatly hampered our national cohesion and delayed our political, social and economic transformation. ... I renounce all the evil foundations and covenants that were laid in idolatry and witchcraft. I renounce all the satanic influence on this nation. And I hereby covenant Uganda to you, to walk in your ways and experience all your blessings forever.

In this prayer, Museveni portrays himself and the NRM as acting to create a new, reconstructed, transformed Uganda, moving away from the past, in line with a future of prosperity and regeneration. He uses the language of baptism and rebirth in the final lines to mark his departure from the past and connect to the grace of his citizens. Pentecostals reacted with excitement, suggesting that national healing and progress can be achieved when leaders acknowledge God's supremacy and that God will answer his prayers. This marks a distinctive vision of leadership and accountability, based on a capacity to act and accomplish personal transformation.

Pentecostals have focused on their visions of personal and public integrity. In particular, the Ugandan Pentecostal urban youth have been campaigning for the moral renewal of the nation. This movement, called the "Joseph Generation," associated with the Hebrew figure Joseph because he refused the duplicitous courtship of his Egyptian master's wife and later became the leader in Egypt, but the beginning of his journey was marked by the moral strength that allows him to resist temptations (Maxwell, 2013). Again we see the connection between individual moral transformation and the mission to save the whole of Uganda through a moral revolution. These efforts sometimes get translated into efforts to secure new legislation, such as the push for the Anti-Homosexuality Act (Gusman, 2009; Downie, 2015; Grossman, 2015; Bompani, 2016).

In sum, although all Christian denominations in the competitive authoritarian regime context have been largely silent on the president and the ruling party, Mainline Christians have taken a stand on procedural and structural issues of poverty, election irregularities and term limits, and working on the peace process in northern Uganda. Catholics and Anglicans have been focused on social justice and collective development issues. In contrast, Pentecostals in Uganda have focused on attaining leadership positions and their relation to political leadership, and sought out active engagement strategies to influence their state based upon their moral views and transformative strategies. Moreover, their engagement in politics promotes a nationalist discourse of public regeneration in the country (Bompani, 2016). Yet the Pentecostal focus on spiritually transforming politics means they ignore the structural challenges that lead to the very corruption and poverty they wish to combat (Asamoah-Gyadu, 2005).

Forms of Political Engagement in Zambia

Zambia has transitioned from a nominally Presbyterian president, to the first Pentecostal president, and then to a series of Catholic and Protestant successors. Additionally, it has transitioned from a single-party state to a fragmented multiparty, fragile democracy, with significant regional divisions. It is also a case in which Pentecostal churches have strong international ties and have engaged in more extensive social service provision, more in the way of Catholics in other sub-Saharan Africa countries. Yet, despite their dramatic gains and reversals in proximity to power by government, Pentecostals retain similar modes of engagement across time, and despite their involvement in social service provision, Pentecostals in Zambia have also retained a focus on leadership traits and leadership development. Mainline Protestants are diverse and smaller in number in Zambia than in Kenya and Uganda, and exhibit lower levels of hierarchy and centralization, but here too, patterns of political engagement remain consistent across time and consistent with the patterns in the other country case studies.

In Zambia, the Catholic Church was highly engaged in the anticolonial struggle for independence as an issue of social justice, with Catholic clergy speaking out against the structural repression of the colonial state (Phiri, 1997). President Kenneth Kaunda was the founding father at independence and a Presbyterian who made great use of his father's missionary and pastor service to confer legitimacy on his government (Gifford, 1998). In his early years, Kaunda referred to biblical passages and used Christian rhetoric to express compassion and integrity (Gifford, 1998). During the postindependence period of multiparty pluralistic competition, all churches were largely silent: the mission churches, including Catholic churches, focused largely on their service provision work in education and health.

As Kaunda consolidated a single-party regime and became increasingly authoritarian, members and leaders of the Mainline churches became more vocal in their opposition. The Catholic Episcopal Conference of Zambia (ECZ) and the Mainline Christian Council of Zambia (CCZ) jointly operated a weekly newspaper, *National Mirror*. In the late 1980s and early 1990s, it began to publish a wide range of background articles on African governance, economic crises, university students' grievances, donor critiques, interviews with former detainees, and full-page advertisements from the opposition Movement for Multiparty Democracy (MMD), none of which was appearing in the sole alternatives of the government-party-owned circulations (Gifford, 1998). Catholics vocally joined the opposition critique, partnering with civil society organizations and the powerful labor unions. The Catholics' pastoral letter calling for an end of the single-party state was particularly powerful in the early 1990s as a nonpartisan but prodemocracy voice (Phiri, 1997, 336). This position of non-partisan critique also led the Catholic churches to a key role in the meditation process of the democratic transition (as in Benin, Burkina Faso, and elsewhere where Catholic church leaders were called upon to help negotiate a regime change and institutional reforms, in part because they were seen as neutral players who were not interested in political leadership themselves).

In contrast, the Pentecostals were most concerned about Kaunda's declaration of scientific socialism and increasing interest in Indian spirituality, which gave the impression that he had forsaken Christianity (Burgess, 2014, 304). A group of pastors denounced these links and voiced concern over his ability to lead (Gifford, 1998, 192). The Pentecostals' concern was over the connection between the mindset and faith of leaders and material outcomes: they feared Kaunda's turn away from Christianity might result in national impoverishment.

In the transition to multiparty democracy in 1991, in the months before the election, the Mainline Protestant and Catholic churches contributed to mediation and a peaceful transition by joining to form the Christian Churches Monitoring group, which focused on procedures and systems surrounding the election. Zambia's diverse coalition of opposition coalesced within the MMD, and out of the trade union leadership emerged the presidential candidate, Frederick Chiluba, a Pentecostal (Mwanakatwe, 1994). Kaunda was increasingly characterized as oppressive, whereas Chiluba's Pentecostal backers portrayed his leadership characteristics as a true spirit-filled believer, about to bring his people to freedom after years of fruitless wandering in the wilderness. Not long after taking office, Chiluba unilaterally declared Zambia to be a Christian nation. His lack of consultation and preparation around this declaration drew a hostile response from Catholics and Mainline Protestants, as the declaration itself appeared to be a form of individual covenant that Chiluba later described as his own promise to God (Phiri, 1997). Chiluba's speech began as a prayer of personal dedication and then evolved into a presidential declaration. Having begun with "Dear God," followed by a commitment to the renunciation of evil and wrongdoing (obviously associated with the former government), the prayer then became an official statement directed in part to the national television audience:

On behalf of the nation I have entered into a covenant law with the living God. And therefore I want to make the following declaration. I declare today that I submit myself as president to the lordship of Jesus Christ. I likewise submit the government and the entire nation of Zambia to the lordship of Jesus Christ. I further declare that Zambia is a Christian nation that will seek to be governed by the righteous principles of the word of God. 2 Chronicles 7:14 says "If my people who are called by my name will humble themselves and pray and seek my face and turn from their wicked ways, then will I hear from heaven and forgive their sin and will heal their land." (Chiluba, quoted in Phiri 1997).

Mainline Protestants and Catholics immediately criticized the move, which was a result of Chiluba's personal religious orientation rather than an outcome of the churches' influence on the country's political life.

Pentecostals were at first supportive and used the public declaration to further catalyze a more energetic and extensive evangelical political engagement with leadership (Phiri, 2003). But less than a year later, the Evangelical Fellowship of Zambia (EFZ) pulled back from energetically and explicitly supporting Chiluba (Phiri, 2003). This instance shows that Pentecostals focus on critically evaluating the traits of leaders even when those leaders are vocally part of their in-group.

This critical stance toward Chiluba remained a critique of his leadership traits and did not transfer to broader pushes for structural or institutional reform. Chiluba's declaration was very personal, and in it he set up the individual criteria by which his presidency should be judged. The Christian nation concept he articulated gave Pentecostals a clear basis on which to evaluate Chiluba, and some Pentecostal leaders found him wanting, after corruption scandals marred his focus on morality and transformed leadership. But when it came to the institutional issue of a constitutional amendment allowing a third presidential term, "many church leaders hesitated to emphasize these issues" (Okite, 2001). Instead, other leaders sought to offer themselves as replacements. A rising political challenger was a fellow Pentecostal, Nevers Mumba, who pronounced his moral strength to pursue his own political career (Cheyeka, Hinfelaar, and Udelhoven, 2014, 1042). Reverend Masupa explained in 2010 that Pentecostals try to guide leadership and find the best leaders but do not look to change the system:

As ICOZ [the Independent Church of Zambia], we contribute to the shaping of the spiritual, social, and political development of Zambia. We play the role of advisers and we also play the prophetic role. We do not engage in struggling, contentions, protest with the governing authority, which would lead to civil strife or anarchy. We don't protest whatever the national constitutions stipulates ... We do not agitate for change of government. We would rather provide alternatives [for leadership]. (Cheyeka, Hinfelaar, and Udelhoven, 2014, 1034).

This quote supports the notion that Pentecostals participate in God's action through supporting leaders and seeking leadership positions but not through change in government institutions and systems. In contrast, the Catholics and Mainline Christians were engaged during this time in the activist Oasis Forum – a loose alliance of the major church bodies, the women's movement, and the Law Association of Zambia – to make sure that laws were in place to crush Chiluba's third term bid (Cheyeka, 2016).

More recently, in Zambia, as elsewhere, Catholics and Mainline Christians have focused on the structural sources of underdevelopment, corruption, and poverty. Pentecostals also voice concern about these issues, but continue to differ in how they pursue such valence goals. Mainline religious organizations have focused on the delivery of social services, sanctioning politicians, and addressing institutional social justice (Burgess, 2015, 178). The *Zambia Post's* editorial content reflected this deeply systemic and structural orientation of the Catholic Church in assessing "its rightful place in the governance of our country": "The Catholic Church in our country, by its nature, has consistently stood up against injustice for the disadvantaged, the vulnerable and the powerless to press for a fair, just and humane society for all" (Post, Zambia, 2004). The Catholics have also been focused on this issue of development and worked collectively on the Jubilee 2000 campaign to cancel the debts of developing countries. The Church focused on the potential injustices involved in forcing poor people, unable to afford the basics of life, to pay interest on loans from which they never profited. It also challenged political leaders not to simply create scapegoats from decisions of the prior governments but to act responsibly as a means of maintaining concern for the poor (Carmody, 2002).

By contrast, the Pentecostal churches have been involved in development and governance issues through seeking to build human capital, giving managerial skills to members to stress each citizen's own responsibility for development. Again, the valence issues are similar, seeking social and economic change (Wood and Warren, 2002; Freeman, 2012). But the forms of political participation focus on training leaders in particular, for "best practices" in approaching government officials to seek services and "building a cohort of Christian leaders who have a record in local office, understand community needs, and eventually can run for district council or Parliament" (Patterson and Kuperus, 2016, 331). In addition, Pentecostal organizations have been working with politicians to have them declare their intentions of good leadership, through a Memorandum of Understanding. The Pentecostal agenda here is to stimulate leaders to articulate their own plans for development and transformation of the community (Patterson and Kuperus, 2016). This approach focuses on cultivating the intrinsic motivations of individual leaders to pursue good governance.

The Zambian case also illustrates how Pentecostals have tended to take a different approach to solving political problems even when they are equally engaged in social service provision alongside Catholic and Mainline Protestant churches. For instance, the Jubilee Center is a Pentecostal faith-based NGO in Zambia that aims to mobilize citizens through "training community leaders and empowering ordinary people to improve the quality of life in their communities" (Burgess, 2015, 179; also, Patterson and Kuperus, 2016). Studies of the Jubilee Center suggest that "they are also indirectly impacting development through reforming cultural values" (Burgess, 2015). The Jubilee Centre's vision is for church leaders and members to be "transformed into agents of change" (Jubilee Centre, 2006). Through the Church Mobilization Programme, it works in urban communities to train local leaders and empower congregations to respond proactively to the AIDS epidemic. By focusing on self-worth, Pentecostals are seen to have higher capacity to foster participation than secular NGOs in bringing about effective and sustainable social change (Freeman, 2012, 24–25; Patterson and Kuperus, 2016). The Centre also runs a leadership program called "Will the Church Save Zambia?" which provides a platform for challenging Pentecostals to deepen their engagement with the poor (Burgess, 2015, 188). The Centre seeks to address issues of good governance and corruption by developing leaders from within (Burgess, 2015). The Jubilee Centre also helps pastors from smaller churches (who were often intimidated by the prospect of engaging with politicians) to "recognize the resources available within their congregations and communities, and to realize that they have the power and agency." The organization is an interesting parallel to the Catholic focus on service provision; while both denominations seek to provide services, their approaches vary dramatically.

During the presidency of Michael Sata (2011–2014), who was a Catholic, Catholics were offered more access to public sector employment and to serve on technical or advisory committees within the government (Cheyeka, 2012). Yet this closeness to the state did not inhibit their inclinations to press for structural and institutional reform, particularly around the core themes of democracy and development. The Catholic bishops raised concerns about the irregular process in legislative by-elections (*Lusaka Times*, 2013). Catholic priests raised concerns about institutions and policies around market trading that were not addressing the plight of the poor (Phiri, 2012).

In contrast, during this period, Pentecostals, who were more blatantly excluded from prominent positions in government, sought to cultivate personal relationships with politicians and to seek renewed, intrinsically motivated leadership. Pentecostals sought to meet with Sata at the State House immediately following his victory in late November 2011. A delegation of twenty-six Pentecostal pastors told the new president that "as Church leaders, they believed that God raises His anointed in various seasons and assured the President that they would continue to pray to God for guidance and give him wisdom in his leadership" (Cheyeka, 2016, 162). The approach taken by the Pentecostals is well summarized by Nevers Mumba. In the manifesto of his political organization, he wrote:

Bad people cannot achieve good governance. Good governance demands good governors. It takes a leadership of morality and integrity to bring healing to Zambia. The only hope for Zambia is to insist on putting into office leaders of proven morality whose values are faith-based and anchored in Godly values. NCC's objective is that there will never be good governance without good governors. The delivery of goods and services to the citizens is dependent on the morality of its leaders.

This approach is centered on getting virtuous leaders into office and on cultivating relationships with existing leaders so that citizens can engage in self-help. The approach is not about institutional or structural reform.

In sum, these differences in orientations toward citizenship reflect similar patterns across the three countries in very different historical periods and organizational contexts. In Kenya, Uganda, and Zambia, it is clear that the modes of participation undertaken by Catholic and Mainline

Protestant laity and religious leaders alike demonstrate their engagement in critique at key moments. Although often reluctant, their efforts mobilize the polity to hold governments accountable, to identify structural and systemic reforms, to change institutions, and to work for social justice. In contrast, Pentecostals seek to transform themselves, and in doing so, the nation, by becoming and selecting moral leaders. The consequences for regime type, liberty, and human development are complex. Pentecostals are pushing forward new types of leaders, from different backgrounds (women, ethnic minorities, nonelite families). But they largely have not mobilized for institutional reform or redress of structural barriers to equality and development. These domains remain the work of the reluctant reformers.

In the next section, we compare brief descriptions of parallel phenomena across a set of anglophone cases through a newspaper analysis. These data provide additional evidence that these differential modes of political engagement persist across political and organizational contexts.

NEWSPAPER ANALYSES ACROSS SUB-SAHARAN AFRICA

To create a broader empirical map of what Pentecostal, Mainline Protestant, and Catholic religious leaders and followers are doing in the public realm, we turned to newspaper archives to create an original database tracking the activities of these two denominations. We add this analysis to the preceding case studies because it allows us to examine a larger set of countries and offers a broader set of political issue areas around which denominations might mobilize. First, including a larger set of cases provides some check on our case study findings because it includes other important cases with very large Pentecostal populations and/or high religious pluralism, such as Nigeria, Ghana, Malawi, and Tanzania. We selected Kenya, Uganda, and Zambia for the case studies in order to leverage a most-different design, but looking at other significant, out-of-sample countries is a useful additional test of our arguments. Second, although the case studies provide more detailed accounts of religious actors' engagement in certain domains documented through interviews and secondary sources, the newspaper database allowed us to gather information across a larger range of political issue areas. By comparing Pentecostal, Mainline Protestant, and Catholic engagement around the same issues areas (e.g., development, elections, violence, corruption, and other specific policy debates), we are able to compare whether and how Pentecostals, Mainline Protestants, and Catholics approach parallel issues.

We searched Access World News, Factiva, and All Africa archives of national and international newspapers from anglophone countries in sub-Saharan Africa.[18] We searched for all time periods, and the earliest relevant entry was from 2005. We thus collected records from 2005 through 2017. We employed a key word search for either Pentecost*, Catholic*, and all main Protestant denominations, along with a term for politic* and/or civic* and/or elect* in order to capture articles discussing any actions in the political or civic arena. The search yielded hundreds of articles with some reference to each denomination, but less than 25 percent of the articles included specific mentions of religious leaders' or lay members' actions or statements. From the search results, we coded 100 articles for each denomination that had relevant actions of religious actors engaging in the public arena to map the empirical variation.[19] We then also coded any relevant articles before 2011, to maximize our historical reach (which is limited by the low prevalence of newspaper archives in the prior decade). The articles are often statements of fact about what a particular religious leader or lay member said, or wrote, or a meeting they attended. We searched across both state-run media outlets and newspapers that position themselves as opposition.[20] Although it is possible that state-run newspapers might limit coverage of particularly critical statements by religious leaders, the opposition papers often pick them up. A state-run paper might also feature the president's response to religious-political action, in which case we would capture the original action as well. Although we might expect more authoritarian contexts to have more repression of the media and limit critical coverage, this would ostensibly apply equally to actions coming from any religious denomination, so the relative difference in modes of political engagement across denominations is still instructive.

Another type of bias in newspaper reporting is the tendency to cover public events and activities of religious or political elites, rather than

---

[18] We did not restrict the search to anglophone countries, but the nature of the search terms and database population meant that all entries were in anglophone countries. This is in keeping with our focus on former British colonies where religious pluralism within Christianity in particular flourished during and after the colonial period.

[19] One hundred in each denomination was our ex ante target, but it was also the case that this largely exhausted all of the relevant articles in the three newspaper archives; as we neared our target, the remaining search results were yielding exceedingly few relevant articles.

[20] See also Bleck and Van de Walle (2013) regarding newspaper database opportunities and constraints.

quotidian activities of the churches or actions of ordinary citizens. In addition, certain forms of participation, such as personal requests of public officials, are not likely to be covered in the news, whereas mass protests are.

It is thus all the more striking that we do observe the political statements and activities of Pentecostals, who at times explicitly call for leadership development, and refer to the need for leaders to have strong faith and Christian values. For example, in 2015 the Ghana News Agency ran the article titled "Christian Youth Being Equipped to Help Develop Africa." In it, the Reverend Dr. Peter Kyei, Rector of the Pentecost University College (PUC), declared a mission:

to help catalyze the building of leaders of integrity to transform Ghana into a first premier country, shaped by God-centered values especially through partnership between the State and the Church ... [through] a moral vision for Africa based on deeply personalized spiritual values as well as to develop a framework for Africa's development that is holistic. Reverend Kyei, therefore, urged the youth to eschew laziness and untruthfulness and rather embrace moral values that would portray them as good citizens as they reflect the change in their families, workplaces, communities and society in general. "Character and morality are strongly linked to spirituality. We need a standard of the perfection demonstrated by Jesus Christ to measure ours with. He offers help to those who ask him for help to live by high moral standards," he told the participants.

This article captures a particular approach to politics – of developing leadership characters and intrinsic motivations – even though one might expect these types of strategies to be less often covered in national media.

Within each article, research assistants recorded all relevant activities for any religiously identified actor or action, quoting the text of the articles in full. Given the variety of newspaper archives, search terms, countries, and dates we were covering, the search results yielded a diverse array of events, and no single event has more than two different articles referring to it. Our findings are not likely skewed by particular reactions to only a few salient events, or by Pentecostals, Mainline Protestants, or Catholics being repeatedly portrayed as pursuing a particular strategy around a single event or issue. Using the text of the article, the authors then independently coded each entry dichotomously into two categories: (1) criticism of institutions and structures, pressure for institutional or legislative reform, protest, and/or pushing for mechanisms of monitoring or sanctioning (extrinsic incentives) to promote good governance; and (2) requests to public officials for services or assistance, officeseeking, leadership development, and commentary on desirable leadership traits. Each entry could receive a 0 or a 1 for either or both categories. Occasionally, there were article entries that received a 0 in both categories, such as general calls for peace, declarations of nonpartisanship, and encouragement to vote. At times, pronouncements were made through interreligious councils that included both Pentecostals and Catholics, in which case both denominations were coded as having engaged in that form of participation. Some article entries also received a 1 in both categories, such as a searing critique of the current government's policies coupled with a character assessment of particular politicians. But the vast majority of all entries fell into one category or another (95 percent Mainline Protestants, 96 percent of Catholics, 90 percent of Pentecostals), suggesting distinct patterns of political engagement.

We also sought to assess how each set of actors engaged in different domains, because it is possible that certain forms of engagement inevitably correspond with particular issue domains, such that the difference is not in religious denominations' strategies vis-à-vis the state, but rather in the particular issues that religious denominations prioritize. To assess this possibility, we code each article entry by issue area, identifying four key domains for all articles: governance and policy issues (i.e., valence priorities such as development, good governance and jobs; Bleck and Van de Walle, 2013), elections (including debates over third terms, constitutional revisions related to election procedure and Electoral Commission processes, voter registration, as well as candidate assessments and partisan statements), mediation (between conflicting parties or civil war), and violence (including discussions of interethnic violence, patterns of war violence, reactions to violent encounters between members of the government and citizens, etc). Certainly, there are certain issues that newspapers will cover with more frequency than others, and it is not surprising that a good deal of coverage is over elections and related statements about candidates, campaigns, parties, and electoral process. That is precisely why it is useful to compare Pentecostal, Mainline Protestant, and Catholic forms of engagement by issue domain, so that we can analyze where and how each denomination is getting involved. The following analysis suggests that Mainline Protestants, Catholics, and Pentecostals are largely not engaging in different domains of politics (though there does seem to be some more action by Mainline Protestants and Catholics around issues of mediation and violence). Rather, the analysis suggests that the denominations pursue different paths toward addressing the same issues.

For example, religious affiliates expressing interest in elections might focus on institutional changes necessary to reform the process for voter registration; they might even make a critique of the regime as being too institutionally authoritarian, thereby advocating for structural reforms and regime transition. Alternatively, they might focus on the qualities and characteristics of particular leaders, assessing their characters, strength of faith, and individual values or motivations. These are both responses to the same issue area (elections), but involve very different modes of participation. In Zimbabwe in 2017, an article entitled "Catholic Bishops Say 'It Is a Sin Not to Vote', Urge People to Boot Out 'Evil' Zanu-PF," explained that Catholic leaders were urging people to address failures in the party and the political system as a whole, and were urging citizens to find institutional solutions to the problem, through voter education programs that focused on the legal infrastructure: "Father Rungano emphasized that Zimbabweans should be educated on the importance of voting and protecting that vote ... Father Rungano and Bishop Ancelimo Magaya of the Zimbabwe Divine Destiny Church have openly criticized the ruling Zanu PF party for failure to respect the rule of law as well as failure to govern the country" (New Zimbabwe, 2017)

In contrast, in a 2018 article in the Herald (Harare), entitled "The Cult of Nelson Chamisa's Personality," the newest leader of the opposition party Movement for Democratic Change was described as seen by his Pentecostal followers (and compared to his predecessor and party founder, Mainline Christian Morgan Tsvangirai, whose background as a trade unionist was described). In focusing on leadership and the personal characteristics that candidates can bring to elections, Chamisa (a Pentecostal) was described not in policy terms, but in contrast to Tsvangirai himself:

Chamisa comes to the fray on the basis of his personality and young age. The chief attribute of Chamisa being young will help explain his leadership of the opposition in the past few months and how this will affect his future politics. In the last election, MDC-Alliance's main selling point was his age as well as purported charisma. He was variably referred to as a boy or the young man: as in, Why don't we give the young man a chance? or Let the boy do the work, etc.

Chamisa, a Pentecostal, also played up the character branding, and "acted out the quintessential youth ... performing physical stunts colloquially known as press-ups to demonstrate his vitality. On the other hand, his messaging was couched in the tradition of young charismatic preachers who promise heaven on earth." Pentecostal supporters created the hashtag #GodIsInIt, suggesting that his leadership plans for the country are imbued in a religious mysticism. This contrast is striking, given that Catholics in Zimbabwe have played multiple roles, as some of the long-time autocratic ruler Robert Mugabe's closest confidants (such as Father Mukonori), and as prominent critics (such as Archbishop Ncube) (Economist, 2017; Farley, 2017). These two patterns don't reflect steady candidate positions of the denominations in the rapidly changing electoral scene of Zimbabwe's politics from 2016 to 2018 but rather different modes of participation by religious members and leaders that are more broadly reflected within denominations (Maxwell, 2000).

These patterns are evident throughout the newspaper database, in actions by religious leaders, and where we were able to identify lay activists by specific denominational affiliation. Where lay Pentecostals are identified in the news media, they are frequently candidates running for office and engaged in discussions about leadership traits. A 2014 article from Nigeria discusses Omowunmi Olatunji-Edet, "one of the stylish female politicians in the Lagos State House of Assembly" (Sun, 2014). In the ensuing interview with her, the article quotes her as explaining,

[My time in] the Pentecostal Fellowship of Nigeria (PFN) began sensitizing Christians to go into politics, and I heeded the call; which is what led me into politics.

In Ghana in 2016, a Pentecostal member of Parliament told congregants that he "prayed to God to help Nana Akufo-Addo to win the 2016 elections. According to him, God had answered his prayers." In these examples, lay Pentecostals focus on leadership traits and on running for office. Catholic laity, on the other hand, are more frequently mentioned in connection with pushes for reform. In 2017 in the Democratic Republic of Congo, the *Cape Times* reported

Last month, about 40 leaders of citizens' movements, civil society organisations, Catholic Church representatives, and other independent Congolese leaders launched the 'Manifesto of the Congolese Citizen' ... to discuss the "return of constitutional order" to the DRC ... They made the case that Kabila had violated the country's constitution by using "force and financial corruption" to stay in power and "entrench his regime of depredation, pauperisation, and the pillaging of the country's resources for the benefit of himself, his family, his sycophants, and his foreign allies in Africa and beyond" (Frykberg, 2017).

The focus on limiting executive power through the constitution displays a focus on extrinsic and institutional constraints rather than on leadership characteristics alone.

Figures 6.1 through 6.3 present these aggregate patterns of political engagement by religious denomination and by issue domain. On the y-axes, the graphs show the total number of articles per issue that fall into

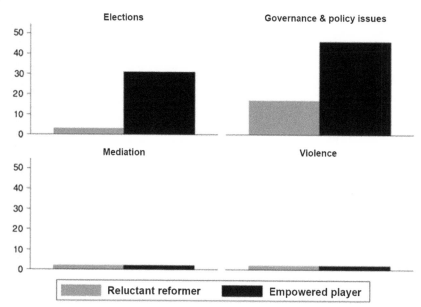

FIGURE 6.1 Newspaper database of political actions: Pentecostals.
Note: Y-axes show a count of the total number of articles.

either category of institutional criticism and pressures for reform ("Reluctant Reformer") or requests for services, office-seeking and assessments
of politicians' individual character traits ("Empowered Player").

The main finding is that Pentecostals, on the one hand, and Mainline Protestants and Catholics, on the other, tend to engage in politics through different modes: Pentecostals are more often engaged in
requests, officeseeking, and assessments of individual leaders' characters
(Figure 6.1); Catholics and Mainline Protestants are more often engaged
in institutional critiques and pressures for structural reform (Figures 6.2
and 6.3). Even with regard to the same issue areas (elections, governance,
violence, and so on), Pentecostals, in comparison to Mainline Protestants
and Catholics, are pursuing different paths toward engagement in the
public arena. In discussions of governance, for example, Catholics
and Mainline Protestants engage by making institutional critiques and
suggesting reforms (increased monitoring, increased penalties for poorly
performing politicians), while Pentecostals engage in this domain by
discussing the importance of good leadership (strong faith, Christian
character) to provide economic development, and the morality and
characteristics of political leaders necessary to address public health

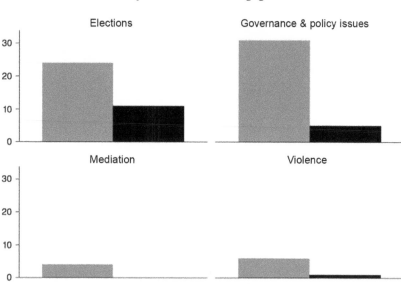

FIGURE 6.2 Newspaper database of political actions: Catholics.
Note: Y-axes show a count of the total number of articles.

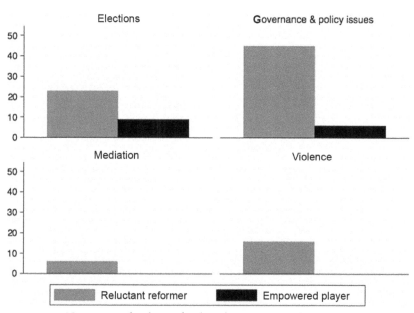

FIGURE 6.3 Newspaper database of political actions: Mainline Protestants.
Note: Y-axes show a count of the total number of articles.

rather than criticizing laws, institutions, or the state as a whole. The Pentecostal focus on leadership, morality, and characteristics of politicians is the solution to provide economic development, address public health, or constitutional reforms *rather than* criticizing laws, institutions, or governments, as the Catholics and Mainlines tend to do. For example, Pentecostals are referenced forty-six times as extolling leadership traits that relate to good governance, or seeking office themselves and developing the next generation of leaders to impact governance, compared to only seventeen instances where they make some kind of critique about the systems, structures, and institutions and advocate for reforms. By contrast, Catholics and Mainline Protestants, respectively, are discussing governance and policy structural reforms in thirty-one and thirty-six instances, and in only five and six instances they raise specific issues about particular leaders' traits.

Even in the domain of elections, in which one might expect mostly discussions of individual candidates, Catholics and Mainline Protestants more often discussed structural issues (free and fair elections, monitoring and sanctioning politicians through votes) that needed to be addressed, and more often critiqued the political class in general for their positions or actions rather than highlighting individual candidate characters (twenty-four and eighteen entries, respectively, versus eleven and six references to individual character traits or officeseeking). The Pentecostal types of engagement did not critique the system at large; rather, they highlighted character or moral flaws in particular individuals and called for internal transformation as the way to good governance. They were not disengaged or other-world-focused during this time period but were instead taking on highly visible roles as candidates for political office, and as citizens interacting with political leaders, seeking to guide and transform political leaders and to transform themselves. They seek national transformation by identifying "transformed" leaders. Catholics and Mainline Protestants, in contrast, when they act, channeled their political engagement into highlighting issues of structural injustice and pressing for institutional reform. In this archival record, the newspaper accounts provide a snapshot of religious actors of different denominations engaging differently in the political arena, even around the same issue areas.

SUMMARY

How does religious messaging shape political participation? We have explored this question at the individual level in previous chapters. Here, we have sought to explore patterns of group-level political behavior as they are observed in the world, in different contexts and countries. Investigating this historical and contemporary evidence helps us understand whether certain repertoires of action that we can isolate among individuals in the laboratory also have implications in the broader political arena and shape substantive governance outcomes. We cannot fully separate lay behavior from clergy behavior in this chapter, or identify the causal effects of sermons on behavior. Instead, we built upon our insights from the laboratory, focus groups, and survey analysis, and described patterns of political engagement by denomination, that are consistent with findings in previous chapters, which persist around similar issues, despite variation in church–state relations over time and country.

In this chapter, we explored institutionally and demographically diverse case studies in Kenya, Uganda, and Zambia, and looked at newspaper accounts of religious actor political activities throughout anglophone Africa. These analyses illustrated how Catholics, Mainline Protestants, and Pentecostals engage in politics in ways consistent with the metaphysical world views communicated in their sermons. Through a most-different case comparison design, the case studies highlighted that, despite variation in political-strategic environments, church organization, and access to international resources, the forms of political engagement undertaken by laity and clergy of different denominations remained consistent with our overarching arguments. We are not arguing that Catholics and Mainline Protestants never pursue leadership or engage in personal transformation, or that Pentecostals never press for large-scale structural reform. Yet, across time and space in recent decades, Pentecostals and Mainline Christians have tended to engage in distinctive forms of political participation even around the same issue areas. These forms of participation are consistent with the religious message they deliver in their pulpits.

7

Implications and Conclusions

We live in a time when religion – in all its forms, practices, experiences, and content – is highly salient to most people in the world (James, 2003; Toft, Philpott, and Shah, 2011). Although modernization theorists once suggested that religion was retreating from the world stage, religion continues to be ubiquitous even in the face of urbanization and industrialization. Indeed, by many estimates, people are even more religious in much of the world today than they were a couple of decades ago. In sub-Saharan Africa, the patterns are striking. In most countries, 80 to 90 percent of the population report that religion is a very important part of their lives. These shares have been increasing over time. When people say that religion is very important to them, they typically mean that one of the world religions (Christianity, Islam) plays a central role in their lives. Whereas at the turn of the twentieth century fewer than a quarter of people living in sub-Saharan Africa practiced Christianity or Islam, now the share is about 86 percent, according to the Pew Forum, with about 57 percent of people in sub-Saharan Africa practicing Christianity and about 29 percent practicing Islam, with syncretic incorporation of traditional beliefs and practices. In African cities and rural areas alike, houses of worship are everywhere. People attend worship services frequently, and sermons are broadcast on radio, television, and smartphones.

However, at the same time that religiosity has persisted and even increased, formal separations between religious organizations and states have become more widespread in the current age than in previous ones (Fox, 2015). Today, religious leaders typically do not operate with the backing of the coercive arm of the state. Religious messages are ubiquitous but are tools for priming and persuasion rather than coercive commands.

With fewer state religions, faith traditions compete with one another within the same polity, as do denominations and sections within the same faith tradition. Contemporary religious leaders are not guaranteed citizen compliance. More often, they operate in religiously plural and religiously competitive environments.

How do we make sense of the role of religion in politics in this day and age? Popular discourse often quickly connects religiosity and religious teachings to modes of political engagement, but social scientists are more cautious. Amid religious pluralism, individuals can self-select into a house of worship whose teachings and modes of practice accord with their preexisting political views and inclinations. Without direct links to the coercive arm of the state, nothing requires individuals to pay attention to and adopt the views or directions they hear during worship. Furthermore, when most people in a society are religious, important theories about the differences between religious and nonreligious people (that they may have access to tighter social networks, gain politically relevant skills, or have internalized moral obligations to contribute to the public good) provide little leverage over variation in political behavior.

To grapple with questions about religious-political influence in the contemporary era, we have turned in this book to Christian practices in contemporary sub-Saharan Africa and to a particular component of that set of religious practices: sermons. We focused on sermons because they are an important part of the religious experience in the setting we examine but also a crucial component of many world religions. Sermons certainly do not represent all forms of Christian religious teachings or of all forms of exposure to Christian ideas. For example, we did not look at the consequences of reading theological texts, or of engaging in theological training. But sermons do constitute a common, and core, way in which Christians (as well as Muslims and Jews) are exposed to the metaphysical ideas and scriptural interpretations of their faith. By focusing on the sermonic content of particular religions in a particular geographic and temporal setting, we did not treat religion as one unified "thing." For instance, we did not take a denomination's official doctrine and assume that it would represent the content of the messages to which ordinary members of that denomination would be exposed on a regular basis. Instead, we paid particular attention to observing and describing differences in sermon content as they were delivered in contemporary houses of worship. Our approach was thus empirically grounded in a specific context, even though the phenomena we focus on – sermons, and their metaphysical representations of the world – are sufficiently general that scholars of other places and of other religions might apply our approach elsewhere.

Taking sermons as they are in this contemporary moment, we showed in this book that sermons can change the ways listeners participate in politics, even when the messages are not explicitly political. We did not seek to explain why particular sermons are being delivered, or why Pentecostalism and other new religious movements have become popular over time. Instead, we provided new evidence about the influence of their spread. We argued that sermons provide *metaphysical instruction*: guidance about how the physical and spiritual worlds work, what the sources of earthly problems are, and whether individuals can enact personal and social change in this world. These metaphysical questions are difficult to answer on one's own, the answers are hard to verify, and yet having some handle on these questions seems crucial to deciding whether and how to respond to political problems. Thus, how sermons answer these deep metaphysical questions can shape how people diagnose and respond to political problems: whether they see political change as imminently possible or unlikely; whether they see the routes to political change as operating through leaders' characters, intrinsic motivations, and strength of faith, or, alternatively, through structural change and extrinsic incentives. These diagnoses in turn inform whether and how citizens participate in politics.

To test these contentions about religion as metaphysical instruction, we focused on the *content* of sermons, rather than on the ways in which they are delivered or received. We described sermon content, then took that content to the lab, isolating it from the charisma and cadence of the preacher, and from the postures listeners take when they hear them. Using this strategy, and with the advantages of random assignment, we found that sermon content affected how people participated in politics and responded to political scenarios. We found that people respond to teachings that are not their own. They also respond, and often more robustly, to teachings whose messages they find appealing and familiar – to sermons that they would have self-selected into in their daily lives. For example, the effect of exposure to a Pentecostal-like sermon was strongest among self-identified Pentecostals. Such findings from the lab studies mean, first, that sermons have an independent influence on political behavior. They are not simply symptomatic of people's political inclinations. Indeed, even people who might not ordinarily self-select into hearing a particular sermon are affected by it. And yet, second, sermons also strongly affect the behavior of those who *do* self-select into hearing them, which means that sermons' political influence does not stem solely from incidental exposure. Rather, the most common form of sermon exposure (self-selected exposure) is also politically consequential.

We also found consistent evidence in survey data, in focus groups, and in the historical record. These data sources did not allow us to isolate content from the manner and environment in which sermons are delivered, but the results were nevertheless consistent with the lab findings, suggesting that our lab findings are indicative of real-world behavioral responses to religious content. We focused in this book mostly on "effects of causes" – that is, we interrogate the consequences of exposure to religious content, rather than seek to find the sole or primary driver of variation in political participation ("causes of effects"). Thus, for the most part, we did not benchmark the size of religious content's influence on political participation against the extent of influence of other possible drivers of political participation. However, in examining the survey data in Chapter 5, we showed that divergences in political behavior across denominations just after sermon exposure are larger than the divergences in political behavior across people with different demographic characteristics commonly given as explanations for political participation. This finding suggests that readers interested in the primary causes of political participation, rather in the consequences of religious content, should also be intrigued by our argument and results.

Our focus on sermon content as metaphysical instruction treats religion as content-full rather than content-free. Some scholarship treats religion simply as a group boundary marker. Religion can be a socially and politically salient cleavage, but this approach ignores the content of religion: its communication, practices, and ideas. Some scholarship treats religion as a proxy for tight social networks, organizational resources and skills, or social service provision. Religion is often all of these things, but these approaches also ignore the ideational content of religion. We hope to have encouraged scholars to continue to treat religion as content-full, because exposure to ideational content – often through sermons – is a central part of religious experience for people around the world. Furthermore, religious messages can provide important leverage over variation in political behavior even when these other aspects of religion cannot. In the empirical contexts we examined in this book, many of these other components of religious practice – access to religious social networks and skills, belief in God, and strength of attachment to religious social identities – do not vary dramatically across individuals and groups, or are not politically salient. Sermon content does vary and can provide explanatory leverage over variation in individual and group political behavior.

A content-full approach to religion also avoids treating religion as unitary. It does not assume that religion writ large has uniform behavioral consequences: that it always promotes cooperation and prosocial behavior, for instance. Instead, a content-full approach demands that we first observe and describe the content of religious ideas being communicated in a particular time and place before theorizing and testing for religious influence on political behavior.

A focus on exposure to sermon content also demands that we grapple with the potential ebb and flow of religious influence on political behavior. Ordinary people seek guidance from sermons, and as we have sought to demonstrate, they are moved by what they hear. But the kind of metaphysical guidance provided in sermons may be difficult to hold at the forefront of one's mind for long periods of time. For instance, sustaining an expectation of imminent material change (as promised by the Pentecostal sermons) may be difficult as people return to the business of daily life and see their conditions in fact remain largely unchanged. Likewise, sustaining an awareness of the structural and institutional sources of earthly problems that the Catholic and Mainline Protestant sermons reference may also be difficult. These structural and institutional sources are difficult to observe in daily life – our own actions and those of individuals are much more obvious. Indeed, most metaphysical claims made in sermons are not easily verified empirically, nor are they meant to be. But this aspect of religious metaphysical instruction may mean that its influence is short-lived, unless recharged. In religiously plural environments, people may also frequently encounter countervailing messages, either purposefully or incidentally, that dissipate the salience of the Sunday sermon. They may hear different religious messages on the radio, public transportation, or in conversation with others. As a result, the influence of any particular religious message may be short-lived, to be resurrected again with the next exposure. We showed evidence of this ebb and flow in Chapter 5.

The short duration of sermons' influence does not mean that such influence is unimportant. Instead, this insight about duration tells us more about the conditions under which religious ideas are likely to influence political behavior. First, religion's influence on political participation, through religious ideas, is likely to be important among people who listen frequently to sermons. Some churches organize midweek worship services in order to recharge the salience of their messages in the minds of congregants. We expect a strong, sustained impact of religious teachings on political behavior from these houses of worship and among people who participate in those recharging opportunities.

Second, religious teachings may be exploited for their short-term effects. When political entrepreneurs provide opportunities for action (meetings, candidate sign-ups, rallies) soon after citizens are exposed to sermons, the sermons can "tee" people up to respond to opportunities in ways consistent with the metaphysical messages in the sermons. In other words, the links between religious messages and political behavior might be strong not just among people who listen to sermons frequently but also where opportunities for political participation occur just after weekly worship services. For instance, in countries with significant numbers of Christians, we should pay attention to the links between religious ideas and political participation on Sundays and Mondays. In countries with significant numbers of Muslims, we should pay attention to the link between religious ideas and political participation on Fridays and Saturdays.

Other scholars have called this century "God's Century" (Toft, Philpott, and Shah, 2011), because it is a century marked by high religiosity across the globe. It is also a century of unprecedented separation between church and state, and of religious pluralism. In this era, we have documented one of the ways religion continues to exert an influence over political behavior. Ordinary citizens turn to sermons for guidance around deep questions about how the world works. Through sermons and other forms of communication, religious associations communicate a metaphysical understanding of the world. That metaphysical understanding of the world need not be political, required, or coercive. Instead, because it shapes listeners' understanding of cause and effect, of causal attribution and of human agency, it can shape how citizens respond to political problems and opportunities, at least in the short term. The influence of religion as metaphysical world view can be catalyzed into political action if opportunities are presented just after citizens are exposed to the sermon, or its influence can be recharged through repeated exposure to such ideas. A focus on sermons thus helps us understand variation in political behavior in highly religious contexts, and generates observable implications about the institutional and temporal patterns of religious-political engagement.

But what, if anything, can our analysis tell us about the nature and future of politics in sub-Saharan Africa? How far are these findings likely to travel? And what does our focus on sermons leave out? How might different aspects of religion be brought together to enrich our understanding of religion's role in shaping political engagement specifically, and politics more generally?

CONSEQUENCES FOR CONTEMPORARY AFRICAN POLITICS

In this book, we argued that one of the ways religion can influence political behavior is by providing metaphysical ideas about how the world works. Specifically, we argued that contemporary Pentecostal sermons, that communicate an individual- and faith-centered view of what causes problems in the world, influence ordinary citizens to feel efficacious and empowered, and to take actions – make requests of public officials, cultivate leaders' faith and intrinsic motivations for serving the public interest, run for office – that seek political change through personal and personnel change. Those exposed to Pentecostal sermons tend to become *empowered players* within the existing political game. By contrast, Mainline Protestant and Catholic sermons that communicate a view of the world that is much less individual-focused and much less optimistic about immediate material change move citizens to take a more critical view of existing institutions, structures, and elite's extrinsic incentives – to view the system as unfair and see the need for structural and legislative reform – while leaving them feeling no more empowered or efficacious. They become *reluctant reformers*.

Empowered players and reluctant reformers are unlikely to form the basis of large-scale social movements for radical reform. The sermons we observed did not provide a form of liberation theology – which, historically, drew attention to structural injustice *and* stressed the importance, and efficacy, of individual action (Levine and Mainwaring, 1989). The world views communicated in the sermons we observed generally either turned attention to individual characters, rather than toward structural injustice, or, though turning attention to structural injustice, gave listeners little hope that change could be achieved. They were thus not the kinds of religious teachings likely to lead to dramatic challenges to existing institutions. Relatedly, Marshall (2009) argues that Pentecostalism is "fundamentally ambivalent with regard to the neo-liberal state"(209). Although she observes that Pentecostal leaders and followers often describe a kind of "radical" project of conversion and self-mastery, this project does not equate with a large-scale reenvisioning of state institutions or systems of power. Sermon content could change over time, of course, and we would expect a corresponding change in modes of political engagement. But in the moment we observe, dominant religious teachings within contemporary Christianity largely stop short of pushing listeners toward radical activism.

Nevertheless, the sermons we observed have perhaps more subtle implications for politics. For instance, relative to Catholic and Mainline

Protestant churches, Pentecostal churches may find more favor with incumbent regimes, because their sermons, although moving and empowering, do not incline people toward structural, regime, and institutional criticism. Pentecostal sermons might move people to criticize the characters of individual leaders, but they are unlikely to take issue with the structures that brought them to power. And if individual leaders can demonstrate personal transformation or conversion, they are likely to win the support of people regularly exposed to Pentecostal sermons, even if their extrinsic incentives for serving citizens' interests remain unchanged. Indeed, in contexts of weak capacity, it may be appealing to politicians to compete over who has "good character" rather than who has good policies (Bleck and Van de Walle, 2013; Grossman, 2015), so incumbents might prefer the dimension of competition suggested by Pentecostal sermons. By contrast, even if Catholic and Mainline Protestant sermons do not seem to make people feel dramatically more efficacious, they do move people toward institutional criticism and toward creating and enforcing structural constraints on government leaders. Such latent pressures for structural reform might be more concerning to incumbents than Pentecostals' desires for leaders of strong character. If Mainline Protestant and Catholic adherents were to overcome their reluctance to take concrete action, they might present a real threat to incumbent regimes. Consistent with these ideas, Sperber (2016) finds that contemporary incumbents in Africa have instituted policies or used patronage to favor Pentecostal churches over Mainline Protestant and Catholic churches. She argues that incumbents have done so in order to reduce the influence of Mainline Protestant and Catholic churches, who might be more likely at some point to press for democratic reforms.

Yet, though more forgiving toward incumbent regimes, Pentecostal sermons do have the potential to change the composition of political candidate pools by making listeners of all backgrounds feel more empowered to take political action, and even to run for office themselves. Although these new candidates might not push for large-scale reform of institutions and regimes, to the extent that the sermons empower less conventional candidacies – of women or members of marginalized groups – Pentecostal sermons could portend increases in descriptive representation. This potential for changing the candidate pool might be troubling to incumbents, who might jealously guard their positions in office; but if, as the analyses in this book suggest, these new candidates are likely to play by the rules of the game, the challenge may be less severe than any future collective mobilization of Mainline Protestant and Catholics. Thus, a more subtle change in who participates (as citizens and as candidates) might be brought about by the increasing popularity of Pentecostal sermons.

Taken together, these observations should caution us not to make claims that "religion" uniformly does one thing: e.g., is good or bad for democracy, is good or bad for cooperation or for social change. If, as Gibson (1995) wrote, the ideal democratic citizen "believes in individual liberty and is politically tolerant, has a certain distrust of political authority but at the same time is trusting of fellow citizens, is obedient but nonetheless willing to assert rights against the state, and views the state as constrained by legality" (55), then religion in this book is neither "good" nor "bad" for democracy. One set of sermons we examined emphasizes individuality, energizes citizens to be engaged with their representatives, and encourages them to "buy into" political institutions. But at the same time, that set of religious teachings depresses citizens' inclinations to make institutional critiques against the state – encouraging them instead to focus on individual characters and on getting the right people into positions of power. The other set of religious teachings increases skepticism of political institutions and authority and, in a sense, encourages citizens to assert their rights against the state. But that set of teachings does little to energize listeners as individuals or to ensure their "buy-in" to the political system. Each of these sets of sermons enhances some aspects of democratic culture while ignoring or detracting from others.

SCOPE CONDITIONS

How far does this approach to studying religion's influence on political behavior travel? Is it a way to study only Christianity in sub-Saharan Africa, or does it apply to the study of other traditions and other places? Would we expect the same consequences of exposure to sermons on political engagement in other contexts?

Although we ground the book in a specific context, we expect the general approach in the book to travel widely, at least to faith traditions in which sermons are an important part of religious experience. Some religions – such as Hinduism and Buddhism – focus more on practice than on elite messaging (Chhibber, 2014), so the approach in this book may be less helpful there.[1] To the extent that the effect of practice on

---

[1] We thank Lily Tsai for this point.

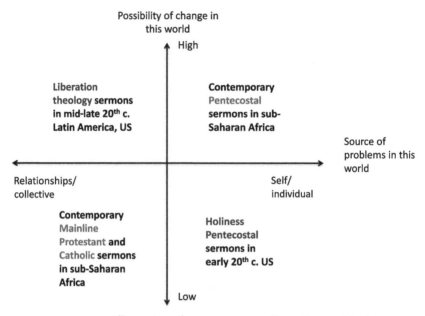

FIGURE 7.1 Illustration of sermon content dimensions revisited.

behavior operates through different mechanisms,[2] other approaches may be better suited to the study of such traditions. Yet, with some exceptions, sermons are a core feature of many prominent world religions. A plurality of the world's population is Christian, and we certainly expect the analytic utility of examining sermon content to extend to places where Christianity is prevalent. Some examples are again given in Figure 7.1. In Islam and Judaism as well, listening to sermons is a key part of lay religious experience and practice (Hirschkind, 2001). We expect that our arguments that sermons can provide metaphysical instruction, thereby inclining people to particular levels and modes of political participation, would apply also in places where Islam and Judaism are prevalent. A public discourse has already arisen around the effects of Friday sermons on participation in protest (Mackay, 2011; Maher, 2014). Our approach and findings in this book suggest that that discourse is picking up on a real empirical phenomenon.

The differences in sermon content we have described in this book touch on deep questions about the human condition that almost all religions

---

[2] For instance, practice might operate through physical conditioning or through the generation of common knowledge (Chwe, 2013).

grapple with: What is the relationship between the spiritual and physical worlds? What causes earthly problems? How does my inner life relate to my outer circumstances? Some world religions provide similar answers to the ones we observed in this book. For instance, Østebø (2015) observes themes in Sufi and Salafi sermons in contemporary West Africa that are very similar to Catholic and Pentecostal sermons, respectively. He finds that Sufi preaching places greater emphasis on problems happening systematically to people no matter their individual strength of faith, while Salafi sermons draw a tighter connection between internal faith and material circumstances.[3] Others have noted that, perhaps in response to the expansion of Pentecostalism in the last few decades, some imams in Nigeria have also adopted preaching themes that emphasize a direct link between individual faith and material change (Adogame and Shankar, 2012). Even when the answers are not exactly the same, other world religions grapple with similar questions. Scholars of Judaism, for instance, point to disagreements about the sources of earthly problems as an important theme distinguishing sermons (Simkovich, 2016). The thematic variation that we observe in this book comes from a particular faith tradition and context, but it likely has parallels in other faith traditions.

Although we expect the general approach to travel widely, some of our specific findings may be circumscribed by context, especially by levels of religious pluralism and religiosity, and by the lower political salience of religious identity cleavages. Our empirical findings are mostly drawn from places that are both highly religious and religiously plural, and where religion is not highly politically salient compared to other social identity cleavages. In this context, we found no evidence of backlash from people who heard a sermon that was not of their primary denomination (Bechtel et al., 2015). Indeed, Christians of all denominational affiliations typically responded *in the same direction* to treatment messages. That people responded to hearing sermons at all may be characteristic of a highly religious environment, where sermons are sought out and authoritative. Where religiosity is low and the religious–secular divide politicized, nontheists may not be open to metaphysical instructions that rely on religious concepts and terms (Bechtel et al., 2015; Shariff et al., 2016). In more secular contexts, one might expect to find little effect, or even a backlash, among secular individuals exposed to religious messages

---

[3] See also Meyer and Sounaye (2017); Sounaye (2014, 2017); Gumi and Tsiga (1992).

because secular individuals face a conflict between upholding their identities as nonreligious people and listening openly to religious teachings. Moreover, in a context of religious pluralism and relatively fluid social boundaries between different Christian denominations, study participants in this book may have had no reason to defy the messages they heard from denominations other than their own. By contrast, where differences in religious content instead *coincide* perfectly with political cleavages, one might expect that listeners would reject "out-group" messages as inappropriate for members of their in-group. Where political identity cleavages do not coincide with differences in religious content, listeners can be open to messages from different houses of worship without defying their group identities, but where political identity cleavages do coincide with differences in religious content, people may be more likely to reject out-group messages in order to affirm their own group allegiances. Their reactions to in-group sermons might be amplified, but their reactions to out-group sermons might be depressed or even reversed.

Whether our findings about the weekly ebb and flow of religious influence are specific to religiously plural environments is less clear. On the one hand, in less pluralistic environments, people typically encounter fewer religious messages other than their own, incidentally or by choice, so the influence of any one set of religious teachings is likely to have more "staying power" because listeners come into relatively little contact with countervailing messages outside of their own house of worship (Bartels, 2014). On the other hand, more religiously plural environments tend to be characterized by higher levels of interreligious competition (Iannaccone, 1990), such that religious leaders invest more heavily in creating opportunities to "recharge" the world views of their followers during the week, in order to beat out the competition. If religious organizations in plural environments succeed in recharging the world views of their followers more often than religious organizations in less pluralistic settings, our descriptions of the short-term effects of religious teachings on political behavior in this book might actually be an *underestimate* of the ebb and flow of religious influence more generally.

In sum, our approach of focusing on sermon content is likely to have broad applicability. Although some of our findings about the impact of specific religious teachings on political engagement might be specific to highly religious, religiously plural, and nonreligiously divided contexts, some of them might be even more evident in more religiously polarized or less pluralistic parts of the world.

UNBUNDLING RELIGION: STEPS FORWARD

This book analyzes religious influence through an examination of sermon content. This approach has its advantages and can help us understand many different religious traditions in different parts of the globe. But as we discussed several times, religion is also a bundle of things: social networks, social identity, resources, skills, and organization, as well as metaphysical ideas expressed through sermons. How do arguments about religious ideational content interact with arguments about other aspects of religion? In the introduction of the book, we outlined several approaches other scholars have taken to unbundle religion.

We suggest these other aspects of religion are likely to *interact* with the influence of religious messages, either amplifying or reducing the effects of religious teachings on political behavior. Future studies of religion and politics should thus treat religion as content-full and then examine how the influence of religion's content *interacts* with its other institutional and social features. As Djupe and Grant (2001) observed, although the organizational resources and skills that come with religious experience have received more attention in social science research, there is no necessary link between them and political views and action. Instead, "some cognitive or social process must occur before members apply church-gained skills to political endeavors" (Djupe and Gilbert, 2009, 179; cited in Glazier, 2015).[4] Religious teachings provide some of this link, shaping congregants' understanding of the world such that they apply their skills and organizational resources to politics in a particular way. Future research on the interaction of teachings and other aspects of religion would help to fully square this circle.

Having made the case in this book that exposure to religious content *can* have important consequences for political engagement, we suggest future research grapple with how religious teachings, skills, identity, networks, and organization jointly shape political behavior. In Table 7.1, we revisit the other institutional and social features of religion that we highlighted in the book's introduction, and we suggest ways in which they might interact with religious teaching content to influence political behavior. In many instances, we expect these other aspects of religion to amplify the effects of exposure to sermons. For instance, Djupe and Gilbert (2009) argue that, if anything, tighter social networks among parishioners likely

---

[4] See also Harris, 1994.

TABLE 7.1 *Possible interactions across aspects of religion.*

Variable	Interaction with content
Social network	Tight social networks likely amplify and sustain the effects of religious teachings as listeners find that others also hold those world views and hear them repeated (Djupe and Gilbert, 2009).
Social identity	Where religious content coincides with strong identity boundaries, the influence of in-group religious teachings may be amplified but the influence of out-group teachings dampened or reversed.
Firm competing for members	In pluralistic contexts, competition among religious leaders and organizations for followers may be particularly intense such that religious leaders invest additional effort not only in trying to appeal to new members but in recharging the world views of existing members. In such contexts, we might expect to see less decay in religious teachings' influence over the course of the week.
Organizing skills	The provision of organizational resources and skills would likely strengthen the connection between religious teaching content and political behavior, because it would give listeners further tools to act on the posture toward the state that the teachings encourage.
Source of social welfare	When modes of social welfare provision complement religious teaching content, social welfare provision is likely to amplify and sustain the influence of the teachings by providing repeated exposure to that world view and providing opportunity for listeners to come together collectively.
Elite directives/ mobilization	Explicit political directives may substitute for the kinds of sermonic influences described in this book; our approach underscores that religious teachings need not be explicitly political to exert influence over political behavior.
Set of practices	In religions that do not include sermons as a regular feature, sets of practices may substitute as a mechanism of conveying content; in religions with sermons as a core feature, sets of practices may lessen the ebb and flow of religious content influence by serving as reminders of recent teachings or may amplify content influence by generating common knowledge about it (Chwe, 2013).

amplify the effect of messages from the pulpit on political behavior. Djupe and Gilbert (2009) emphasize explicitly political cues from the pulpit when making this argument, but we expect the same would be true of nonpolitical sermons. As in the focus groups we conducted in Nairobi, where congregants bolstered each other's religious views when they referenced recent sermons, tight social networks are likely to amplify and "recharge" the effects of religious teachings on political behavior. Similarly, we expect that the provision of organizational resources and skills amplifies the effects of religious teachings on political behavior. As the content of the teachings shapes how people are inclined to engage in politics, the provision of organizational resources and skills facilitates the translation of those inclinations into action. Finally, we expect that intense competition for members among houses of worship, following a political economy conception of religious associations as firms (Iannaccone, 1990; Gill, 2008), could lead to more durable effects of religious teachings on behavior, as religious leaders invest more in mechanisms for frequently "recharging" the influence of their teachings on political behavior.

In some instances, we expect the interaction of religion's other features with the content of religious teaching would have mixed consequences. For example, we expect that the politicization of a religious identity cleavage would amplify the influence of in-group religious teachings on political behavior but depress the influence of out-group religious teachings on political behavior. When politicized social identity cleavages coincide with differences in religious teachings, individuals are likely to view the world views of their house of worship not only as *appealing* but also as *obligatory* and as characteristic of the world view of a prototypical in-group member that they want to emulate. In this situation, listeners are likely to be strongly influenced by in-group religious messages, and perhaps also to have that influence recharged frequently through interaction with other in-group members. However, they are likely to dismiss or react strongly *against* out-group religious teachings, which are not in keeping with their efforts to conform to in-group norms (Bechtel et al., 2015).

Weber observed that ideational theories need not *displace* other types of explanations, such as those based on interests. He famously observed that interest-based explanations are incredibly important but that "very frequently the 'world images' that have been created by 'ideas' have, *like switchmen, determined the tracks along which action has been pushed* by the dynamic of interest," (Weber, 1993, 280, emphasis added). That is, both types of explanations give us insight into social phenomena, additively and in interaction with one another.

We see our focus on sermons as a complement to, rather than a substitute for, other perspectives on religion's role in shaping political participation.[5] Religious teachings, and other ideational and cultural forces, can shape how people pursue their interests and engage in the political world around them. Even when citizens share the same end goals, religious teachings can shape the *routes* through which they pursue those interests – e.g., whether they pursue their interests with a focus on personal and leadership transformation or on reforming political structures and institutions. Religious teachings can also shape how vigorously people act on those interests. Other aspects of religion – social networks, identity, resources and skills, leaders' incentives, and so forth – are likely to moderate and, in many cases, amplify these effects. These other aspects of religion should be thought about in interaction with religion's ideational content.

BEYOND ELECTORAL PARTICIPATION

Comparative politics research on political participation and political behavior has paid a lot of attention to electoral behavior. A rich body of literature seeks to explain voter turnout and vote choice. To the extent that political science research has sought to understand the role of religion in politics, the focus has often been on understanding religion as a tool of social identity (in-group/out-group) mobilization around parties and candidates during elections (Wilkinson, 2006; Dancygier, 2017) or as an explanation for why particular political *issues* become salient in elections (Grossman, 2015; McCauley, 2015a, 2017). In some parts of the world – e.g., the United States – particular religious denominations have become "issue owners" or aligned with particular parties and mobilized partisan bloc votes (Putnam and Campbell, 2012; Koter, 2013).

In this book, we have drawn particular attention to religion's role in shaping how people participate outside of elections, how they conceive of their own role as citizens, and whether they engage in leadership development, critiques, or movements for institutional change. The participation we sought to explain was not limited to electoral behavior. We examined the possibility for critique against institutions, evaluating leaders' characters and strengths of faith, and assessing one's role as a citizen and member of society in quotidian practices. Political participation in and outside of elections varies not just in occurrence but also in kind (Verba

---

[5] See Collier (2017) for the argument that cultural explanations in general should be thought of as complements of interest-based explanations.

and Nie, 1972; Barnes and Kaase, 1979; Claggett and Pollock, 2006). Citizens can stay out of public life altogether, or they can participate to varying degrees and with various postures toward the state – sometimes participating within the rules of the game, sometimes demanding reform of those rules and structures. As Claggett and Pollock (2006) characterize it, sometimes citizens participate by *following existing rules and institutions*, and sometimes they participate instead by *challenging these rules and institutions*. Exposure to religious communication is one driver of such variation. Even outside of elections, it can shape how people think about their role as citizens and about appropriate routes to political change.

Indeed, the patterns in our study underscore that we should be looking for the influence of religion not *only* on issue positions and vote choice, or *only* through explicit political endorsements of policy issues or candidates. Sermons in our study context were more apolitical during elections than one might expect. They typically did not include endorsements of particular candidates or parties; nor did they focus on particular policy issues. In Nairobi, these patterns may have been due to religious leaders' reticence to stoke interethnic conflict in the period following the 2007–2008 elections, in which there was such violence (Deacon, 2015), but they nevertheless illustrate that even where churches do not explicitly mobilize voters, their activities are consequential for politics. As others and we have shown, vote choice in Kenya correlates highly with ethnicity (tribe-language), regardless of what religious practice voters engage in. We also do not see much divergence across religious practices in terms of issue positions. Instead, religious teachings influence other features of political life, particularly the role that citizens see for themselves outside of the electoral cycle: whether they seek to change the characters of or the external constraints on the winners of those elections; whether they see government institutions as fair or unfair; whether they take to the streets or seek voice within prescribed venues for citizen–government interaction; whether they prepare for leadership positions themselves.

Religion can of course also affect voter and issue mobilization, but we should pay more attention to nonelectoral forms of participation as well. Their configurations are important to understand because they have different implications for the nature and outcomes of state–society relations. Some forms of nonelectoral participation (contacting and making requests of officials) likely help the system, however flawed, function smoothly and do not pose dramatic challenges to incumbents. By contrast, other forms of participation (pushes for institutional reform, disobedi-

ence, protest) draw attention to structural shortcomings of existing institutions and policies and, in that pursuit, generate conflict between citizens
and officials. These variations in citizen–state relationships harken back
to Hirschman (1970)'s distinctions between exit, voice, and loyalty. One
could argue that the Pentecostal teachings discussed in this book promote
more loyal forms of public engagement – accepting existing rules and
trying to promote individual transformation within them – whereas the
Mainline Protestant and Catholic teachings we discuss lend themselves
toward voice. Other religious teachings – such as the holiness doctrines
of Pentecostal churches in the United States at the turn of the twentieth
century–likely cultivate withdrawal and disengagement. Without attention to the full constellation of public engagement during and outside of
electoral cycles, we cannot fully grasp state–society relations.

RELIGIOUS TEACHINGS AS PART OF A FAMILY
OF METAPHYSICAL MESSAGES

Religion is not alone in providing metaphysical discussions and instruction. Secular sources can provide such guidance as well. Secular self-help
books discuss how individuals can or cannot enact change in their lives.
University courses discuss cause and effect, as well as the individual and
structural sources of empirical patterns (poverty, inequality, and the like).
Novels can contribute to our notions of how the world works, and of our
place in it (Martin, 2018).

Thus, many of the arguments in this book could be applied to
nonreligious messages. Secular messages that frame earthly problems as
individually rather than structurally attributable should also encourage
citizen behavior that is more acceptant of existing political structures but
critical of individual characters, whereas secular messages that convey a
structural world view should lead people to more critical postures toward
political institutions and structures of power. Secular messages aimed at
boosting self-efficacy can increase willingness to participate in politics
(Lieberman and Zhou, 2017). Secular metaphysical discussions, though
powerful in the moment, can also recede quickly from the forefront of
people's minds (Hill et al., 2013; Bartels, 2014). In this sense, religious
teachings are not sui generis, but rather a case of the larger category
of metaphysical communication. Indeed, many features of religion have
secular equivalents. Social networks, social identity, organization, skills,

and resources are found in secular organizations. Religious teachings bear a family resemblance to secular metaphysical messages too, in this regard.

On the other hand, it is in many ways the *content* of religion that makes it religious. Within any given context, people internalize what it means to be religious within a web of cultural traditions and shared knowledge, and these contexts provide particular understandings of what is unique about religion. The sermons we examine integrate understandings of the present, physical world with understandings of the divine and of the afterlife, which similar secular messages do not. For example, in the Pentecostal teachings, imminent change is possible because God rewards individual faith both in this life and in the next; in the Mainline Protestant and Catholic teachings, God rewards actions to address structural injustice only in the next life, rather than in this one, depressing the possibility of imminent material change. In other words, the sermons we describe in this book hang together through a religious logic that is understood as such by its believers. When we take religious content seriously, we inevitably have to describe and grapple with conceptions of the divine as they are understood in context and with logics of how the spiritual and physical worlds operate and interact. Although sermons may be one case in a larger category of metaphysical instruction and of elite messaging, they are a case that cannot be fully described or understood without taking contextually grounded conceptions of the spiritual world seriously.

Religious teachings are one of the most ubiquitous and regular forms of elite communication in the world. They are thus worthy of study simply so that scholars of political communication have a better understanding of elite messaging effects from one of their most common forms. Certain types of logics may be more straightforwardly expressed with the backing of religious concepts that have meaning and substance to believers in that context: positive thinking and material change might be difficult to link together without conceptions of the divine. For all of these reasons, we should be incorporating religious communication into more general lines of research on political communication.

* * *

Just as Weber argued that religious teachings do not need to be explicitly economic to have economic consequences, this book has argued that religious teachings do not need to be explicitly political to have political implications. Sermons engage in metaphysical discussions that can then shape citizens' responses to political affairs absent any mention of specific leaders, policies, or political issues and absent explicit political directions

(Ellis and Ter Haar, 1998). The specific metaphysical answers religion provides can shape citizens' attributions of responsibility for political problems as well as their sense of agency to enact political change. These inclinations can then be catalyzed into particular types of political action.

The prediction of many modernization scholars was that religion would gradually lose its place and importance in the public sphere as societies urbanize and industrialize. Instead, religion continues to play a major role in many countries, through heterogeneous practices, beliefs, messages, and experiences. In many parts of the world, people are more religious now than ever. Religion continues to be a major presence in the most dense and complex cities around the world. Religions – both new and old – seem to keep pace with the concerns and anxieties of individuals in urbanizing environments such that religion remains as important as ever.

That religion is still such a core part of the lives of ordinary citizens demands a rigorous grappling with the role that religion plays in shaping social and political behavior. It demands a grappling with the role of religion in politics, even where religious content is not explicitly political and even where religions are increasingly separated from the arm of the state. This book has taken up calls for more research in this vein (Bellin, 2008; Grzymala-Busse, 2016, 2012) and argued for treating religion as content-full. We have paid particular attention to the influence of sermons on ordinary citizens' political engagement since sermons are such a central part of lay religious experience. We showed how exposure to sermons – as one form in which religious teachings are communicated – can shape political engagement even when that communication is not explicitly political, when almost everyone is religious, and when religious identity attachments are not the primary identities structuring candidate and policy preferences. In addressing deep metaphysical questions, sermons can influence listeners' inclination to criticize existing institutions, structures, and rules of the game, or to seek individual and personnel transformation within that system. Like the influence of other forms of elite communication, the influence of sermons requires reinforcement to sustain their effect, but if we want to improve our understanding of political participation and state–society relations, we should be paying attention to it. This book has provided a template for how to do so – one that is not specific to Africa or to Christianity – and we call for more research in this vein to address the diversity and complexity that religion presents in the contemporary world.

References

ACHAP, Africa Christian Health Associations Platform. 2008. Contribution of Christian Health Networks to the National Health Sector in Select African Countries. Technical report Africa Christian Health Associations Platform website.

Adida, Claire, Jessica Gottlieb, Erica Kramon, and Gwyneth McClendon. 2017. "Reducing or Reinforcing In-Group Preferences? An Experiment on Information and Ethnic Voting." *Quarterly Journal of Political Science* 12(4): 437–477.

Adogame, Afe, Roswith Gerloff, and Klaus Hock. 2008. *Christianity in Africa and the African Diaspora: The Appropriation of a Scattered Heritage*. A&C Black.

Adogame, Afe and Shobana Shankar. 2012. *Religion on the Move!: New Dynamics of Religious Expansion in a Globalizing World*. Brill Academic Publishers.

Alava, Henni and Jimmy Spire Ssentongo. 2016. "Religious (De) Politicisation in Uganda's 2016 Elections." *Journal of Eastern African Studies* 10(4): 677–692.

Ankrah, Canon Kodwo E. 1998. *Development and the Church of Uganda: Mission, Myths and Metaphors*. Action Publishers.

ARHAP, African Religious Health Assets Programme. 2006. Appreciating Assets: The Contribution of Religion to Universal Access in Africa. Technical report African Religious Health Assets Programme, report for the World Health Organization Cape Town.

2008. The Contribution of Religious Entities to Health in Sub-Saharan Africa. Technical report African Religious Health Assets Programme, Study commissioned by the B&M Gates Foundation Cape Town.

Asamoah-Gyadu, Johnson Kwabena. 2005. *African Charismatics: Current Developments within Independent Indigenous Pentecostalism in Ghana*. Brill Academic Publishers.

Atuhair, Scovia, Alex Ashaba, and Felix Basiime. 2018. "Uganda: Bishop Tells President Museveni to Step Down Peacefull." *The Monitor* 02. http://allafrica.com/stories/201802100159.html.

Barkan, Joel D. 2008. "Legislatures on the Rise?" *Journal of Democracy* 19(2):124–137.

Barnes, Samuel and Max Kaase. 1979. *Political Action: Mass Participation in Five Western Democracies.* Sage.

Barro, Robert, Jason Hwang, and Rachel McCleary. 2010. "Religious Conversion in 40 Countries." *Journal for the Scientific Study of Religion* 49(1):15–36.

Bartels, Larry M. 2014. "Remembering to Forget: A Note on the Duration of Campaign Advertising Effects." *Political Communication* 31(4):532–544.

Bassett, Carolyn. 2008. "The South African People's Budget Campaign as a Challenge to Neoliberal Policy Framework and Methodology." In *Neoliberalism and Globalization in Africa*, ed. Joseph Mensah. Springer, pp. 221–239.

Bassi, Anna and K. Williams. 2017. "Weather, Risk and Voting: An Experimental Analysis of the Effect of Weather on Vote Choice." *Journal of Experimental Political Science* 6(1):17–32.

Bechtel, Michael M., Jens Hainmueller, Dominik Hangartner, and Marc Helbling. 2015. "Reality Bites: The Limits of Framing Effects for Salient and Contested Policy Issues." *Political Science Research and Methods* 3(3):683–695.

Beck, Linda. 2008. *Brokering Democracy in Africa: The Rise of Clientelist Democracy in Senegal.* Springer.

Bellin, Eva. 2008. "Faith in Politics: New Trends in the Study of Religion and Politics." *World Politics* 60(2):315–347.

Ben-Nun Bloom, Pazit, Gizem Arikan, and Marie Courtemanche. 2015. "Religious Social Identity, Religious Belief, and Anti-Immigration Sentiment." *American Political Science Review* 109(02):203–221.

Benn, Christoph. 2003. "Why Religious Health Assets Matter. " *ARHAP: Assets and Agency Colloquium, Assets and Agency Colloquium, African Religious Health Assets Programme (ARHAP)* 40:3–11.

Benoit, Kenneth, Drew Conway, Benjamin Lauderdale, and Michael Laver. 2016. "Crowd-Sourced Text Analysis: Reproducible and Agile Production of Political Data." *American Political Science Review* 110(2):278–295.

Berge, Lars Ivar Oppedal, et al. 2017. "Ethnically Biased? Experimental Evidence from Kenya." *Working Paper.*

Blair, Graeme, Rebecca Littman, and Elizabeth Levy Paluck. 2019. "Motivating the Adoption of New Community-Minded Behaviors: An Empirical Test in Nigeria." Science Advances 5(3) DOI: 10.1126/sciadv.aaau5175.

Bleck, Jaimie and Nicolas Van de Walle. 2013. "Valence Issues in African Elections: Navigating Uncertainty and the Weight of the Past." *Comparative Political Studies* 46(11):1394–1421.

Boas, Taylor Chase. 2014. "Pastor Paulo vs. Doctor Carlos: Professional Titles as Voting Heuristics in Brazil." *Journal of Politics in Latin America* 6(2):39–72.

Bompani, Barbara. 2016. "'For God and for My Country': Pentecostal-Charismatic Churches and the Framing of a New Political Discourse in Uganda." In *Public Religion and the Politics of Homosexuality in Africa*, eds. Adriaan van Klinken and Ezra Chitando. Ashgate, pp. 19–34.

Bongmba, Elias Kifon. 2012. *The Wiley-Blackwell Companion to African Religions*. Vol. 58. John Wiley & Sons.

Botha, Nico and Peter Maruping. 2013. "Reformed Christianity and the Confession of Accra: A Conversation about Unavoidable Questions in the Quest for Justice." *Studia Historiae Ecclesiasticae* 39: www.scielo.org.za/scielo.php?script=sci_arttext&pid=S1017-04992013000100009&lng=en&tlng=en.

Brady, Henry E., Sidney Verba, and Kay Lehman Schlozman. 1995. "Beyond SES: A Resource Model of Political Participation." *American Political Science Review* 89(2):271–294.

Branch, Daniel. 2010. "Kenya's Referendum: 'In the Name of God, No!'." *Open Democracy* August 17. www.opendemocracy.net/en/kenyas-referendum-in-name-of-god-no/.

Brass, Paul R. 1997. *Theft of an Idol: Text and Context in the Representation of Collective Violence*. Princeton University Press.

Bratton, Michael and Mwangi S. Kimenyi. 2008. "Voting in Kenya: Putting Ethnicity in Perspective." *Journal of Eastern African Studies* 2(2):272–289.

Bratton, Michael and Nicholas Van de Walle. 1997. *Democratic Experiments in Africa: Regime Transitions in Comparative Perspective*. Cambridge University Press.

Bryan, Gharad T., James J. Choi, and Dean Karlan. 2018. Randomizing Religion: The Impact of Protestant Evangelism on Economic Outcomes. Working Paper National Bureau of Economic Research.

Burgess, Richard. 2014. "Pentecostals and Politics in Nigeria and Zambia."

2015. "Pentecostals and Politics in Nigeria and Zambia: An Historical Perspective." In *Pentecostalism in Africa*. ed. Martin Lindhardt. Brill, pp. 291–321.

Burgess, Richard. 2015. "Pentecostalism and Democracy in Nigeria." *Nova Religio: The Journal of Alternative and Emergent Religions* 18(3):38–62.

Cagé, Julia and Valeria Rueda. 2016. "The Long-Term Effects of the Printing Press in Sub-Saharan Africa." *American Economic Journal: Applied Economics* 8(3):69–99.

Callaghy, Thomas M. 1987. "The State as Lame Leviathan: The Patrimonial Administrative State in Africa." In *The African State in Transition*, ed. Zaki Ergas. Palgrave Macmillan Limited, pp. 87–116.

Cammett, Melani. 2014. *Compassionate Communalism: Welfare and Sectarianism in Lebanon*. Cornell University Press.

Cammett, Melani and Sukriti Issar. 2010. "Bricks and Mortar Clientelism: Sectarianism and the Logics of Welfare Allocation in Lebanon." *World Politics* 62(3):381–421.

Campbell, David E. 2004. "Acts of Faith: Churches and Political Engagement." *Political Behavior* 26(2):155–180.

Caprara, Gian Vittorio, Michele Vecchione, Cristina Capanna, and Minou Mebane. 2009. "Perceived Political Self-Efficacy: Theory, Assessment, and Applications." *European Journal of Social Psychology* 39:1002–1020.

Carbone, Giovanni M. 2003. "Political Parties in a 'No-Party Democracy': Hegemony and Opposition under 'Movement Democracy' in Uganda." *Party Politics* 9(4):485–501.

Carmody, Brendan. 2002. "The Catholic Church and Zambia's Elections." *America* 186(7):13–15.

Carney, Jay. 2017. "Faithful Citizenship in the USA and Uganda: A Comparative Analysis of Recent Catholic Pastoral Letters on Politics." *Journal of Religion and Society* 14:80–95.

Chaves, Mark. 1993. "Denominations as Dual Structures: An Organizational Analysis." *Sociology of Religion* 54(2):147–169.

Cheyeka, Austin. 2012. "A Layman's Appreciation of the Indigenous Roman Catholic Diocesan Priest in a 'Church in Transition' in Zambia." *Journal of Contemporary Issues* 29:17–32.

2016. "Zambia, a "Christian Nation" in Post Movement for Multiparty Democracy (MMD) Era, 2011–2016." *International Journal of Humanities and Social Science* 6(7):159–172.

Cheyeka, Austin, Marja Hinfelaar, and Bernhard Udelhoven. 2014. "The Changing Face of Zambia's Christianity and Its Implications for the Public Sphere: A Case Study of Bauleni Township, Lusaka." *Journal of Southern African Studies* 40(5):1031–1045.

Chhibber, Pradeep. 2014. *Religious Practice and Democracy in India.* Cambridge University Press.

Chhibber, Pradeep and Jasjeet S. Sekhon. 2015. "The Asymmetric Role of Religious Appeals in India." *Working Paper.*

Chwe, Michael Suk-Young. 2013. *Rational Ritual: Culture, Coordination, and Common Knowledge.* Princeton University Press.

Cilliers, Jacobus, Oeindrila Dube, and Bilal Siddiqi. 2015. "The White-Man Effect: How Foreigner Presence Affects Behavior in Experiments." *Journal of Economic Behavior & Organization* 118:397–414.

Claggett, William and Philip H. Pollock. 2006. "The Modes of Participation Revisited, 1980–2004." *Political Research Quarterly* 59(4):593–600.

Collier, Paul. 2017. "Culture, Politics, and Economic Development." *Annual Review of Political Science* 20:111–125.

Comaroff, Jean. 2012. "Pentecostalism, Populism and the New Politics of Affect." In *Pentecostalism and Development: Churches, NGOs and Social Change in Africa*, ed. Dena Freeman. Palgrave Macmillan, pp. 41–66. p. 41.

Cooke, Jennifer G. 2015. *Religious Authority and the State in Africa.* Rowman & Littlefield.

Cooper, Barbara M. 2006. *Evangelical Christians in the Muslim Sahel.* Indiana University Press.

Cottee, Simon. 2016. "What's the Right Way to Think about Religion and ISIS?" *The Atlantic*, July 12.

Dancygier, Rafaela M. 2017. *Dilemmas of Inclusion: Muslims in European Politics.* Princeton University Press.

Daughton, James Patrick and James Patrick Daughton. 2008. *An Empire Divided: Religion, Republicanism, and the Making of French Colonialism, 1880–1914.* Oxford University Press.

De La O, Ana Lorena and Jonathan A. Rodden. 2008. "Does Religion Distract the Poor?: Income and Issue Voting around the World." *Comparative Political Studies* 41(4):437.

Deacon, Gregory. 2015. "Driving the Devil Out: Kenya's Born-Again Election." *Journal of Religion in Africa* 45(2):200–220.

Deacon, Gregory and Gabrielle Lynch. 2013. "Allowing Satan in? Moving toward a Political Economy of Neo-Pentecostalism in Kenya." *Journal of Religion in Africa* 43(2):108–130.

DiMaggio, Paul. 1997. "Culture and Cognition." *Annual Review of Sociology* 23(1):263–287.

Djupe, Paul A. and Brian R. Calfano. 2013a. *God Talk: Experimenting with the Religious Causes of Public Opinion*. Temple University Press.

2013b. "Divine Intervention? The Influence of Religious Value Communication on US Intervention Policy." *Political Behavior* 35(4):643–663.

Djupe, Paul A. and Christopher P. Gilbert. 2003. *The Prophetic Pulpit: Clergy, Churches, and Communities in American Politics*. Rowman & Littlefield.

2009. *The Political Influence of Churches*. Cambridge University Press.

Djupe, Paul A. and J. Tobin Grant. 2001. "Religious Institutions and Political Participation in America." *Journal for the Scientific Study of Religion* 40(2): 303–314.

Dowd, Robert A. 2015. *Christianity, Islam, and Liberal Democracy: Lessons from Sub-Saharan Africa*. Oxford University Press.

Dowd, Robert A. and Michael Driessen. 2008. "Ethnically Dominated Party Systems and the Quality of Democracy: Evidence from Sub-Saharan Africa." *Afrobarometer Working Paper # 92*.

Downie, Richard. 2015. "Religion and the State in Uganda: Co-optation and Compromise." In *Religious Authority and the State in Africa*, ed. Jennifer Cooke, Center for Strategic and International Studies. Rowman & Littlefield, pp. 29–48.

Driskell, Robyn, Elizabeth Embry, and Larry Lyon. 2008. "Faith and Politics: The Influence of Religious Beliefs on Political Participation." *Social Science Quarterly* 89(2):294–314.

Durkheim, Emile. 1912. *The Elementary Forms of Religious Life*. Oxford University Press.

Economist. 2006. "Hallelujah! The Rise of Pentecostalism Could Change the Face of Kenya." July 22:46.

2017. "The Impact of Religion on Mugabe: The Best and Worst of Organized Christianity." *The Economist*, November 20.

Ekeh, Peter P. 1975. "Colonialism and the Two Publics in Africa: A Theoretical Statement." *Comparative Studies in Society and History* 17(1):91–112.

Ellis, Stephen and Gerrie Ter Haar. 1998. "Religion and Politics in Sub-Saharan Africa." *Journal of Modern African Studies* 36(2):175–201.

Elolia, Samuel K. 2012. "Religion and the Road to Democracy in Kenya." In *Religion, Conflict, and Democracy in Modern Africa: The Role of Civil Society in Political Engagement*, ed. Samuel K. Elolia. Wipf and Stock Publishers, pp. 101–130.

England, Andrew. 2005. "Self-Help Books Take a Grip on Kenya's Middle Class." *Financial Times*, 18 October.

Englebert, Pierre. 2002. *State Legitimacy and Development in Africa*. Lynne Rienner Publishers.

Englund, Harri. 2011. *Christianity and Public Culture in Africa*. Ohio University Press.

Enke, Benjamin. 2017. Kinship Systems, Cooperation and the Evolution of Culture. Working Paper National Bureau of Economic Research.

Fantini, Emanuele. 2013. "Transgression and Acquiescence: The Moral Conflict of Pentecostals in Their Relationship with the Ethiopian State." *PentecoStudies* 12:198–223.

Farley, Harry. 2017. "Zimbabwe: Who Is the Catholic Priest behind Robert Mugabe." *Christian Today*, November.

Fernandes, Sujatha. 2009. "Ethnicity, Civil Society, and the Church: The Politics of Evangelical Christianity in Northeast India." In *Evangelical Christianity and Democracy in Asia*, ed. David Lumsdaine. Oxford University Press, pp. 131–153.

Fox, Jonathan. 2015. *Political Secularism, Religion, and the State: A Time Series Analysis of Worldwide Data*. Cambridge University Press.

Freeman, Dana. 2012. "The Pentecostal Ethic and the Spirit of Development." In *Pentecostalism and Development: Churches, NGOs and Social Change in Africa*, ed. Dana Freeman. Palgrave Macmillan, pp. 1–40.

Freston, Paul. 2001. *Evangelicals and Politics in Asia, Africa, and Latin America*. Cambridge University Press.

2013. "Pentecostals and Politics in Latin America." *Spirit and Power: The Growth and Global Impact of Pentecostalism*, pp. 101–118.

Frykberg, Mel. 2017. "Congo Opposition Leader Set to Challenge Kabila." Cape Times, September 4.

Gakuru, Griphus. 2016. "The Church of Uganda and Speaking Truth to Power: Lessons from Nathan the Prophet." *Mission Theology in the Anglican Communion*. www.missiontheologyanglican.org/article-mt/church-of-uganda-speaking-truth-to-power-lessons-from-nathan-the-prophet/.

Gallego, Francisco A. and Robert Woodberry. 2010. "Christian Missionaries and Education in Former African Colonies: How Competition Mattered." *Journal of African Economies* 19(3):294–329.

Garrard, D.J. 2003. Kenya. In *The New International Dictionary of Pentecostal and Charismatic Movements*, eds. M. Stanley Burgess and E. Van Der Maas. Zondervan, pp. 150–155.

Garrow, David J. 1986. *Bearing the Cross: Martin Luther King Jr., and the Southern Christian Leadership Conference*. Open Road Media.

Geertz, Clifford. 1973. *The Interpretation of Cultures*. Basic Books.

Gerber, Alan S., James G. Gimpel, Donald P. Green, and Daron R. Shaw. 2011. "How Large and Long-Lasting Are the Persuasive Effects of Televised Campaign Ads? Results from a Randomized Field Experiment." *American Political Science Review* 105(01):135–150.

Gerring, John. 2006. *Case Study Research: Principles and Practices*. Cambridge University Press.

Ghana News Agency. 2015. "Christian Youth Being Equipped to Help Develop Africa." August 28.

Ghanian Times. 2016. "Grace Baptist Church Launches Anti-Corruption Campaign." *Ghanaian Times*, September 2.

Gibson, James. 1995. "The Resilience of Mass Support for Democratic Institutions and Pro Nascent Russian and Ukrainian Democracies." In *Political Culture and in Russia and the New States of Eurasia*, ed. V. Tismaneanu. M. E. Sharpe, pp. 53–111.

Gifford, Paul. 1991. *The New Crusaders: Christianity and the New Right in Southern Africa*. Pluto Press.

1994. "Some Recent Developments in African Christianity." *African Affairs* 93:513–534.

1995. *The Christian Churches and the Democratisation of Africa*. Brill Academic Publishers.

1998. "Chiluba's Christian Nation: Christianity as a Factor in Zambian Politics 1991–1996." *Journal of Contemporary Religion* 13(3):363–381.

2004. *Ghana's New Christianity: Pentecostalism in a Globalizing Economy*. Indiana University Press.

2009. *Christianity, Politics and Public Life in Kenya*. C. Hurst & Co.

2015. *Christianity, Development and Modernity in Africa*. Hurst.

Giles, Jim and Michael Hopkin. 2005. "Psychologists Warn of More Suicide Attacks in the Wake of London Bombs." *Nature* 436(7049):308–309.

Gill, Anthony. 2001. "Religion and Comparative Politics." *Annual Review of Political Science* 4(1):117–138.

2004. "Weber in Latin America: Is Protestant Growth Enabling the Consolidation of Democratic Capitalism?" *Democratization* 11(4):42–65.

2008. *Rendering unto Caesar: The Catholic Church and the State in Latin America*. University of Chicago Press.

Githae, Wanjohi. 2016. "Kenya: New Rules Seek to Rein in Errant Religious Leaders." *Daily Nation*, 3 January. https://allafrica.com/stories/201601042090.html.

Glazier, Rebecca A. 2013. "Divine Direction: How Providential Religious Beliefs Shape Foreign Policy Attitudes." *Foreign Policy Analysis* 9(2):127–142.

2015. "Bridging Religion and Politics: The Impact of Providential Religious Beliefs on Political Activity." *Politics and Religion* 8(3):458–487.

Gonzalez, David. 2007. "A Sliver of a Storefront, a Faith on the Rise." *New York Times*, January 14.

Grimmer, Justin and Brandon M. Stewart. 2013. "Text as Data: The Promise and Pitfalls of Automatic Content Analysis Methods for Political Texts." *Political Analysis* 21(3):267–297.

Grossman, Guy. 2015. "The Political Saliency of LGBTs in Sub-Saharan Africa." *Journal of Politics* 77(2):337–351.

Grossman, Guy, Macartan Humphreys, and Gabriella Sacramone-Lutz. 2014. "'I wld like u WMP to extend electricity 2 our village': On Information Technology and Interest Articulation." *American Political Science Review* 108(03):688–705.

Grzymala-Busse, Anna. 2012. "Why Comparative Politics Should Take Religion (More) Seriously." *Annual Review of Political Science* 15:421–442.

2015. *Nations under God: How Churches Use Moral Authority to Influence Policy*. Princeton University Press.

2016. "The Difficulty with Doctrine: How Religion Can Influence Politics." *Government and Opposition* 51(2):327.

Gumi, Abubakar Mahmud and Ismaila Abubakar Tsiga. 1992. Where I Stand. Spectrum Books.

Gusman, Alessandro. 2009. "HIV/AIDS, Pentecostal Churches, and the 'Joseph Generation' in Uganda." *Africa Today* 56(1):67–86.

Güth, James L., John C. Green, Corwin E. Smidt, Lyman A. Kellstedt, and Margaret M. Poloma. 1997. *The Bully Pulpit: The Politics of Protestant Clergy*. University Press of Kansas.

Güth, James L., Lyman A. Kellstedt, John C. Green and Corwin E. Smidt. 2002. "A Distant Thunder? Religious Mobilization in the 2000 Elections. In *Interest Group politics*. Vol. 6, eds. Allan J. Cigler and Burdett A. Loomis. CQ Press, pp. 161–184.

Gyimah-Boadi, Emmanuel and Daniel Armah Attoh. 2009. "Are Democratic Citizens Emerging in Africa?" *Afrobarometer Working Paper Series*.

Habyarimana, James, Macartan Humphreys, Daniel N. Posner, and Jeremy M. Weinstein. 2009. *Coethnicity: Diversity and the Dilemmas of Collective Action*. Russell Sage Foundation.

Hale, Christopher W. 2018. "Religious Institutions and Collective Action: The Catholic Church and Political Activism in Indigenous Chiapas and Yucatán." *Politics and Religion* 11(1):27–54.

Hall, Stuart. 1980. "Cultural Studies: Two Paradigms." *Media, Culture & Society* 2(1):57–72.

Harris, Fredrick C. 1994. "Something Within: Religion as a Mobilizer of African-American Political Activism." *Journal of Politics* 56:42–68.

Harvey, Paul. 2016. "Civil Rights Movements and Religion in America." *Oxford Research Encyclopedia of Religion*, ed. John Barton. Oxford University Press. DOI: 10.1093/acrefore/9780199340378.013.492.

Haynes, Jeffrey. 1996. *Religion and Politics in Africa*. Zed Books.

Herald (Harare). 2018. "The Cult of Nelson Chamisa's Personality." November 28.

Hill, Seth J., James Lo, Lynn Vavreck, and John Zaller. 2013. "How Quickly We Forget: The Duration of Persuasion Effects from Mass Communication." *Political Communication* 30(4):521–547.

Hirschkind, Charles. 2001. "The Ethics of Listening: Cassette-Sermon Audition in Contemporary Egypt." *American Ethnologist* 28(3):623–649.

Hirschman, Albert O. 1970. *Exit, Voice, and Loyalty: Responses to Decline in Firms, Organizations, and States*. Vol. 25. Harvard University Press.

Holbein, John B. 2017. "Childhood Skill Development and Adult Political Participation." *American Political Science Review* 111(3):572–583.

Horowitz, Donald L. 1985. *Ethnic Groups in Conflict*. University of California Press.

Huckfeldt, R. Robert and John Sprague. 1995. *Citizens, Politics and Social Communication: Information and Influence in an Election Campaign.* Cambridge University Press.

Huntington, Samuel P. 1997. *The Clash of Civilizations and the Remaking of World Order.* Penguin Books India.

Hurd, Elizabeth Shakman. 2015. *Beyond Religious Freedom: The New Global Politics of Religion.* Princeton University Press.

Iannaccone, Laurence R. 1990. "Religious Practice: A Human Capital Approach." *Journal for the Scientific Study of Religion* 29(3):297–314.

Inglehart, Ronald and Pippa Norris. 2011. *Sacred and Secular.* Cambridge University Press.

Isichei, Elizabeth. 1995. *A History of Christianity in Africa: From Antiquity to the Present.* Wm. B. Eerdmans Publishing.

James, William. 2003. *The Varieties of Religious Experience: A Study in Human Nature.* Routledge.

Jennings, Michael. 2014. Bridging the Local and the Global: Faith-Based Organisations and the Emergence of the Non-State Provider Sector in Tanzania. In *The Politics of Non-State Social Welfare in the Global South*, eds. Lauren Maclean and Melani Cammett. Cornell University Press, pp. 119–136.

Jo, Donghee. 2017. "Better the Devil You Know: An Online Experiment on News Consumption." *Working Paper Massachusetts Institute of Technology.*

Johnson, Todd M. and Gina A. Zerlo, eds. 2015. *World Christian Database.* Brill.

Jones-Correa, Michael A. and David L. Leal. 2001. "Political Participation: Does Religion Matter?" *Political Research Quarterly* 54(4):751–770.

Jost, John T., Carlee Beth Hawkins, Brian A. Nosek, et al. 2014. "Belief in a Just God (and a Just Society): A System Justification Perspective on Religious Ideology." *Journal of Theoretical and Philosophical Psychology* 34(1):56.

Jost, John T., Julia Becker, Danny Osborne, and Vivienne Badaan. 2017. "Missing in (Collective) Action: Ideology, System Justification, and the Motivational Antecedents of Two Types of Protest Behavior." *Current Directions in Psychological Science* 26(2):99–108.

Jubilee Centre. 2006. "Memorandum of Understanding: Engaging Politicians in Community Development." http://mczambia. http://files.wordpress.com/2007/02/jc-case-study-memorandum-of-understanding.pdf.

Kabukuru, Wanjohi. 2013. "Uhuru and the Catholic Connection." *New African* 257. https://newafricanmagazine.com/news-analysis/politics/uhuru-and-the-catholic-connection/.

Kalu, Ogbu. 2008. *African Pentecostalism.* Oxford University Press.

2013. *African Christianity: An African Story.* Deptartment of Church History, University of Pretoria.

Kalyvas, Stathis N. 1996. *The Rise of Christian Democracy in Europe.* Cornell University Press.

Karanja, John. 2008. "Evangelical Attitudes toward Democracy in Kenya." In *Evangelical Christianity and Democracy in Africa*, ed. Terence O. Ranger. Oxford University Press, pp. 67–93.

Kasozi, A. 1994. *Social Origins of Violence in Uganda, 1964–1985.* McGill-Queen's Press-MQUP.

Kassimir, Ronald. 1998. "The Social Power of Religious Organization and Civil Society: The Catholic Church in Uganda." *Commonwealth & Comparative Politics* 36(2):54–83.

Katongole, M. Emmanuel. 2012. "Violence and Social Imagination: Rethinking Religion and Politics in Africa?" In *Religion Conflict and Democracy in Modern Africa: The Role of Civil Society in Political Engagement,* ed. Samuel L. Eliola. Wipf & Stock, pp. 21–50.

Kavulla, Travis R. 2008. "'Our Enemies Are God's Enemies': The Religion and Politics of Bishop Margaret Wanjiru, MP." *Journal of Eastern African Studies* 2(2):254–263.

Kellstedt, Lyman A. and Corwin E. Smidt. 1993. "Doctrinal Beliefs and Political Behavior: Views of the Bible. In *Rediscovering the Religious Factor in American Politics,* eds. David C. Leege and Lyman A. Kellstedt. Routledge, pp. 177–198.

Kellstedt, Lyman A. and John C. Green. 1993. "Knowing God's Many People: Denominational Preference and Political Behavior." In *Rediscovering the Religious Factor in American Politics,* eds. David Leege and Lyman Kellstedt. Rutledge, pp. 53–71.

Kenyatta, Jomo. 2015. *Facing Mount Kenya: The Traditional Life of the Gikuyu.* Vol. 219. East African Educational Publishers.

Kirsch, Thomas G. 2003. "Church, Bureaucracy, and State: Bureaucratic Formalization in a Pentecostal Church of Zambia." *Zeitschrift für Ethnologie* 128(2):213–231.

Kiwanuka, M. Semakula. 1970. "Colonial Policies and Administrations in Africa: The Myths of the Contrasts." *African Historical Studies* 3(2):295–315.

Knighton, Ben. 2009. *Religion and Politics in Kenya: Essays in Honor of a Meddlesome Priest.* Springer.

Kombo, James and Julius Gogo. 2012. "The Role of the Church in the Provision of Early Childhood Education in Nairobi Province, Kenya." *Daystar University Working Paper Series 2012/004.*

Koter, Dominika. 2013. "King Makers: Local Leaders and Ethnic Politics in Africa." *World Politics* 65(2):187–232.

Krosnick, Jon A. 1989. "Attitude Importance and Attitude Accessibility." *Personality and Social Psychology Bulletin* 15(3):297–308.

Krosnick, Jon A., David S. Boninger, Yao C. Chuang, Matthew K. Berent, and Catherine G Carnot. 1993. "Attitude Strength: One Construct or Many Related Constructs?" *Journal of Personality and Social Psychology* 65(6):1132.

Kunda, Ziva. 1990. "The Case for Motivated Reasoning." *Psychological Bulletin* 108(3):480.

Laitin, David D. 1986. *Hegemony and Culture: Politics and Change among the Yoruba.* University of Chicago Press.

Leeper, Thomas J. 2016. "How Does Treatment Self-Selection Affect Inferences about Political Communication?" *Journal of Experimental Political Science* 4(1):21–33.

Leight, Jessica, Rohini Pande, and Laura Ralston. 2016. "Value for Money in Purchasing Votes? Vote-Buying and Voting Behavior in the Laboratory." *USAID Research and Innovation Grants Working Paper Series.*

Levine, Daniel and Scott Mainwaring. 1989. "Religion and Popular Protest in Latin America: Contrasting Experiences." In *Power and Popular Protest: Latin American Social Movements*, ed. Susan Eckstein. University of California Press, pp. 203–240.

Levine, Daniel H. 1986. *Religion and Political Conflict in Latin America.* UNC Press Books.

Levitsky, Steven and Lucan A. Way. 2010. *Competitive Authoritarianism: Hybrid Regimes after the Cold War.* Cambridge University Press.

Levitt, Steven D. and John A. List. 2007. "What Do Laboratory Experiments Measuring Social Preferences Reveal about the Real World?" *Journal of Economic Perspectives* 21(2):153–174.

Lewis, Valerie A., Carol Ann MacGregor, and Robert D. Putnam. 2013. "Religion, Networks, and Neighborliness: The Impact of Religious Social Networks on Civic Engagement." *Social Science Research* 42(2):331–346.

Lieberman, Evan S. 2009. *Boundaries of Contagion: How Ethnic Politics Have Shaped Government Responses to AIDS.* Princeton University Press.

Lieberman, Evan S. and Yang-Yang Zhou. 2017. "Efficacy and Active Citizenship in Development: Experimental Evidence on Validated Participation in Tanzania." *Working Paper Princeton University.*

Lipset, Seymour Martin and Stein Rokkan. 1967. *Party Systems and Voter Alignments: Cross-National Perspectives.* Free Press.

Lloyd, John. 2008. "Uganda's Controversial Pastors." *Financial Times,* October 24.

Logan, Carolyn and Robert Sentamu. 2007. "Kenyans and Democracy: What Do They Really Want from It Anyway?" *Afrobarometer Working Paper Series* 70.

Longman, Timothy. 2009. *Christianity and Genocide in Rwanda.* Cambridge University Press.

Lowes, Sara, Nathan Nunn, James A. Robinson, and Jonathan L. Weigel. 2017. "The Evolution of Culture and Institutions: Evidence from the Kuba Kingdom." *Econometrica* 85(4):1065–1091.

Luhrmann, Tanya M. 2012. *When God Talks Back: Understanding the American Evangelical Relationship with God.* Vintage.

Lusaka Times. 2013. "President Michael Sata Response to Catholic Bishops' Pastoral Letter." *Lusaka Times,* February 1.

Mackay, Mairi. 2011. "Prayer and Politics: How Friday Became the Middle East's Day of Protest." *CNN,* June 17.

Maher, Ahmed. 2014. "Egypt Mosques: Weekly Sermon Themes Set by Government." *BBC World News* 31 January.

Maluleke, Tinyiko Sam. 1997. "Half a Century of African Christian Theologies: Elements of the Emerging Agenda for the Twenty-First Century." *Journal of Theology for Southern Africa* 99:4–23.

Manson, Katrina. 2014. "Thousands Gather for Kenyan Rally." *Financial Times,* July 7.

Margolis, Michele F. 2017. "How Politics Affects Religion: Partisanship, Social-ization, and Religiosity in America." *Journal of Politics* 80(1):30–43.

Marshall, Ruth. 2009. *Political Spiritualities: The Pentecostal Revolution in Nigeria*. University of Chicago Press.

Martin, Cathie Jo. 2018. "Imagine All the People: Literature, Society and Cross-National Variation in Education Systems." *World Politics* 70(3):398–442.

Martin, David. 1990. *Tongues of Fire: The Explosion of Protestantism in Latin America*. Basil Blackwell.

    2002. *Pentecostalism: The World Their Parish*. Blackwell Publishers.

Martin, Lucy. 2014. "Taxation, Loss Aversion, and Accountability: Theory and Experimental Evidence for Taxation's Effect on Citizen Behavior." *Working Paper Yale University*.

Masoud, Tarek, Amaney Jamal, and Elizabeth Nugent. 2016. "Using the Qur'ān to Empower Arab Women? Theory and Experimental Evidence from Egypt." *Comparative Political Studies* 49(12):1555–1598.

Mathangani, Patrick. 2003. "How Bishops Rate Kibaki." *East African Standard*, November 26:1–2.

Maupeu, Hervé. 2007. "The Role of Religious Institutions." In *The General Elections in Kenya, 2007*, ed. Jerome Lafargue. Mkuki Na Nyota Publishers, p. 311.

Maxwell, David. 2000. "'Catch the Cockerel before Dawn': Pentecostalism and Politics in Post-Colonial Zimbabwe." *Africa* 70(2):249–277.

    2013. "Social Mobility and Politics in African Pentecostal Modernity." In *Global Pentecostalism in the 21st Century*, ed. Robert W. Hefner. Indiana University Press, pp. 91–114.

McCauley, John. 2015a. "The Political Mobilization of Ethnic and Religious Identities in Africa." *American Political Science Review* 108(04):801–816.

McCauley, John F. 2013. "Africa's New Big Man Rule? Pentecostalism and Patronage in Ghana." *African Affairs* 112:1–21.

    2014. "Pentecostalism as an Informal Political Institution: Experimental Evidence from Ghana." *Politics and Religion* 7(04):761–787.

    2017. *The Logic of Ethnic and Religious Conflict in Africa*. Cambridge University Press.

McCauley, John F. and Daniel N. Posner. 2017. "The Political Sources of Religious Identification: Evidence from the Burkina Faso–Côte d'Ivoire Border." *British Journal of Political Science* 49(2):421–444.

McCauley, Robert N. 2015b. "Maturationally Natural Cognition Impedes Professional Science and Facilitates Popular Religion." In *Religion and Science as Forms of Life: Anthropological Insights into Reason and Unreason*, eds. Carles Salazar and Joan Bestard. Berghahn Books, pp. 25–48.

McClendon, Gwyneth and Rachel Beatty Riedl. 2015. "Religion as a Stimulant of Political Participation: Experimental Evidence from Nairobi, Kenya." *Journal of Politics* 77(4):1045–1057.

McClendon, Gwyneth and Rachel Beatty Riedl. 2016. "Individualism and Empowerment in Pentecostal Sermons: New Evidence from Nairobi, Kenya." *African Affairs* 115(458):119–144.

Meyer, Birgit. 1998. "Make a Complete Break with the Past: Memory and Postcolonial Modernity in Ghanaian Pentecostal Discourse." In *Memory and the Postcolony: African Anthropology and the Critique of Power*, ed. Richard Werbner. Zed Books, pp. 182–208.

2004. "Christianity in Africa: From African Independent to Pentecostal-Charismatic Churches." *Annual Review of Anthropology* 33:447–474.

Meyer, Birgit and Abdoulaye Sounaye. 2017. "Sermon in the City: Christian and Islamic Preaching in West Africa." *Journal of Religion in Africa* 47(1):1–8.

Miller, Donald. 2013. Pentecostalism as a Global Phenomenon. In *Spirit and Power: The Growth and Global Impact of Pentecostalism*, eds. Donald E. Miller, Kimon H. Sargeant, and Richard Flory. Oxford University Press, pp. 1–24.

Miller, Donald and Tetsunao Yamamori. 2007. *Global Pentecostalism: The New Face of Christian Social Engagement*. University of California Press.

Miller, Donald E. 2009. "Progressive Pentecostalism: An Emergent Trend in Global Christianity." *Journal of Beliefs & Values* 30(3):275–287.

Morrell, M.E. 2005. "Deliberation, Democratic Decision-Making and Internal Political Efficacy." *Political Behavior* 27(1):49–69.

Munro, Iron. 2010. "Two Explosions Kill 5, Wound 75 at Kenya Political Rally." *Associated Press*, June 14.

Mwanakatwe, John M. 1994. *End of Kaunda Era*. Multimedia Zambia.

Mwaura, Philomena Njeri and Constansia Mumma Martinon. 2010. "Political Violence in Kenya and Local Churches' Responses: The Case of the 2007 Post-Election Crisis." *Review of Faith & International Affairs* 8(1):39–46.

New Vision. 2012. "For the Sins of Uganda, I Repent – Museveni." *New Vision*, October 18.

2016. "The Voice of Peace in the 2016 Polls." *New Vision* February 29.

New Zimbabwe. 2017. "Catholic Bishops Say 'It Is a Sin Not to Vote,' Urge People to Boot Out 'Evil' ZANU-PF." New Zimbabwe August 15.

Ngong, David. 2014. "African Pentecostalism and Religious Pluralism." In *Pentecostal Theology in Africa*, ed. Clifton Clark. Wipf and Stock Publishers, pp. 193–208.

Ngunyi, Mutahi G. 1995. "Religious Institutions and Political Liberalisation in Kenya." In *Markets, Civil Society and Democracy in Kenya*, ed. Peter Gibbon. Nordiska Afrikainstitutet, pp. 121–177.

Nielsen, Richard. 2015. "Ethics for Experimental Manipulation of Religion." In *Ethical Challenges in Political Science Experiments*, ed. Scott Desposato. Routledge, pp. 42–65.

Niemi, Richard G., Stephen C. Craig, and Franco Mattei. 1991. "Measuring Internal Political Efficacy in the 1988 National Election Study." *American Political Science Review* 85(4):1407–1413.

Norenzayan, Ara. 2013. *Big Gods: How Religion Transformed Cooperation and Conflict*. Princeton University Press.

Nunn, Nathan. 2010. "Religious Conversion in Colonial Africa." *American Economic Review Papers and Proceedings* 100:147–152.

Okite, Odhiambo. 2001. "Zambia: Church Leaders Publicly Oppose Third Term for Christian President." *Christianity Today*, April 23.

Olupona, Jacob K. and Sulayman S. Nyang. 1993. *Religious Plurality in Africa: Essays in Honour of John S. Mbiti.* Walter de Gruyter.

Opalo, Kennedy. 2014. "The Long Road to Institutionalization: The Kenyan Parliament and the 2013 Elections." *Journal of Eastern African Studies* 8(1):63–77.

Østebø, Terje. 2015. "African Salafism: Religious Purity and the Politicization of Purity." *Islamic Africa* 6:1–29.

Paller, Jeffrey W. 2014. "Informal Institutions and Personal Rule in Urban Ghana." *African Studies Review* 57(3):123–142.

Paluck, Betsy and Joan Ricart-Huguet. 2019. "When the Sorting Hat Sorts Randomly: A Natural Experiment on Culture." Princeton University *Working Paper.*

Pape, Robert. 2005. *Dying to Win: The Strategic Logic of Suicide Terrorism.* Random House.

Parsitau, Damaris S. 2014. "The Civic and Public Roles of Neo-Pentecostal Churches in Kenya (1970–2010)." PhD thesis Kenyatta University.

Patheos, Religion Library. 2018. "Ethics and Community." URL: www.patheos .com/library/presbyterian/ethics-morality-community/leadershipclergy.

Patterson, Amy S. and Tracy Kuperus. 2016. "Mobilizing the Faithful: Organizational Autonomy, Visionary Pastors, and Citizenship in South Africa and Zambia." *African Affairs* 115(459):318–341.

Pearson-Merkowitz, Shanna and James G. Gimpel. 2017. "Religion and Political Socialization." In *The Oxford Handbook of Religion and American Politics*, eds. Corwin Smidt, Lyman Kellstedt, and James L. Guth. Oxford University Press, pp. 164–190.

Pew. 2006. "Spirit and Power: A Ten-Country Survey of Pentecostals." *Technical report Pew Forum on Religion and Public Life.*

Philpott, Daniel. 2007. "Explaining the Political Ambivalence of Religion." *American Political Science Review* 101(3):505.

Phiri, Chris. 2012. "Michael Sata: Zambia's No. 1 Enemy of Freedom of Expression." *Zambia Reports*, August 7.

Phiri, Isaac. 1997. "When Churches Preach Politics: A Comparative Analysis of the Political Role of Churches in South Africa, Zimbabwe, and Zambia." PhD thesis Northern Illinois University.

Phiri, Isabel Apawo. 2003. "President Frederick JT Chiluba of Zambia: The Christian Nation and Democracy." *Journal of Religion in Africa* 33(4): 401–428.

Pirouet, M. Louise. 1980. "Religion in Uganda under Amin." *Journal of Religion in Africa* 11(1):13–29.

Posner, Daniel N. 2005. *Institutions and Ethnic Politics in Africa.* Cambridge University Press.

Post (Zambia). 2004. "Let's Reflect, Meditate Deeply on Poverty." *The Post (Zambia)* January 31.

Putnam, Robert and David Campbell. 2010. *American Grace: How Religion Divides and Unites Us.* Simon and Schuster.

Quinley, Harold E. 1974. *The Prophetic Clergy: Social Activism among Protestant Ministers.* Wiley.

Rambo, Lewis R. 1993. *Understanding Religious Conversion*. Yale University Press.

Ranger, Terence O. 2008. *Evangelical Christianity and Democracy in Africa*. Oxford University Press.

Rhodes, Christopher Edward. 2015. "Political Christianity: Internal Organization, Preferences and Church Political Activity." PhD thesis Harvard University.

Richard, Rive. 1987. *'Buckingham Palace', District Six*. New Africa Books.

Riedl, Rachel Beatty. 2016. "Strong Parties, Weak Parties." In *Parties, Movements, and Democracy in the Developing World*, eds. Nancy Bermeo and Deborah J. Yashar. Cambridge Studies in Contentious Politics. Cambridge University Press, pp. 122–156.

Roberts, Margaret E., Brandon M. Stewart, Dustin Tingley, et al. 2014. "Structural Topic Models for Open-Ended Survey Responses." *American Journal of Political Science* 58(4):1064–1082.

Robinson, Amanda Lea. 2016. "Nationalism and Ethnic-Based Trust: Evidence from an African Border Region." *Comparative Political Studies* 49(14):1819–1854.

Sabar-Friedman, Galia. 1995 "'Politics' and 'Power' in the Kenyan Public Discourse and Recent Events: The Church of the Province of Kenya (CPK)." *Canadian Journal of African Studies* 9(3–4):429–453.

Sabar-Friedman, Galia. 1997. "Church and State in Kenya 1986–1992: The Churches' Involvement in the Game of Change." *African Affairs* 96(382): 25–52.

Sachs, Natan. 2010. "Shame and Religious Prosociality." *APSA 2010 Annual Meeting Paper*.

Scacco, Alexandra and Shana S Warren. 2018. "Can Social Contact Reduce Prejudice and Discrimination? Evidence from a Field Experiment in Nigeria." *American Political Science Review* 112(3):654–677.

Scheve, Kenneth and David Stasavage. 2006. "Religion and Preferences for Social Insurance." *Quarterly Journal of Political Science* 1(3):255–286.

Seawright, Jason. 2016. *Multi-Method Social Science: Combining Qualitative and Quantitative Tools*. Cambridge University Press.

Seawright, Jason and John Gerring. 2008. "Case Selection Techniques in Case Study Research: A Menu of Qualitative and Quantitative Options." *Political Research Quarterly* 61(2):294–308.

Seay, Laura E. 2013. "Effective Responses: Protestants, Catholics and the Provision of Health Care in the Post-War Kivus." *Review of African Political Economy* 40(135):83–97.

Sen, Maya and Omar Wasow. 2016. "Race as a Bundle of Sticks: Designs that Estimate Effects of Seemingly Immutable Characteristics." *Annual Review of Political Science* 19:499–522.

Shariff, Azim F., Aiyana K. Willard, Teresa Andersen, and Ara Norenzayan. 2016. "Religious Priming: A Meta-Analysis with a Focus on Prosociality." *Personality and Social Psychology Review* 20(1):27–48.

Shariff, Azim F. and Ara Norenzayan. 2007. "God Is Watching You: Priming God Concepts Increases Prosocial Behavior in an Anonymous Economic Game." *Psychological Science* 18(9):803–809.

Shariff, Azim F., Jared Piazza, and Stephanie R. Kramer. 2014. "Morality and the Religious Mind: Why Theists and Nontheists Differ." *Trends in Cognitive Sciences* 18(9):439–441.

Shorter, Aylward. 1985. *Jesus and the Witchdoctor: An Approach to Healing and Wholeness*. Burns & Oates.

Shurden, Walter B. 2018. "Turning Points in Baptist History." *Baptist History and Heritage Society*. URL: www.centerforbaptiststudies.org/pamphlets/style/turningpoints.htm.

Simkovich, Malka Z. 2016. Geography-Based Giving in Jewish Tradition. In *Poverty and Wealth in Judaism, Christianity, and Islam*, eds. Nathan R. Kollar and Muhammad Shafiq. Palgrave Macmillan, pp. 245–261.

Smith, Amy Erica. 2017. "Democratic Talk in Church: Religion and Political Socialization in the Context of Urban Inequality." *World Development* 99:441–451.

Snyder, Charles R., Cheri Harris, John R. Anderson, et al. 1991. "The Will and the Ways: Development and Validation of an Individual-Differences Measure of Hope." *Journal of Personality and Social Psychology* 60(4):570.

Sounaye, Abdoulaye. 2014. "Mobile Sunna: Islam, Small Media and Community in Niger." *Social Compass* 61(1):21–29.

    2017. "Salafi Aesthetics: Preaching among the Sunnance in Niamey, Niger." *Journal of Religion in Africa* 47(1):9–41.

Sperber, Elizabeth Sheridan. 2016. "Deus ex Machina? New Religious Movements in African Politics." PhD thesis Columbia University.

Sperber, Elizabeth and Erin Hern. 2018. "Pentecostal Identity and Citizen Engagement in Sub-Saharan Africa: New Evidence from Zambia." *Politics and Religion* 11(4):830–862.

State. 2015. "Sierra Leone International Religious Freedom Report." *US State Department Report*.

Stewart, Brandon, Molly Roberts, and Dustin Tingley. 2014. stm: R Package for Structural Topic Models. Technical report Harvard University.

Sun. 2014. "KWAM I Helped Me Win Election – Olatunji-Edet, Lagos Lawmaker." December 10.

Sundkler, Bengt and Christopher Steed. 2000. *A History of the Church in Africa*. Cambridge University Press.

Swidler, Ann. 1986. "Culture in Action: Symbols and Strategies." *American Sociological Review* 51(2):273–286.

Taber, Charles S. and Milton Lodge. 2006. "Motivated Skepticism in the Evaluation of Political Beliefs." *American Journal of Political Science* 50(3):755–769.

Tesler, Michael. 2015. "Priming Predispositions and Changing Policy Positions: An account of When Mass Opinion Is Primed or Changed." *American Journal of Political Science* 59(4):806–824.

Tesler, Michael and John Zaller. 2017. "The Power of Political Communication." In *The Oxford Handbook of Political Communication*, eds. Kate Kenski and Kathleen Hall Jamieson. Oxford University Press, p. 69.

Thachil, Tariq. 2014. *Elite Parties, Poor Voters: How Social Services Win Votes in India*. Cambridge University Press.

Throup, David. 2015. "Politics, Religious Engagement, and Extremism in Kenya." In *Religious Authority and the State in Africa*, eds. Jennifer Cooke and Richard Downie, Center for Strategic and International Studies. Rowman & Littlefield, pp. 29–48.

Time. 2005. "Pope John Paul II." *Time Magazine* 165(15).

Toft, Monica Duffy, Daniel Philpott, and Timothy Samuel Shah. 2011. *God's Century: Resurgent Religion and Global Politics*. WW Norton & Company.

Togarasei, Lovemore. 2011. "The Pentecostal Gospel of Prosperity in African Contexts of Poverty: An Appraisal." *Exchange* 40(4):336–350.

Trejo, Guillermo. 2009. "Religious Competition and Ethnic Mobilization in Latin America: Why the Catholic Church Promotes Indigenous Movements in Mexico." *American Political Science Review* 103(03):323–342.

Trinitapoli, Jenny. 2009. "Malawi Religion Project: Sermon Reports Data, 2004." *Database Description*.

Trinitapoli, Jenny and Alexander Weinreb. 2012. *Religion and AIDS in Africa*. Oxford University Press.

Tunón, Guadalupe. 2017. "When the Church Votes Left: How Progressive Religion Hurts Gender Equality." *Working Paper, University of California, Berkeley*.

UEC. 2005. Towards a Democratic and Peaceful Uganda Based on the Common Good: On the Transition from the Movement System of Governance to Multiparty Politics. Technical report Pastoral Letter of the Catholic Bishops of Uganda Kampala, Uganda.

2012. Fifty Years of Independence: Celebrating Our Heritage. Technical report Pastoral Letter of the Catholic Bishops of Uganda Kampala, Uganda.

Valentino, Nicholas A., Vincent L. Hutchings, Antoine J. Banks and Anne K. Davis. 2008. "Is a Worried Citizen a Good Citizen? Emotions, Political Information Seeking, and Learning via the Internet." *Political Psychology* 29(2):247–273.

Van de Walle, Nicolas. 2003. "Presidentialism and Clientelism in Africa's Emerging Party Systems." *Journal of Modern African Studies* 41(2):297–321.

Van Wyk, Ilana. 2014. *The Universal Church of the Kingdom of God in South Africa: A Church of Strangers*. Cambridge University Press.

Varshney, Ashutosh. 2003. *Ethnic Conflict and Civic Life: Hindus and Muslims in India*. Yale University Press.

Verba, Sidney, Kay Lehman Schlozman, and Henry E. Brady. 1995. *Voice and Equality: Civic Voluntarism in American Politics*. Harvard University Press.

Verba, Sidney and Norman H. Nie. 1972. *Participation in America*. Harper & Row.

Villalón, Leonardo A. 2010. "From Argument to Negotiation: Constructing Democracy in African Muslim Contexts." *Comparative Politics* 42(4): 375–393.

Wald, Kenneth D., Dennis E. Owen, and Samuel S. Hill. 1988. "Churches as Political Communities." *American Political Science Review* 82(02):531–548.

Wantchekon, Leonard, Marko Klašnja, and Natalija Novta. 2014. "Education and Human Capital Externalities: Evidence from Colonial Benin." *Quarterly Journal of Economics* 130(2):703–757.

Wanyeki, L. Muthoni. 2010. "How Did Our Religious Leaders Sink So Low?" *The East African* 04. URL: www.theeastafrican.co.ke/oped/comment/How-did-our-religious-leaders-sink-so-low/434750-901536-ykybwez/index.html.

Warner, Carolyn M. 2000. *Confessions of an Interest Group: The Catholic Church and Political Parties in Europe.* Princeton University Press.

Warner, Carolyn M., Ramazan Kılınç, Christopher W. Hale, Adam B. Cohen, and Kathryn A. Johnson. 2015. "Religion and Public Goods Provision: Experimental and Interview Evidence from Catholicism and Islam in Europe." *Comparative Politics* 47(2):189–209.

Washington Times. 2007. "Pentecostalism and Politics." *Washington Times*, January 21.

Watson, David, Lee A. Clark, and Auke Tellegen. 1988. "Development and Validation of Brief Measures of Positive and Negative Affect: The PANAS Scales." *Journal of Personality and Social Psychology* 54(6):1063.

Weber, Max. 1934. *The Protestant Ethic and the Spirit of Capitalism.* Charles Scribner's and Sons.

    1993. *The Sociology of Religion.* Beacon Press.

Wielhouwer, Peter. 2009. "Religion and American Political Participation." In *The Oxford Handbook of Religion and American Politics*, eds. Corwin Smidt, Lyman A. Kellstedt, and James L. Guth. Oxford University Press. DOI: 10.1093/oxfordhb/9780195326529.003.0014.

Wilkinson, Steven I. 2006. *Votes and Violence: Electoral Competition and Ethnic Riots in India.* Cambridge University Press.

Wilkinson, Sue. 1998. "Focus Group Methodology: A Review." *International Journal of Social Research Methodology* 1(3):181–203.

Wittenberg, Jason. 2006. *Crucibles of Political Loyalty: Church Institutions and Electoral Continuity in Hungary.* Cambridge University Press.

Wood, Richard L. and Mark R. Warren. 2002. "A Different Face of Faith-Based Politics: Social Capital and Community Organizing in the Public Arena." *International Journal of Sociology and Social Policy* 22(9/10):6–54.

Woodberry, R. 2013. "Pentecostalism and Democracy: Is There a relationship." In *Spirit and Power: The Growth and Global Impact of Pentecostalism*, eds. Donald E. Miller, Kimon H. Sargeant, and Richard Flory. Oxford University Press, pp. 119–137.

Woodberry, Robert. 2008. "Pentecostalism and Economic Development." In *Markets, Morals and Religion*, ed. Jonathan B. Imber. Transaction Publishers, pp. 157–177.

Woodberry, Robert D. 2006. "The Economic Consequences of Pentecostal Belief." *Society* 44(1):29–35.

Yoder, Paton. 2003. "The Amish View of the State." In *The Amish and the State*, ed. Donald B. Kraybill. Johns Hopkins University Press, pp. 23–42.

Young, Crawford. 1994. *The African Colonial State in Comparative Perspective.* Yale University Press.

   2012. *The Postcolonial State in Africa: Fifty Years of Independence, 1960–2010.* University of Wisconsin Press.

Zaller, John. 1996. "The Myth of Massive Media Impact Revived: New Support for a Discredited Idea." In *Political Persuasion and Attitude Change* 17, eds. Diana C. Mutz, Paul M. Sniderman, and Richard A. Brody. University of Michigan Press, pp. 17–78.

Zimba, Thomas. 2011. "President Sata and Evangelicals." *Zambian Watchdog,* November 20.

Index